THE WORLD'S GREAT
STEALTH
AND
RECONNAISSANCE
AIRCRAFT

SMITHMARK

THE WORLD'S GREAT
STEALTH
AND
RECONNAISSANCE
AIRCRAFT

This edition published in 1991 by SMITHMARK Publishers Inc., 112 Madison Avenue, New York, NY 10016.

SMITHMARK books are available for bulk purchase for sales promotion and premium use. For details write or telephone the Manager of Special Sales, SMITHMARK Publishers Inc., 112 Madison Avenue, New York, NY 10016. (212) 532-6600

Printed in Hong Kong

ISBN: 0-8317-9558-1

Pictures were supplied by:

Bruce Bailey, Boeing, David Donald, Malcolm English, Peter Foster, Grumman Corporation, Denys Hughes, Japanese Air Self-Defence Force, Lockheed, Jon Lake, Robert L. Lawson Collection, McDonnell Douglas, Military Aircraft Photographs, Ministry of Defence, Bob Monro, Robert Monro Snr, Lindsay Peacock, RAF News, Royal Netherlands Navy, Terry Senior, Robbie Shaw, Andrew Thomas, US Air Force, US Army, US Department of Defense, US Navy.

Special thanks to TRH Pictures

Production controller: Alastair Gourlay
Production assistant: Darren Ketteringham
Design: George Keyes

Previous pages: Six Lockheed S-3 Vikings pictured during an anti-submarine warfare training exercise.

CONTENTS

UK   **BAe Nimrod**   7

USA   **Lockheed SR-71 Blackbird**   19
          Grumman E-2 Hawkeye   31
          Lockheed P-3 Orion   43
          Boeing E-3 Sentry   55
          Lockheed S-3 Viking   67
          Boeing RC-135   79
          Grumman EA-6B Prowler   91
          Grumman EF-111A Raven   103
          McDonnell Douglas RF-4 Phantom   115
          Grumman OV-1 Mohawk   127
          Lockheed U-2/TR-1   139
          Northrop B-2   151
          Lockheed F-117   163
          Advanced Tactical Fighter - YF-22/23   173

USSR **Tupolev Tu-142 'Bear'**   187

The BAE NIMROD

engined prototype on 23 June 1976 and were developed in three trials conversions of MR.Mk 1s which first flew in March 1978, May 1978 and March 1979. In fact, the latter followed the initial 'production' conversion, which was airborne at Woodford on 13 February 1979 before being handed-over to No. 201 Squadron on 23 August of the same year. Plans to transform 32 aircraft into what is known as Nimrod MR.Mk 2 standard were subsequently amended to cover all 35 available airframes (11 more were reserved for the AEW.Mk 3 programme), the last of which was completed in 1985. The Kinloss Wing disposed of its final MR.Mk 1 in October 1982 and No. 42 Squadron began crew training on the MR.Mk 2 in June 1983.

Whilst the MR.Mk 2 conversion programme adds some 2722 kg (6,000 lb) to the aircraft's empty weight, external signs of change are restricted to a deleted cabin window, new intakes and ducts around the rear fuselage, and changes in the positioning of some aerials. Internally, it is a very different story, and it is no exaggeration to say that the leap in capability between the two marks of Nimrod is greater than that separating the Shackleton MR.Mk 3 from Nimrod MR.Mk 1. Out has gone the ASV Mk 21 radar handed down by the Shackleton, to be replaced by the EMI ARI 5980 Searchwater unit, whilst processing of sonobuoy signals is now entrusted to a twin Marconi AQS 901 installation.

Paint job

Independently of the MR.Mk 2 programme, Nimrods have undergone other changes of external appearance, beginning early in 1977 with the application of an experimental camouflage finish to a Kinloss aircraft. After some modification, this was adopted by the whole fleet between 1980 and 1982, the white top giving way to a brownish-grey tone known as hemp. In the spring of 1985 (somewhat later than planned) Loral 1017A ESM pods began to appear on Nimrod wingtips, following aerodynamic trials begun in 1979 to clear the fitment for flight.

For participation in the Falklands war against Argentina, in 1982, when Nimrods operated up to 6440 km (4,000 miles) from their advanced base at Ascension Island, several changes were rapidly introduced. These concerned the MR.Mk 2, which relieved MR.Mk 1s after the first few days. To augment their Mk 44 or Mk 46 homing torpedoes, aircraft were issued with the Marconi Stingray in advance of its planned service-entry date. Clearance was also received to carry 1,000-lb (454-kg) bombs; Hunting BL755 cluster bombs; and the McDonnell Douglas AGM-84A Harpoon anti-ship missile, the last-mentioned coming just too late for operational deployment. Even air-to-air armament was provided in the form of a pair of AIM-9G Sidewinders on each of the two underwing pylons in case the Nimrod met an Argentine maritime reconnaissance aircraft. An inflight-refuelling probe extended the Nimrod's radius of action and allowed flights of up to 19 hours' duration, some of which were close to the enemy coastline. Less perilous, but still appreciated by British

airmen, were missions co-ordinating refuelling link-ups by other aircraft over the featureless South Atlantic and providing SAR cover in the event of a ditching.

The Nimrod R.Mk 1s operated by No. 51 Squadron also saw service during the Falklands war, flying from Ascension, and perhaps from bases in Brazil or Chile. The first of the three Nimrod R.Mk 1s built was delivered to Wyton in July 1971, but modifications for the new role took over two years and flight trials did not start until late 1973. The first operational flight of a No. 51 Squadron Nimrod took place on 3 May 1974, and the type was formally commissioned one week later, on 10 May. The aircraft offered a considerable increase in capability over the de Havilland Comet Mk 2Rs previously used, although a handful of English Electric Canberras were retained for another two years until further modifications could be made to the Nimrods.

R.Mk 1 radomes

Visually, the Nimrod R.Mk 1 differs from the standard maritime patrol aircraft in having a conical spiral aerial in a short radome in place of the MAD boom, with similar radomes in the nose of each leading-edge tank. The weapons bay of the R.Mk 1 is thought to be sealed and may contain a large aerial or other Elint equipment. Since their introduction in 1974 the three aircraft have received further modifications and now have an even more distinctive appearance. Increased internal equipment is thought to be responsible for the blanking off of all but a few fuselage windows, and the aircraft have sprouted an 'antenna farm' on the under fuselage reminiscent of that carried by some Lockheed TR-1s and U-2Rs. This may indicate the installation of American equipment. One Nimrod R.Mk 1 was probed for the Falklands war, by which time all had received wingtip ESM pods, long before the rest of the Nimrod fleet. These changes in configuration led the 1984-5 edition of *Jane's All The World's Aircraft* to give the aircraft a new designation, R.Mk.2, but this has not been officially confirmed and must remain a matter of speculation. The role of No. 51 Squadron has not been officially ad-

More interest than information surrounds the sinister Nimrod R.Mk 1s flown by No. 51 Sqn. They fly Elint sorties around the periphery of WarPac countries from RAF Wyton, Cambridgeshire.

mitted, usually being described as 'radar calibration'. Newspaper reports describe the unit as 'GCHQ's squadron of Nimrods' 'funded by the Foreign Office', and since the Nimrod R.Mk 1s have also been intercepted by Swedish fighters over the Baltic it seems certain that the actual role is the gathering of electronic intelligence.

Remarkably, only one Nimrod of any kind has been lost in a flying accident in 16 years of operations, and that to a multiple birdstrike shortly after take-off, for which the aircraft can hardly be held responsible. The 34 remaining maritime Nimrods, repackaged with advanced avionics in defiance of the adage which maintains that an old (sea) dog cannot be taught new tricks, have sufficient airframe life remaining for service up to the end of the century. Without doubt, they will be kept well occupied until then on the vital task of patrolling the waters which surround the UK.

Glossary

CTS Central Tactical System
Elint Electronic intelligence
ESM Electronic Support Measures
MAD Magnetic Anomaly Detector
OCU Operational Conversion Unit
SAR Search And Rescue

Nimrods first acquired inflight-refuelling probes during the Falklands war, enabling them to carry out patrols of 19 hours' duration. Crews continue to practise their use, but Nimrod's normal endurance of up to 12 hours is usually adequate.

British Aerospace Nimrod MR.Mk 2P RAF Kinloss Nimrod Wing

ESM pod
On both wingtips is a pod supplied by Loral Electric of the USA. It contains several spiral helix receiver aerials for reception from all directions of unknown or hostile signals. Each passive receiver is tuned to one waveband. An alternative to ESM (electronic surveillance measures) is EWSM (electronic warfare support measures). Introduction of these pods has been delayed by financial constraints

Slot
As on the Comet 4 series, a fixed slot aft of the tank fairing improves airflow over the wing downstream

IFF
Several small blade aerials serve the identification friend or foe transponder system, enabling the Nimrod to identify friendly platforms on land, sea and air

ADF
Achilles heel of the Comet I airliner the cut-out in the pressure cabin for automatic direction finder loop aeri the Nimrod this radio device, which indicates bearings of ground statior has unlimited fatigue life

Searchlight
Valuable at night, this 70 million candlepower searchlight is mounted on the front of the external fuel tank on the right wing. A product of Strong Electric, it is fed by the cable carried over the top of the tank

Inflight-refuelling probe
Added in an urgent modification during the Falklands campaign in 1982, this fixed inflight-refuelling probe passes received fuel around the inside of the pressurized fuselage and thence into the main wing tanks

Taxi light
These lamps are used both for landing and to illuminate ground ahead during taxiing. The crew can control the wing root and nose lights individually

Radar
Under the nose is the Thorn-EMI Searchwater main radar, specially developed for this application and with its own associated Ferranti digital computer.

Pitot head
This sensor measures pitot (dynamic or ram pressure) for the air-data system, including the airspeed indicators

Structural joint
Along this line are joine the circular- section pressurized fuse and the and we bay below un systems cor

HF
Twin wires serve the duplicated HF (high frequency) radios, which provide voice contact over global distances. The original MR.Mk 1 aircraft had a single HF set

Aerials
These three large blade aerials serve the three main VHF/UHF radio communications equipments

Upward light
This brilliant occulting red beacon is the upward identification and anti-collision light

Loran
The Decca Loran installation is one of the longest-established radio navigation aids, indicating position by time-difference of reception from multiple ground stations at great distances

was
the
l. On

s,

Landing light
The most powerful lights on the aircraft are outboard of the engines. In many aircraft such lights are hinged and retract, but these are fixed

Air inlet
Between the main engine air inlets is an intake to a duct serving an environmental-control heat exchanger between each pair of engines. Fresh air taken in here cools hot air bled from the engine compressors

Weapon doors
These huge hydraulically-driven doors cover the vast unpressurized weapons bay. Here they are open

d
n
lage
eapon
pressurized
partments

Nimrod: mighty hunter

Nimrod's sleek, airliner-type appearance and innocuous colour scheme belies the fact that it is a highly capable warplane, designed to kill enemy submarines that would pose a threat to Britain if war ever broke out.

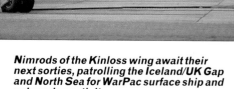

Having suffered grievous losses of merchant navy shipping and Royal Navy warships to submarines in two world wars, the UK appreciates more than most nations the importance of keeping a close watch on the vessels on (and under) the waters which encircle it. By historical accident, it is the RAF which is responsible for the operation of shore-based maritime patrol aircraft, its current equipment for this task being the BAe Nimrod. As the product of an unusual development programme, the Nimrod completed a decade in service before being extensively modernized, so that the aircraft now seen over the Atlantic Ocean and North Sea are far removed in terms of capability from first-generation models.

Ordered by the RAF to replace the venerable Avro Shackleton MR.Mk 3, the Nimrod may be said to have had its birth in June 1964, when Hawker Siddeley at Woodford began work on the HS.801 project. However, conception comes before birth, and in the case of the Nimrod the true origin of the airframe is the de Havilland Comet, the world's first jet airliner. Major changes involved in producing a maritime reconnaissance version included addition of an unpressurized lower fuselage component (giving a 'double-bubble' cross section) to house the weapons bay and radar scanner, a modified fin, and a MAD 'stinger' at the extreme rear. Two prototypes were produced from unsold Comet Mk 4C airframes. The second of these (serialled XV148) was converted to HS.801 standard and fitted with the four Rolls-Royce RB.168 Spey turbofans chosen for the maritime reconnaissance aircraft. Its maiden flight on 23 May 1967 came shortly after the HS.801 was named Nimrod in an allusion to the 'mighty hunter' mentioned in the Book of Genesis, and was rapidly followed, on 31 July, by the first sortie of XV147.

Swift development

Making much use of proven avionics, the Nimrod MR.Mk 1 enjoyed a short development period. Even before the mid-1965 public announcement of government support for the HS.801 project, a contract had been placed for 38 Nimrod MR.Mk 1s, the first of these flying from Woodford on 28 June 1968. Service deliveries began to the Maritime Operational Training Unit (later re-designated No. 236 OCU) at St Mawgan on 2 October 1969. All five squadrons equipped with Nimrods formerly operated Shackletons, and it was to Kinloss that the 13th production aircraft was supplied on 25 June 1970 to begin conversion of Nos 120, 201 and 206 Squadrons. Deliveries then turned again to St Mawgan for the benefit of No. 42 Squadron, with which the 27th example arrived on 3 April 1971 at the beginning of a six-month transformation. The fifth unit, No. 203 Squadron, was assigned to Luqa, Malta, for operations in the Mediterranean, but received its first Nimrod (the 32nd) at Kinloss on 31 July 1971.

The last of the original 38 Nimrods had

Nimrods of the Kinloss wing await their next sorties, patrolling the Iceland/UK Gap and North Sea for WarPac surface ship and submarine activity.

been completed in February 1972 and delivered on 18 September. Further production had by then been guaranteed by the announcement in January 1972 of a requirement for eight more Nimrod MR.Mk 1s as spare and attrition aircraft, and these were ordered two years later, making their first flights from November 1974 onwards. The impending departure of the RAF from Luqa rendered the batch technically superfluous, so three were held back at Woodford for trials work. Now, all except one have been converted to Nimrod AEW.Mk 3 standard. The five delivered to the RAF had improved communications equipment, since standardized in the fleet by retrospective modification.

Nationalization of the aircraft industry in 1977 resulted in British Aerospace becoming the parent of the Nimrod, even though no new aircraft remained to be built. By this time, however, plans were well advanced for a programme of modification to the aircraft, in which advantage would be taken of developments in sensor systems since the mid-1960s. The new avionics had first flown in the Spey-

A pleasing snapshot of a Kinloss Nimrod over the Scottish coast. But the view is deceptive; Nimrod is a potent warplane with a serious job to do.

Nimrod in service units and example aircraft

No. 42 Squadron
Converted: from April 1971
Base: St Mawgan
Task: Maritime reconnaissance
Equipment: Nimrod MR.Mk 2/2P
Example aircraft: XV226, XV229, XV231, XV243, XV250, XZ284

No. 120 Squadron
Converted: from February 1971
Base: Kinloss
Task: Maritime reconnaissance
Equipment: Nimrod MR.Mk 2/2P
Example aircraft: pooled with Nos 201 and 206 Squadrons, e.g. XV227, XV234, XV238, XV246, XV252, XV260

No. 201 Squadron
Converted: from October 1970
Base: Kinloss
Task: Maritime reconnaissance
Equipment: Nimrod MR.Mk 2/2P
Example aircraft: (see No. 120 Squadron)

No. 206 Squadron
Converted: from November 1970
Base: Kinloss
Task: Maritime reconnaissance
Equipment: Nimrod MR.Mk 2/2P
Example aircraft: (see No. 120 Squadron)

No. 51 Squadron
Converted: from October 1973
Base: Wyton
Task: Electronic intelligence-gathering
Equipment: Nimrod R.Mk 1
Example aircraft: XW664, XW665, XW666

No. 236 OCU
Converted: from October 1969
Base: St Mawgan
Task: Crew conversion and (designated **No. 38 Squadron**) maritime reconnaissance
Equipment: Nimrod MR.Mk 2/2P
Example aircraft: (shared with No. 42 Squadron)

No. 51 Sqn's aircraft are the only Nimrods to routinely carry a unit badge, an unusual step for a squadron which shuns publicity so assiduously.

Left: Maritime Nimrods do not display prominent squadron insignia, though the squadron badges do sometimes appear on the forward fuselage. This aircraft is from No. 201 Sqn.

Below: Nimrods seldom carry any markings except during competitions. This one participated in the Fincastle Trophy in 1984, and has been well and truly zapped.

BAe Nimrod variants

Nimrod prototypes: two converted from uncompleted Comet 4C airframes; first retained Avon turbojets, though second had Rolls-Royce Spey turbofans but no avionics; weapons bay and fuel tanks in underfuselage pannier, strengthened landing gear, dorsal fin, radar, ESM and MAD equipment for ASW role

Nimrod MR.Mk 1: initial production variant; 46 ordered, three of these delivered as development aircraft for AEW.Mk 3 programme; one lost in accident, 11 converted to AEW.Mk 3, rest converted to MR.Mk 2

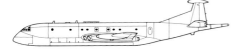

Nimrod R.Mk 1: three aircraft delivered to No. 51 Squadron and converted for Elint missions; radomes in front of wing tanks and in place of MAD boom, various aerials; all now have ESM pods on wingtips

Nimrod R.Mk 1P: one R.Mk 1 given inflight-refuelling capability for Falklands operations; the other two may be modified to this standard at a later date

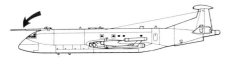

Nimrod MR.Mk 2: 31 converted from MR.Mk 1 incorporating new Marconi Searchwater radar, communications, avionics, and navigational equipment; all will eventually receive Loral ARI18240 wingtip ESM pods; can carry four AIM-9 Sidewinders on twin underwing launchers

Nimrod MR.Mk 2P: all Nimrod MR.Mk 2s will eventually be given refuelling probes and associated aerodynamic modifications; first MR.Mk 2P conversions undertaken for Falklands campaign

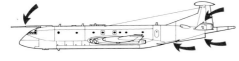

Nimrod AEW.Mk 3: incorporates new GEC radar with newly developed, identically shaped dual-frequency twisted cassegrain antennae at nose and tail giving good all-round coverage; dual IFF interrogators, Loral ESM pods with anti-jamming features; three development and 11 production aircraft converted from Nimrod MR.Mk 1; taller fin

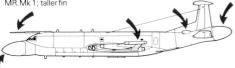

British Aerospace Nimrod MR.Mk 2P cutaway drawing

1 Dielectric radome
2 Glidescope aerial
3 Taxiing lamp
4 Ice detector
5 Beak access panel
6 EMI Searchwater radar scanner
7 Radome hoist point
8 Front pressure bulkhead
9 Windscreen (area enlarged from original Comet)
10 Four windscreen wipers
11 Instrument panel coaming
12 Inflight-refuelling probe
13 Co-pilot's seat
14 Eyebrow window
15 Pilot's seat
16 Pitot head
17 Interrogator set
18 Radar absorbent material
19 Twin nosewheels
20 Nosewheel splash guards
21 Doppler bay
22 Forward radio crate
23 Port DC electrics crate
24 Engineer's station
25 Escape hatch (inoperable with refuelling boom fitted)
26 Scarbe aerials (two)
27 Starboard DC electrics crate
28 Crew entry door
29 IFF aerial (upper)
30 Periscope sextant
31 Equipment systems crate
32 Toilet
33 Ground supply socket
34 Bomb doors ground control
35 Door jack
36 AGM-86A Harpoon anti-ship missile
37 Bomb door
38 Mixed ASW weapons load
39 Tank blow-off
40 Inward opening domed observation window (port)
41 Port beam lookout's seat
42 Starboard beam lookout's seat
43 Inward opening domed observation window (starboard)
44 TACAN aerial
45 Sonics homers (two)
46 ADF loop aerial
47 Navigation equipment rack
48 Blackout curtain
49 Routine navigator's panel and chart table
50 Routine navigator's seat
51 Tactical navigator's displays and control panels
52 Tactical navigator's seat
53 Communications operator
54 AEO's seat
55 Fixed domed window (starboard only)
56 UHF/VHF no. 2
57 Sonics (acoustics) stations
58 UHF/VHF no. 1
59 Sonics operator's seats
60 Equipment cooling ducting
61 Searchwater station crates
62 Searchwater station
63 ASV operator's seat
64 Bulkhead
65 Port AC electrics crate
66 Starboard AC electrics crate
67 ESM/MAD station
68 ESM/MAD operator's seat
69 Machined inner wing skin panel
70 Undercarriage bay upper panel
71 Loran aerial
72 Flow spoiler
73 Wing bumper
74 Searchlight (70 m candle power)
75 External fuel tank
76 Cable trough
77 Fixed slot
78 Integral fuel tanks
79 Skin butt-joint rib
80 Over-wing fuel filler
81 Forward radome
82 Lightning protection strips
83 Starboard ESM pod
84 Access panel
85 Aft radome
86 Lightning protection strips
87 Starboard aileron
88 Aileron tab
89 Flap outer section
90 Airbrake (upper and lower surfaces)
91 Fuel dump pipes
92 Fuel vent
93 Flap inner section
94 Folding door
95 Emergency escape panels
96 Fuselage frames
97 Electrics trough
98 Dinette
99 Galley
100 Partition with folding door
101 Starboard sonobuoy stowage (six frames)
102 Acoustic equipment crates
103 Underfloor bag-type keel tanks
104 Port sonobuoy stowage (two frames)
105 Stores loaders' seats (two)
106 Pressurized launchers
107 Rotary launchers
108 Ready-use oxygen stowage
109 Intercom panel
110 CRT displays (port and starboard)
111 Emergency door (starboard)
112 Escape chute stowage
113 Marine marker stowage
114 Escape rope stowage
115 UHF/VHF no. 3
116 Hat-rack
117 Camera magazine stowage
118 Retro-launcher
119 F.135 camera hatch
120 Equipment rack
121 Equipment cooling fans
122 Rear pressure bulkhead
123 APU
124 Conditioning pack intake (port only)
125 Dorsal fin
126 HF aerial cables (two)
127 Starboard tailplane
128 Auxiliary fins (above and below)
129 VOR aerial
130 Starboard elevator
131 Dielectric fairing
132 Rudder
133 Tailfin structure
134 Tailcone
135 MAD detector head in dielectric end cap
136 Elevator tab
137 Port elevator
138 VOR aerial
139 Tailplane structure
140 Tail bumper/ventral fin
141 Fuselage vent
142 ILS marker aerial no. 2
143 Sonics aerial
144 Tailfin/fuselage frame
145 De-icing conduit
146 Conditioning pack
147 Rudder and elevator linkage
148 APU and aft fuselage access hatch
149 Safe
150 Liquid oxygen pack
151 F.126 camera hatch
152 Intercom panel

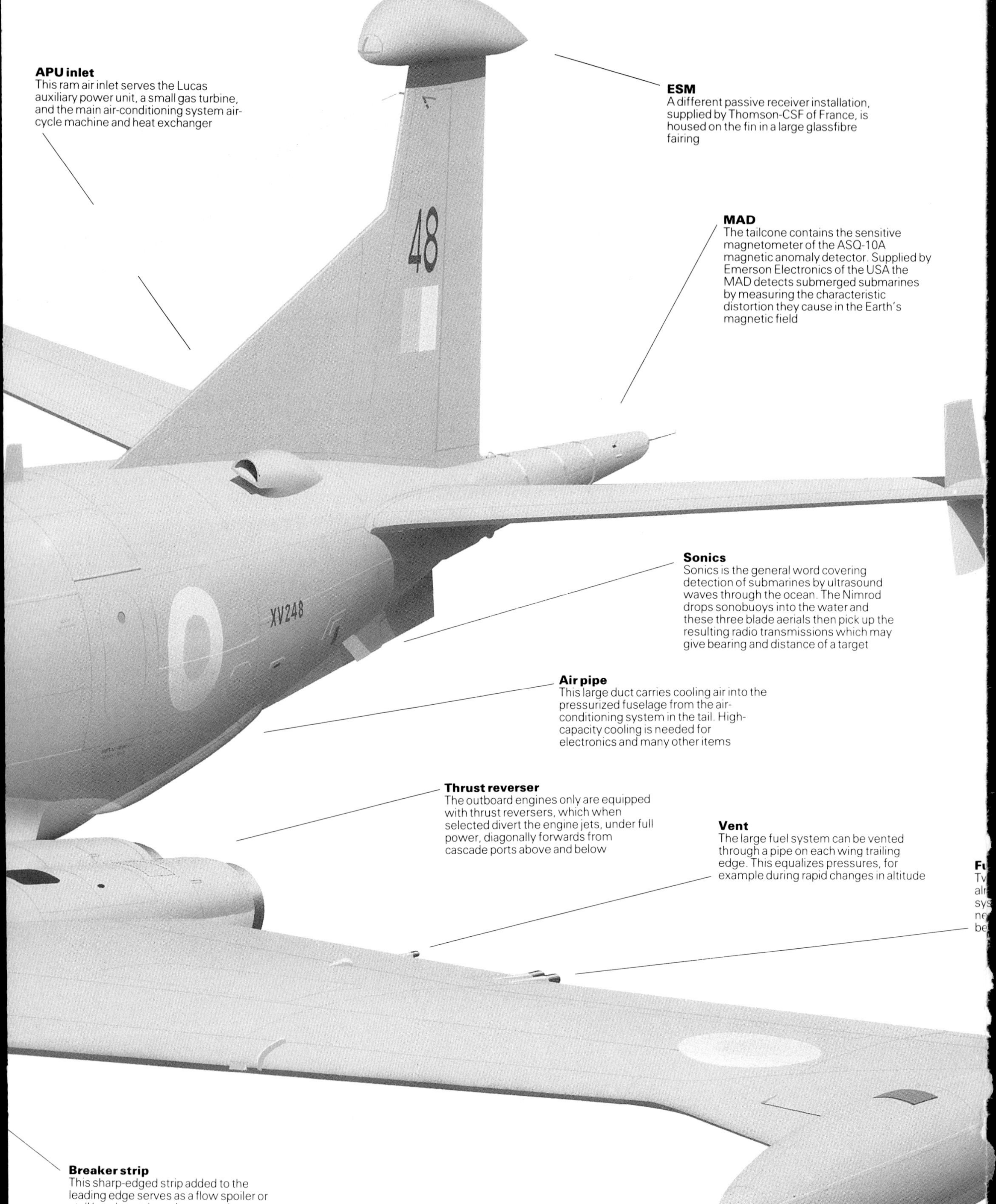

APU inlet
This ram air inlet serves the Lucas auxiliary power unit, a small gas turbine, and the main air-conditioning system air-cycle machine and heat exchanger

ESM
A different passive receiver installation, supplied by Thomson-CSF of France, is housed on the fin in a large glassfibre fairing

MAD
The tailcone contains the sensitive magnetometer of the ASQ-10A magnetic anomaly detector. Supplied by Emerson Electronics of the USA the MAD detects submerged submarines by measuring the characteristic distortion they cause in the Earth's magnetic field

Sonics
Sonics is the general word covering detection of submarines by ultrasound waves through the ocean. The Nimrod drops sonobuoys into the water and these three blade aerials then pick up the resulting radio transmissions which may give bearing and distance of a target

Air pipe
This large duct carries cooling air into the pressurized fuselage from the air-conditioning system in the tail. High-capacity cooling is needed for electronics and many other items

Thrust reverser
The outboard engines only are equipped with thrust reversers, which when selected divert the engine jets, under full power, diagonally forwards from cascade ports above and below

Vent
The large fuel system can be vented through a pipe on each wing trailing edge. This equalizes pressures, for example during rapid changes in altitude

Fu
Tw
al
sys
ne
be

Breaker strip
This sharp-edged strip added to the leading edge serves as a flow spoiler or stall breaker strip and ensures that, should extreme angle of attack be reached, the stall will start here and progress in a controlled manner, leaving the ailerons operative

Extra fins
Three auxiliary fins were added to
improve yaw stability, which in some
conditions became marginal after
installation of the AAR probe

VOR
The tailplane tips each house an aerial for
the VHF omni-directional range receiver.
VOR is a worldwide radio navigation aid
used mainly by civil aircraft which fly
from beacon to beacon along
established airways

uel jettison pipes
win pipes on each wing can dump
most the entire contents of the fuel
tem in minutes. This might be
cessary should an emergency landing
needed soon after take-off

Vortex generators
A row of small inclined vanes, also
known as turbulators, stirs up airflow
ahead of the ailerons and improves
lateral control under all flight conditions.
As on the Comets, the flight controls are
fully powered

Bumper
A tough fairing is added under each
outer-wing external tank because in
severe cross-wind or asymmetric
conditions it is possible to scrape either
tank on the runway

Planned to have entered service in 1982, the AEW version of Nimrod remains plagued with problems. The contractors completed the conversion of the remaining aircraft, but only one has reached RAF Waddington where it will, hopefully, eventually serve with No. 8 Sqn.

British Aerospace Nimrod recognition features

Searchlight in tip of starboard tank

Tailplanes with pronounced dihedral

Distinctive double-bubble fuselage cross-section

Slender MAD boom

Four engines buried in wing roots

Large fuel tanks project from wing leading edge

Large nose with slight point near underside

Large dorsal fin fillet

Large bulbous ESM pod on fin tip

Nimrod is similar in appearance to the Comet and Caravelle airliners. Few aircraft of similar size have wing root engines, notable exceptions being the Tupolev Tu-16 'Badger' and Myasischev M-4 'Bison'

Specification:

Wings
Span	35,00 m	(114 ft 10 in)
Area	197.0 m²	(2,121 sq ft)
Sweep	20° at quarter chord	

Fuselage and tail unit
Accommodation	12	
Length overall (including probe)	39.31 m	(129 ft 1 in)
Height overall	9.06 m	(29 ft 8.5 in)
Tailplane span	14.51 m	(47 ft 7.25 in)

Landing gear
Retractable tricycle landing gear with four-wheel tandem bogie main units and twin nosewheels
Wheelbase	14.24 m	(46 ft 8.5 in)
Wheel track	8.60 m	(28 ft 2.5 in)

Weights
Empty	39009 kg	(86,000 lb)
Maximum take-off	8709 kg	(192,000 lb)
Maximum disposable load	6123 kg	(13,500 lb)
Internal fuel load	38936 kg	(85,840 lb)

Powerplant
Four Rolls Royce RB.168-20 Spey Mk 250 turbofans with reverse thrust on two outer engines
Static thrust, each engine	5507 kg	(12,140 lb)

Performance:

Maximum speed	500 kts	(927 km/h; 576 mph)
Normal transit speed	425 kts	(787 km/h; 489 mph)
Service ceiling	42,000 ft	(12800 m)
Ferry range, unrefuelled	9254 km	(5,750 miles)
Patrol endurance, unrefuelled	12 hours	

Weapons load

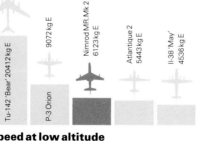

Tu-142 'Bear' 20412 kg E
P-3 Orion 9072 kg E
Nimrod MR.Mk 2 6123 kg E
Atlantique 2 5443 kg E
Il-38 'May' 4536 kg E

Service ceiling

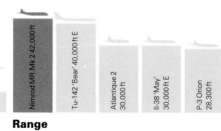

Nimrod MR.Mk 2 42,000 ft
Tu-142 'Bear' 40,000 ft E
Atlantique 2 30,000 ft
Il-38 'May' 30,000 ft E
P-3 Orion 28,300 ft

Speed at high altitude

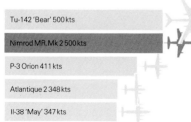

Tu-142 'Bear' 500 kts
Nimrod MR.Mk 2 500 kts
P-3 Orion 411 kts
Atlantique 2 348 kts
Il-38 'May' 347 kts

Speed at low altitude

Nimrod MR.Mk 2 475 kts
Tu-142 'Bear' 450 kts E
P-3 Orion 400 kts
Atlantique 2 320 kts
Il-38 'May' 320 kts E

Range

Tu-142 'Bear' 12550 km
Nimrod MR.Mk 2 9265 km
P-3 Orion 7670 km
Atlantique 2 7300 km
Il-38 'May' 7200 km

The **Nimrod** cockpit clearly shows its **Comet** ancestry, differing only in its more modern navigation and communications equipment. Flight instruments are fully duplicated, with engine instruments and throttle quadrant between the captain and co-pilot. Four windscreen wipers are provided for low-level flight over the sea.

Main entry door
Cooling air duct, outside pressure shell
Tailpipes
Ground-operated doors (rear loading of stores)
Wingroot fillet structure
Dinghy stowage bay

159 Thrust reverser (outboard engines only)
160 Rear spar/fuselage attachment joint
161 Rolls-Royce Spey 250 turbofan engine
162 Inboard engine bay (engine deleted to show detail)
163 Heat exchanger
164 Front spar/fuselage attachment joint
165 Landing/taxi light
166 Engine intakes
167 Ram air to heat exchanger
168 Landing light
169 Flow spoiler
170 Main undercarriage leg pivot fixing

171 Undercarriage well
172 Leading edge ribs
173 Underwing stores pylon
174 Missile launch rails
175 AIM-9 Sidewinder air-to-air missiles
176 Fixed slot
177 External fuel tank
178 Wing bumper
179 Bottom wing skin panel access holes
180 Wing structure
181 Port ESM pod
182 Forward radome

183 Forward high-band aerials
184 Forward low-band aerials
185 Lightning strips
186 Wing de-icing outlet
187 Port navigation light
188 LRU 1
189 Access panels
190 Semi-rigid co-axial cables
191 Aft radome
192 Aft low-band aerials
193 Aft high-band aerials
194 Static dischargers
195 Port aileron
196 Aileron tab
197 Flap outer section
198 Airbrake (upper and lower surfaces)
199 Dump pipes
200 Fuel vent
201 Flap inner section structure

© Pilot Press Limited

The LOCKHEED SR-71 BLACKBIRD

Lockheed SR-71 `Blackbird´

The world's most spectacular aircraft, without equal after two decades, the SR-71 still plays a vital part in the arsenal of the USA. Blackbirds can operate where satellites fail to reach, and often prove more cost-effective in the vital area of reconnaissance.

For 20 years now, the 9th Strategic Reconnaissance Wing (SRW) of the US Air Force has been flying the incredible Lockheed SR-71 'Blackbird' on top-secret worldwide missions. During all that time, Lockheed's exotic thoroughbred has been the world's highest and fastest air-breathing machine. It has never been shot down, despite hundreds of sorties over countries which are (or have been) sufficiently hostile to the US to contemplate such an action, for instance China, Cuba, Egypt, Nicaragua and North Korea.

Flights over the USSR have theoretically been banned since the undertaking given by President Eisenhower in 1960 following the shooting down of Gary Powers' Lockheed U-2. By then, the development of the Lockheed trio of Mach 3 aircraft (A-12, F-12 and SR-71) was well under way. The A-12 first flew in 1962, the YF-12 a year later, and the SR-71 on 23 December 1964. The programme was kept secret until February 1964, when a televised announcement was made by President Johnson.

The A-12 was conceived as a direct replacement for the U-2 in the strategic reconnaissance role. It was a lighter, single-seat forerunner to the SR-71 and was operated by the Central Intelligence Agency until the US Air Force 'Blackbird' became fully operational in 1968. It carried a large camera mounted behind the cockpit as well as electromagnetic-spectrum sensors.

The YF-12 was a spin-off development of a long-range interceptor which was never ordered into production. Its Hughes radar and AIM-47 missiles were later refined into the AWG-9/Phoenix system on the Grumman F-14 Tomcat.

Self-destruct fledgling

A 'mini-Blackbird' was also developed. This was the unmanned D-21 ramjet vehicle which was originally intended to be launched from A-12 'motherships'; the concept was abandoned after a fatal launch accident and the drones were subsequently mated to underwing pylons on two modified Boeing B-52s. The D-21 was designed to fly at even greater speed than the 'Blackbird' over an area of interest before returning to friendly airspace to eject its sensor package into the sea for recovery, the drone itself then self-destructing. There were apparently about 20 test and operational launches before the programme was halted in 1971.

All the development flying for the 'Blackbird' series was carried out at Groom Lake, a remote and secret test site in the Nevada desert. CIA A-12 missions were flown from here, and from Kadena AB, Okinawa. The B-52/D-21 combination also staged out of Eielson AB, Alaska. 'Blackbird' operations finally came out of the closet on 7 January 1966, when the first SR-71 was delivered to Beale AFB, California where new, custom-built facilities awaited it.

View from the tanker: an SR-71A approaches for refuelling. The aircraft has its own special fleet to handle the JP-7 fuel; these tankers are designated KC-135Q, and are operated by the 100th Air Refuelling Wing, deployed around the world for support of SR-71 activities.

Today, the 'Blackbird' still operates from Beale as well as from two permanent overseas detachments at Kadena (Detachment 1, 9th SRW) and Mildenhall (Detachment 4, 9th SRW). The type can also be seen at Lockheed's Palmdale base, where 'Blackbirds' are overhauled. During the South East Asia war, they also operated from Thailand and Korea. Middle East overflights during the 1973 war were staged out of Seymour Johnson AFB, North Carolina.

Although 32 SR-71s were built, only about 10 are in use at any one time: two each at the permanent detachments and five or six at Beale, including a pilot-training SR-71B. In addition, a single aircraft is based at Palmdale for test and development work. Eleven are known to have been written off in accidents, leaving

Bad weather makes the SR-71A look even more sinister. As well as its well-known 'Blackbird' nickname, US servicemen call it the 'Habu', after the Habu pit viper found on Okinawa, from where a detachment operates. The blending of wings, chines and fuselage is more than evident in this shot.

Rudder deflection is shown in this pass by an SR-71 in asymmetric flight, with one afterburner lit. The J58 engines were as radical as the aircraft, being more akin to ramjets at operating speed and altitude. The inlet cone on each engine is controlled by computer, being able to move backwards and forwards for optimum inlet performance.

probably a high-resolution SLAR linked to Elint and Comint receivers. IR and conventional photographic sensors are also in use, including long-range oblique cameras with large focal lengths. The sensors are palletized to fit interchangeably into four underfuselage bays and in the nose. Their output can reportedly be data-linked to ground stations, via satellite uplink if necessary. The 'Blackbird' also carries a state-of-the-art ECM suite.

Each operational mission is planned in meticulous detail. The process begins at least a day ahead with the preparation of sensors and a mission tape, which commands inflight navigation changes and sensor operations. The aircraft preflight takes at least 2½ hours. While the flight crew are suiting-up and pre-breathing the pure oxygen that they will consume throughout the flight, the ground crew are heating up the hydraulic fluid. The crew climb aboard and start engines 40-50 minutes before take-off, and also work through the lengthy check lists.

Moving to the runway, the pilot performs engine trim and other last-minute checks before heading out on a 400-kt (741-km/h;460-mph) climb to 25,000 ft (7620 m). Here a rendezvous is made with a pre-positioned KC-135Q tanker. Once

An aircraft designed for Mach 3+ flight takes a lot of stopping; the SR-71 employs a huge parachute for this task. Once on the ground, the aircraft undergoes a lengthy maintenance session. When the aircraft is cold, the seals shrink to such an extent that the fuel drips out through the tanks and wing skin. Luckily the JP-7 fuel has such a high flashpoint that the danger of fire from the inevitable pool under the aircraft is non-existent.

fully topped up, the 'Blackbird' is ready to climb and accelerate through Mach 1. To enable the high-drag transonic regime to be negotiated quickly, the aircrews perform what they call the 'Dipsy Doodle' manoeuvre. A subsonic climb to 33,000 ft (10060 m) is followed by a 3,000-ft (415-m) descent during which Mach 1 is achieved. The aircraft then resumes its upward course at 450 kts (834 km/h; 518 mph).

Mystery tour

Above 60,000 ft (18290 m) the aircraft is lost from the radar screens as the crew switch off the ATC transponder. Only a select few know where the 'Blackbird' goes next. The USSR is clearly the main target of interest. Mildenhall-based aircraft can easily monitor the Barents and Baltic Sea borders. Sorties from Beale may patrol the periphery of Soviet Asia. 'Blackbirds' from the Kadena detachment regularly overflew China for many years, and they still attract periodic protests for overflying North Korea, which has fired off a number of SA-2 surface-to-air missiles in a vain attempt to down the elusive bird.

A standard mission lasts for 2½ hours, but 5-hour flights involving five refuel-

lings from as many tankers are not uncommon. Such flights demand careful crew planning, because each descent to refuelling height leaves Mach 3 cruise some 320 km (200 miles) away from the contact point. Moreover, the crews must maintain a very specific flight profile on the way down to conserve fuel and keep the inlet/engine combinations working properly.

Once subsonic, the 'Blackbird' handles conventionally, and is agile for such a large aircraft. Upon reaching home base at the end of a mission, pilots often perform one or two circuits and approaches. As well as providing an interesting airshow for onlookers, this procedure allows the airframe to cool down more rapidly so that the groundcrew can quickly move in and service the craft.

Glossary
ATC Air Traffic Control
Comint COMmunications INTelligence
Elint ELectronic INTelligence
IR Infra-Red
RSO Reconnaissance Systems Operator
SLAR Side-Looking Airborne Radar
SRS Strategic Reconnaissance Squadron
SRTS Strategic Reconnaissance Training Squadron
SRW Strategic Reconnaissance Wing

Lockheed SR-71A `Blackbird´
9th Strategic Reconnaissance Wing
Strategic Air Command, US Air Force

Serial number
The only form of identification on the aircraft, since US Air Force titles and insignia were removed in 1982

Rudder
Large, all-moving vertical tail surfaces are needed to counteract the effect of an inlet unstart or engine failure. They are canted inwards to reduce rolling

Power unit
Each rudder power unit moves with the rudder and works against the fixed nacelle. Unique hydraulic systems are used with very high temperature fluid

Leading edge
Temperature here can exceed 427°C (800°F) purely because of kinetic heating in cruising flight. The main wing skins soak at about 303°C

Elevons
Outboard elevons provide roll control; inboard elevons provide pitch control. They do not provide trimming for the aircraft; this is done by pumping fuel forward and aft. An elevon mixer box in the rear fuselage selects the ratios and deflections needed from the inboard and outboard elevons to meet pilot demand

Ejector flaps
These control exhaust airflow and float freely according to engine condition. They are closed on take-off but fully open and nearly white hot at Mach 3

Tertiary doors
These control engine surrounding airflow by opening inwards and admitting fresh air into the nozzle section. They are open at take-off but closed at Mach 3

Engine access
The entire outer wing and outer ha' each engine nacelle fold upwards hinges so that the engine may be worked on or removed

Air data probes
Small pitot probes around the nacelles
measure air data and assist the air-inlet
control system

Stealth
The whole aircraft is designed for
minimal radar reflectivity. The internal
structure forms re-entrant triangles
which 'capture' radar waves and by
repeatedly reflecting them attenuate
them so that there is no reflected wave

J58 engine
The only engine of its kind in the world, a
monster from Pratt & Whitney providing
over 13610 kg (30,000 lb) thrust. The
engine shifts into another cycle at
3220 km/h (2,000 mph), bypassing the
conventional compressor to operate as a
ramjet

Brake parachute housing
This is situated in the top of the fuselage

if of
on

Centrebody bleed louvres
These dump overboard the boundary-
layer air sucked away through the
perforations around the inlet spike

By-pass doors
The first of four sets of doors that fashion
the airflow into and around the engine.
They are closed at high speed unless the
airflow has inadvertently been separated
from the inlet (a phenomenon known as
inlet unstart)

Fuel
There are six large tanks in the fuselage
and wings, but no fuel bladders. The skin
of the aircraft serves as the outer wall of
the tanks. Special high-flashpoint JP-7
fuel is used

about 10 in storage. Aircraft are rotated in and out of storage to equalize flying hours in the fleet.

The appropriately-numbered Strategic Reconnaissance Squadron (SRS) flies this extraordinary two-seat aircraft. Its potential pilots have to have 1,500 hours of jet time, and candidate Reconnaissance Systems Operators (RSOs) must already be well-experienced military navigators. They must pass rigorous physical examinations, searching interviews and background security checks.

The SR-71A's uniquely high speed, altitude and temperature environment make it a complex and demanding aircraft to handle. New pilots are checked out in the Northrop T-38, which has similar handling qualities to the 'Blackbird' at subsonic speeds. They then spend no less than 100 hours in the SR-71 simulator before progressing to the SR-71B trainer, in which they are accompanied by an instructor pilot. RSOs spend even longer in a rear-seat simulator, learning to operate the various reconnaissance sensors as well as the aircraft's unique astro-inertial navigation system. After about eight flights, the trainee pilot is joined in an SR-71A by the trainee RSO, and they fly together from then on as a permanent team, working up to mission-ready status.

Life support system

A small army of support personnel is needed to run the 'Blackbird' operation. The Physiological Support Division looks after the crew's life support system, including the astronaut-type flight suits. The Reconnaissance Technical Squadron looks after the sensors and processes the returned data. A flying training squadron (4029th SRTS) looks after the dozen or more T-38s, which are also used as a proficiency trainer by the wing's operational pilots between their SR-71 flights. Two squadrons of modified Boeing KC-135Q Stratotankers are maintained to refuel the 'Blackbird' with the special JP-7 low-volatility fuel.

The ultimate capability of the SR-71 is still classified. For public consumption, the US Air Force quotes the absolute world speed and altitude records which were gained by 9th SRW machines on 28 July 1976. A speed of 1,904.57 kts (3529.56 km/h; 2,193.17 mph) and sustained height of 85,069 ft (25929 m) were measured on that day.

To attain this remarkable performance, the aircraft was designed essentially as a blended body and delta wing built around two huge Pratt & Whitney engines designated J58. These are rated at around 14742-kg (32,500-lb) thrust in afterburner at sea level. This brute force is harnessed in remarkable fashion by the ingenious inlet, nacelle and ejector design. Many wind-tunnel and flight-test hours were devoted to perfecting this system, which modifies the airflow through the power-plant to suit the wide variety of speeds encountered by complex scheduling of the positions of the inlet spike, ejector flaps and various nacelle-mounted bypass and bleed doors. At Mach 3.2 the engine itself is generating only one-tenth of the total thrust thanks to these devices. They are controlled by an onboard Honeywell computer system which has recently been updated from analog to digital type.

The new system also integrates a number of previously separate computerized controls of the flight regime: this aircraft can be inherently unstable in pitch and yaw. It is mostly flown on autopilot, and even when flown manually an eight-channel stability-augmentation system is kept engaged to smooth out the airframe oscillations.

Since the airframe is subjected to temperatures as high as 500°C (932°F) when cruising, it had to be made of heat-resistant titanium alloys. Nevertheless, allowance still had to be made for expansion, which is why the wing skin has prominent chordwise corrugations, and why the grounded 'Blackbird' leaks copious amounts of fuel: the corrugations smooth out and seal the gaps during flight.

The high-temperature regime demands the use of various other exotic and un-usual materials, ranging from silver-coated tyres to synthetic hydraulic fluid, which goes almost solid below 30°C (86°F).

The long forward fuselage performs a number of aerodynamic functions, and also provides more space for fuel and sensors. Its flat profile helps the 'Blackbird' achieve a low radar cross-section, as does the specially reflective 'iron-ball' black paint that gives the type its nickname. The distinctive all-moving vertical tails are large enough to counteract an asymmetric power situation. Their inward cant reduces the aircraft's rate of roll.

Flexible reconnaissance

But what use is all this wizardry in the age of the all-seeing spy satellite? Expensive as the 'Blackbird' is, it is nevertheless a cheaper, more flexible and more immediately-available method of reconnoitering any new area of interest. Satellites have fixed tracks and orbits which cannot be easily altered and which, moreover, can be determined in advance by the 'other side'. Their lifetime in space is limited, and replacements are costly to launch. Nowadays, they can also be attacked.

The 'Blackbird' suffers from none of these disadvantages. Moreover, even when political considerations preclude its making a direct overflight, its great cruising height enables the onboard sensors to look sideways across a border and still obtain significant data.

The sensor systems are amongst the most closely-held of all 'Blackbird' secrets. All that the USAF will say is that the SR-71A 'is capable of surveying 259000 km² (100,000 square miles) of terrain every hour'. The main sensor is

Destination Baltic Sea, Kola Peninsula or East German border, an SR-71A of Detachment 4, 9th Strategic Reconnaissance Wing, blasts off into typical East Anglian weather from RAF Mildenhall. Following take-off, the aircraft carries out a steep climb to a transitting altitude.

Windshield
The knife-edge windshield is birdproof and made of special high-temperature glasses and plastics laminations. The knife edge reaches 340°C (644°F), one of the hottest parts of the airframe

Pitot tube and air data sensor

Nose sensors
The entire nose is detachable forward of the cockpit so that interchangeable units carrying different sensor combinations may be fitted

Chines
These gain more lift and reduce trim drag as the speed of the aircraft increases. They also improve directional stability and help reduce the aircraft's radar cross-section

ECS
Ahead of the palletized sensor bays, the chines house the high-capacity cockpit environmental control system

Main sensor bays
Four compartments each accept sensors on interchangeable pallets. Equipment can include panoramic and long-range oblique cameras; side-looking radar; infra-red linescan; and Elint/Comint antennae and receivers

Inlet spike
This huge device is hydraulically operated, and progressively retracts into the nacelle once Mach 1.7 is reached in order to correctly position the shock wave. The actuator thrust needed is almost the same as the maximum thrust of the engine

Landing and taxi lights
These are mounted on the steerable nose landing gear

Titanium skin
Ninety-three per cent of the airframe is made of titanium, an expensive and difficult metal with which to work, but highly heat-resistant. The ejector is made of exotic Hastelloy and Rene 41 alloys

Lockheed SR-71 'Blackbird'

A thirsty Blackbird meets up with its accommodating tanker for a dawn refreshment.

Performance: approximate

Maximum speed, Mach 3+ at 78,740 ft (24000 m), or more than 1,737 kts	3220 km/h	2,000 mph	Landing distance at maximum landing weight	1097 m	(3,600 ft)	
Mach 2+ at 30,000 ft (9144 m), or more than 1,146 kts	2124 km/h	1,320 mph	Operational radius, typical Range, Mach 3 at 78,740 ft (24000 m) without inflight refuelling	1931 km 4798 km	(1,200 miles) (2,981 miles)	
Landing speed 150 kts	278 km/h	173 mph	Maximum endurance, Mach 3			
Operational ceiling more than	24000 m	(78,740 ft)	at 78,740 ft (24000 m)			
Take-off distance at 63503-kg (140,000-lb) gross weight	1646 m	(5,400 ft)	without inflight refuelling		1 hour 30 minutes	

Speed at high altitude

Lockheed SR-71A Mach 3.5
MiG-25R 'Foxbat-B/D' Mach 3.2
MiG-25 'Foxbat-A' Mach 2.83
F-15C Eagle Mach 2.5+
Fu-15 'Flagon' Mach 2.5
MiG-23 'Flogger'   Mach 2.35
F-14A Tomcat   Mach 2.34
Lockheed U-2R 380kt

Range

Lockheed SR-71A 5,300+ km
Lockheed U-2R 4,830km
F-15C Eagle 4,630km
F14A Tomcat 3,220km
MiG-25 'Foxbat-A'   2,900km
MiG-25R   'Foxbat B/D' 2,500km E
MiG-23   'Flogger' 2,500km
FU-15   'Flagon' 1,500km E

Operational ceiling

Lockheed U-2R 90,000 ft
MiG-25R 'Foxbat-B/D' 85,000+ ft
MiG-25 'Foxbat-A' 80,000 ft
F-15C Eagle 70,000+ ft
FU-15 'Flagon' 65,000 ft
Lockheed SR-71A 85,000+ ft
MiG-23 'Flogger' 61,000 ft

Lockheed SR-71A Blackbird cutaway drawing key

1 Pitot tube
2 Air data probe
3 Radar warning antennae
4 Nose mission equipment bay
5 Panoramic camera aperture
6 Detachable nose cone joint frame
7 Cockpit front pressure bulkhead
8 Rudder pedals
9 Control column
10 Instrument panel
11 Instrument panel shroud
12 Knife-edged windscreen panels
13 Upward hinged cockpit canopy covers
14 Ejection seat headrest
15 Canopy actuator
16 Pilot's Lockheed 'zero-zero' ejection seat
17 Engine throttle levers
18 Side console panel
19 Fuselage chine close-pitched frame construction
20 Liquid oxygen converters (2)
21 Side console panel
22 Reconnaissance Systems Officer's (RSO) instrument display
23 Cockpit rear pressure bulkhead
24 RSO's Lockheed 'zero-zero' ejection seat
25 Canopy hinge point
26 SR-71B dual control trainer variant, nose profile
27 Raised instructor's rear cockpit
28 Astro navigation star tracker
29 Navigation and communications systems electronic equipment
30 Nosewheel bay
31 Nose undercarriage pivot fixing
32 Landing and taxiing lamps
33 Twin nosewheels (forward retracting)
34 Hydraulic retraction jack
35 Cockpit environmental system equipment bay
36 Air refuelling receptacle (open)
37 Fuselage upper longeron
38 Forward fuselage frame construction
39 Forward fuselage integral fuel tanks

Left: Two aircraft (64-17956 and probably 64-17957) were modified on the production line to SR-71B standard with an extra cockpit for conversion training. Aircraft '57 crashed at Beale in 1968 and was replaced by the SR-71C (64-17981), built up from an old YF-12 rear fuselage and various factory spares, and affectionately dubbed 'The Bastard'. This aircraft has since been withdrawn from service, leaving '56 as the sole two-seater.

Main tyres
These retract inwards to a special compartment surrounded by fuel in order to insulate them from the heat. However, it is still necessary to inflate them with nitrogen and impregnate them with powdered aluminium.

Fuselage fuel
This is the last to be used as it heats up less rapidly than the fuel in the thin wings. Total capacity is over 45000 litres (9,900 gal), but fuel enters the engine at 130 lb/sq in at 316°C (600°F).

Skin corrugations
These chordwise indentations are smoothed out by airframe expansion as the airframe heats up in flight. Surface temperatures reach 260°C (500°F) over much of the airframe and 510°C (950°F) around the engines, the skin heating up much faster than the heavy internal structure.

Crew
Separate cockpits house pilot and reconnaissance systems operator (RSO); there are no flight controls in the rear cockpit, where the RSO is responsible for navigation and sensor systems.

Star tracker
A unique and extremely accurate astro-inertial system gives the aircraft complete independence from ground-based aids. The tracker is slaved to a chronometer and pre-programmed to search for more than 50 stars held in a 'catalogue'.

Inflight-refuelling receptacle
This is compatible with the hi-speed boom of the special KC-135Q tankers

Blue-black paint
Specially formulated to assist in the irradiation of heat from the aircraft's skin, it also helps reduce its radar signature by transmitting electric charges between billions of microscopic iron balls. At cruising speed and altitude, it changes colour to blue

Wings

	16.94 m	(55 ft 7 in)
	167.22 m²	(1,800.0 sq ft)

Fuselage and tail unit

...th overall	32.74 m	(107 ft 5 in)
...ht overall	5.64 m	(18 ft 6 in)

Landing gear

Wheelbase	10.36 m	(34 ft 0 in)
Wheel track	5.18 m	(17 ft 0 in)

Weights (estimated)

Empty	27216 kg	(60,000 lb)
Maximum take-off	65771 kg	(145,000 lb)
Fuel, maximum internal more than	36287 kg	(80,000 lb)

Lockheed SR-71 variants

A-12: twelfth design from the Lockheed drawing boards, and the one which was given the go-ahead by the CIA; single-seat 17237-kg (38,000-lb) aircraft; 13 built, including one two-seat trainer; can be best distinguished from SR-71 by tapering of fuselage chine to a pointed nose

M-12: adaptation of the A-12 to carry and launch the D-21 drone, carrying a second crew member for that purpose; two built

YF-12A: long-range interceptor version with nose-mounted radar (a distinguishing feature) and missiles in fuselage bays; three built for USAF tests; two later used by NASA, although one crashed

YF-12C: an SR-71A which was provided to NASA following the crash of one of its YF-12As

SR-71A: operational two-seat reconnaissance aircraft; 29 built

SR-71B: dual-control trainer with raised second cockpit; 2 built

SR-71C: hybrid dual-control trainer built from parts following the loss of one SR-71B

Lockheed SR-71 in service

This list shows the status of each SR-71 built

64-17950 SR-71A written off Apr 1969
64-17951 SR-71A transferred to NASA as YF-12C 06937; now in store; it has long been thought that this was an SR-71B, but it is likely the aircraft was 17957
64-17952 SR-71A written off Jan 1966
64-17953 SR-71A written off Jan 1967
64-17954 SR-71A written off Feb 1966
64-17955 SR-71A Lockheed test aircraft; based at Palmdale; current
64-17956 SR-71B 9th SRW; current
64-17957 probable SR-71B written off Jan 1968
64-17958 SR-71A 9th SRW; current
64-17959 SR-71A Lockheed test aircraft; stored(?)
64-17960 SR-71A 9th SRW; current
64-17961 SR-71A 9th SRW; stored(?)
64-17962 SR-71A 9th SRW; current
64-17963 SR-71A 9th SRW;
64-17964 SR-71A 9th SRW; current
64-17965 SR-71A written off Oct 1967(?)
64-17966 SR-71A written off Apr 1967(?)
64-17967 SR-71A 9th SRW; current
64-17968 SR-71A 9th SRW; stored(?)
64-17969 SR-71A written off 1970(?)
64-17970 SR-71A written off June 1970
64-17971 SR-71A 9th SRW; current
64-17972 SR-71A 9th SRW; current
64-17973 SR-71A 9th SRW; current
64-17974 SR-71A 9th SRW; current
64-17975 SR-71A 9th SRW; current
64-17976 SR-71A 9th SRW; current
64-17977 SR-71A written off Oct 1968
64-17978 SR-71A written off May 1973
64-17979 SR-71A 9th SRW; current
64-17980 SR-71A 9th SRW; current
64-17981 SR-71C 9th SRW; stored

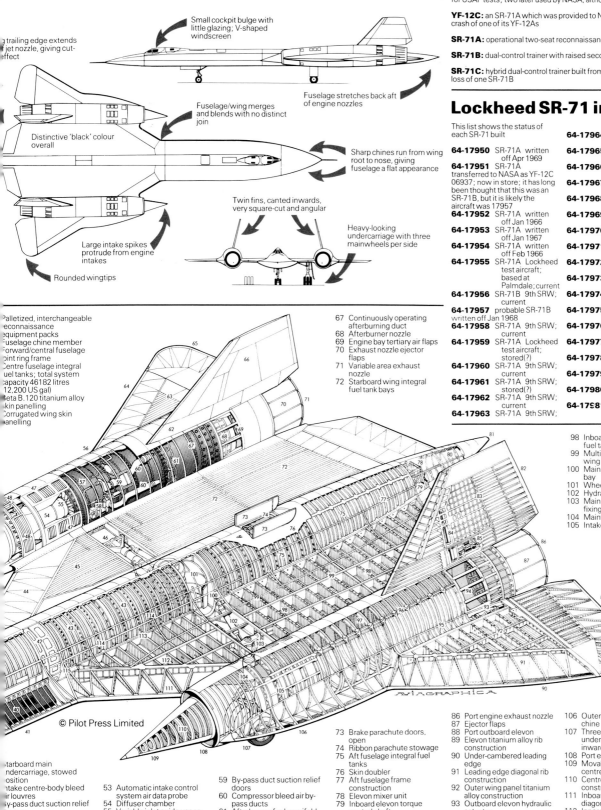

Small cockpit bulge with little glazing; V-shaped windscreen

...g trailing edge extends ...f jet nozzle, giving cut-...effect

Fuselage/wing merges and blends with no distinct join

Fuselage stretches back aft of engine nozzles

Distinctive 'black' colour overall

Sharp chines run from wing root to nose, giving fuselage a flat appearance

Twin fins, canted inwards, very square-cut and angular

Large intake spikes protrude from engine intakes

Heavy-looking undercarriage with three mainwheels per side

Rounded wingtips

...Palletized, interchangeable ...reconnaissance ...equipment packs
...Fuselage chine member
...Forward/central fuselage ...oint ring frame
...Centre fuselage integral ...fuel tanks; total system ...capacity 46182 litres ...(12,200 US gal)
...Beta B.120 titanium alloy ...skin panelling
...Corrugated wing skin ...panelling

67 Continuously operating afterburning duct
68 Afterburner nozzle
69 Engine bay tertiary air flaps
70 Exhaust nozzle ejector flaps
71 Variable area exhaust nozzle
72 Starboard wing integral fuel tank bays

98 Inboard wing panel integral fuel tank bays
99 Multi-spar titanium alloy wing construction
100 Main undercarriage wheel bay
101 Wheel bay heat shield
102 Hydraulic retraction jack
103 Main undercarriage pivot fixing
104 Mainwheel leg strut
105 Intake duct framing

© Pilot Press Limited

AVIAGRAPHICA

...starboard main ...undercarriage, stowed ...osition
...ntake centre-body bleed ...ir louvres
...y-pass duct suction relief ...ouvres
...tarboard engine air intake
...Movable intake conical ...entre-body
...entre-body retracted ...high speed) position
...oundary layer bleed air ...oles

53 Automatic intake control system air data probe
54 Diffuser chamber
55 Variable inlet guide vanes
56 Hinged engine cowling/ outer wing panel
57 Pratt & Whitney JT11D-20B (J58) single spool turbo-ramjet engine
58 Engine accessory equipment
59 By-pass duct suction relief doors
60 Compressor bleed air by-pass ducts
61 Afterburner fuel manifold
62 Tailfin fixed root section
63 Starboard outer wing panel
64 Under-cambered leading edge
65 Outboard, roll control, elevon
66 All-moving starboard fin

73 Brake parachute doors, open
74 Ribbon parachute stowage
75 Aft fuselage integral fuel tanks
76 Skin doubler
77 Aft fuselage frame construction
78 Elevon mixer unit
79 Inboard elevon torque control shaft
80 Tailcone
81 Fuel vent
82 Port all-moving fin
83 Fin rib construction
84 Torque shaft hinge mounting
85 Fin hydraulic actuator

86 Port engine exhaust nozzle
87 Ejector flaps
88 Port outboard elevon
89 Elevon titanium alloy rib construction
90 Under-cambered leading edge
91 Leading edge diagonal rib construction
92 Outer wing panel titanium alloy construction
93 Outboard elevon hydraulic actuator
94 Engine bay tertiary air flaps
95 Engine nacelle/outer wing panel integral construction
96 Engine cowling/wing panel hinge axis
97 Port nacelle ring frame construction

106 Outer wing panel/nacelle chine
107 Three-wheel main undercarriage bogie, inward retracting
108 Port engine air intake
109 Movable intake conical centre-body
110 Centre-body frame construction
111 Inboard leading edge diagonal rib construction
112 Inner wing panel integral fuel tank
113 Wing root/fuselage attachment root rib
114 Close-pitched fuselage titanium alloy frames
115 Wing/fuselage chine blended fairing panels

The GRUMMAN
E-2 HAWKEYE

Hawkeye: Seaborne Sentinel

No matter how impressive the strike power within the modern carrier air wing, effective over-the-horizon AEW and co-ordination of operations are essential if the force is to maintain its optimum capability. The Grumman Hawkeye shoulders these vital responsibilities, ranging far out from the carrier as the airborne 'eyes of the Fleet'.

Originally gaining operational status aboard the USS *Kitty Hawk* (CVA-63) off the coast of Vietnam in autumn 1965, Grumman's distinctive E-2 Hawkeye recently entered its third decade of service and looks set to retain its present position as the US Navy's primary airborne early warning and control platform until well into the next century.

By today's standards, the aircraft that entered service during the mid-1960s were somewhat primitive although at that time they represented a fantastic improvement over the same manufacturer's 1950s-vintage E-1B Tracer. Since then, the Hawkeye has been the subject of considerable updating, taking full advantage of the microchip age to remain an integral part of modern carrierborne aviation. It says much for the basic soundness of the design that it has been able to incorporate without undue difficulty and in what is essentially a most compact airframe the latest developments in AEW technology.

The initial variant of the Hawkeye was the E-2A, production of this model totalling 59 aircraft plus three prototypes, the first of which made its maiden flight on 21 October 1960. This was essentially just an aerodynamic test-bed, and it was not until 19 April 1961 that a full-system aircraft took to the air. Not surprisingly in view of system complexity, research and development took time, and deliveries to fleet units finally got under way in January 1964 when VAW-11 of the Pacific Fleet at North Island, California began to receive the Hawkeye. Subsequently, the E-2A was also assigned to VAW-12 of the Atlantic Fleet at Norfolk, Virginia with effect from February 1966.

Mission-related equipment employed by this original model included General Electric APS-96 search radar, its antenna housed in a massive 7.31-m (24-ft) diameter rotodome carried above the centre fuselage section, this being a distinctive and ever-present feature of succeeding variants of the Hawkeye. Less obvious, but no less vital to the AEW task, was the impressive array of computerized processing equipment, most of which was accommodated in the rather cramped confines of the cabin and all of which was

Though it may seem out of place among the sleek, supersonic jets of modern-day aviation, the Hawkeye, with its deep fuselage, large propellers and ungainly rotodome, is every bit as effective in its intended roles.

necessary in order to present data in a coherent form to the three systems operators. Other members of the five-man crew comprised a pilot and co-pilot, and despite the vast improvements made since the type first flew the Hawkeye still relies on just a five-man crew.

The first major attempt at enhancing capability occurred in the late 1960s, this mainly centering around the on-board computer package. When the Hawkeye made its debut, computer technology dictated the adoption of a system which frequently required physical modi-

A Hawkeye is about to engage one of the trap wires traversing the deck of an aircraft carrier. Prominent in this view is the A-frame arrester hook beneath the rear fuselage.

fication, this often being a most complex process and one which tended to limit overall capability. The advent of the far more flexible digital computer permitted system revision by the means of programme changes, and the Navy was not slow to take advantage of this, initiating an update programme which entailed installation of a Litton L-304 general-purpose computer, the resulting aircraft being known as the E-2B and flying for the first time on 20 February 1969. However, rather than purchase new-build Hawkeyes, it was decided to retrofit this system to existing E-2As, 52 aircraft being brought to E-2B standard by the time this programme terminated in December 1971.

Even as the E-2B project was getting under way, work on a rather more sophisticated version of the Hawkeye was also beginning, this eventually resulting in the appearance of a variant known as the E-2C. Arising mainly from the desire to enhance overland target-detection capability, the E-2C introduced a completely new radar, development of which began as early as 1964. Extensive evaluation of the General Electric APS-111 radar aboard an E-2A between June 1965 and October 1967 proved sufficiently encouraging to warrant further development of the Hawkeye, and this continuing evolutionary process eventually culminated in the E-2C, funding being released for a couple of prototypes in March 1968, these being produced by the simple expedient of modifying two former E-2A test specimens.

Increased capacity

The E-2C made its maiden flight on 20 January 1971, initial evaluation of the pair of prototypes revealing significant increases in overall capability. This led directly to a decision to proceed with the E-2C, production of which began in mid-1971. By then the radar had been further improved into the APS-120, and it was this unit which was installed in production examples, the first of which made its initial flight on 23 September 1972.

Deliveries to the Navy began in December of that year, initially to Atlantic Fleet squadrons stationed at Norfolk, Virginia and the E-2C duly made its operational debut with VAW-123 in September 1974 when it sailed for the Mediterranean aboard the USS *Saratoga* (CV-60). Pacific Fleet units had to wait quite some time before they also began to convert from the considerably less capable E-2B, a process which got under way shortly before the end of the decade.

Subsequent updating of the radar

system led to the appearance of an improved variant of the E-2C in 1976, this utilizing the APS-125 which was somewhat more flexible in that it was able to perform the detection, acquisition and tracking functions automatically while also being more resistant to electronic jamming. Introduced on the 34th production example of the E-2C, the APS-125 radar was retrospectively fitted to earlier aircraft but is itself now in process of being supplanted, the latest examples of the E-2C incorporating General Electric's APS-138 advanced radar processing system, and it seems likely that this will also be retrofitted to older aircraft.

Key features of the newest radar are greater range: detection, identification and tracking can be accomplished over land and sea at ranges approaching 480 km (300 miles) when operating at an altitude of about 30,000 ft (9145 m), and the system also has an expanded computer 'memory', and is able to accomplish triangulation automatically. Passive detection capability has also been greatly enhanced, the E-2C being able to recognize and classify enemy electronic emissions at ranges well in excess of that of the onboard radar.

Currently operational with a total of 15 front-line US Navy squadrons as well as two Reserve Force units, the Hawkeye has the ability to keep pace with developments in the radar and computer fields, and this has resulted in a tremendous increase in the scope of the missions it performs. The type is truly unique in being the only aircraft ever designed from the outset to undertake the task of airborne early warning and control.

Increasing capability has brought with it a commensurate increase in workload, but the advent of new automated processing systems and other mission-related equipment has in many ways simplified the task of the three system operators by

With an operational career on the Hawkeye dating back to the mid-1960s, VAW-114 'Hormel Hawgs' has a record second to none on this AEW workhorse. A 14-year accident-free period has enhanced the E-2's reputation.

freeing them from the necessity to perform routine activities. Thus they are now able to devote virtually all of their attention to monitoring the developing tactical situation which is presented by means of the Hazeltine APA-172 control indicator group in the cabin of the Hawkeye, where the combat information centre officer, the air control officer and the radar operator work.

Each of the three crew stations is identical, these featuring a 25.4-cm (10-in) diameter main radar display screen and a 12.7-cm (5-in) alphanumeric auxiliary display, the former providing data pertaining to target tracks. Independent controls at each station enable crew members to select information relevant to their respective responsibilities, data which can be presented including target symbols, velocity vectors, disposition of friendly fighter forces, surface task forces and waypoints, it being possible for the E-2C to track automatically more than 250 targets while simultaneously controlling some 30 airborne interceptions. Data inputs and requests for information may be made either by means of an alphanumeric keyboard or by light-pen, the latter, for instance, being used to 'hook' a specific F-14 Tomcat interceptor to a specific target, information relating to that target then being automatically fed to the Tomcat's AWG-9 weapons control system by means of a data-link.

Delivery of four Hawkeyes to Israel during 1981 added to an already formidable air force inventory. There can be no doubt that the quartet have proved invaluable in this nation's conflicts with its neighbours, though publicity is rarely given.

Rotodome
The Randtron AN/APA-171 rotodome (radar and IFF antennae) is 7.3 m (24 ft) in diameter and revolves at 6 rpm. The Yagi-type radar aerial (antenna) arrays within the rotodome are interfaced to the onboard avionics suite

Radiator
A large ducted radiator with a ram-air inlet above the forward fuselage contains a Freon vapour cycle cooling radiator. This system removes the large heat load generated by the main radar, and is powerful enough to cool the radar while the aircraft is stationary

Rotodome pylon
The four-legged rotodome pylon has a retractable upper section containing a hydraulic jack which raises the rotodome to the flight position (as shown), or lowers it slightly to facilitate stowage of the Hawkeye in carrier hangar space

RESCUE

VAW123

DANGER → ← DANGER

RESCUE

Nosewheel unit
A forged strut at the rear of the nosewheel oleo transmits the 90-ton pull of the nose gear when catapulting the aircraft into the air. The nose gear is steerable, and for each catapult launch is automatically compressed to reduce the stress on the gear, eliminate wing lift during the catapult stroke and store energy to thrust the nose upwards at the end of the launch

Crew entry
The main crew access door hinges downwards, revealing integral crew access steps

Engine inlets
The engine air inlets have an internal duct which takes air up past the propeller gearbox to the Allison T56-A-425 turboprops further back inside the cowling. The lower inlet provides access to the oil cooling radiator

Wing structure
Cantilever high wing of all-metal construction incorporates a hinged leading edge which provides access to flying and engine controls. The outer panels fold rearwards about a skewed-axis hinge to lie parallel with the rear fuselage, thus greatly reducing the hangar space required by the Hawkeye

Ailerons and flaps
Long-span ailerons and Fowler flaps are power-operated (as are all the power surfaces) with the ailerons automatically drooped when the flaps are lowered

Propellers
Hamilton Standard four-blade, reverse pitch, fully-feathering, constant-speed propellers have composite blades which are foam-filled and incorporate a steel spar within the glassfibre shell. Electric anti-icing units are present in the spinners and blades

Crew distribution
Crew accommodation consists of the pilot and co-pilot on the flight-deck, while the combat information centre officer, air control officer and radar operator occupy the AIDS section of the main cabin

PDS receivers (forward-facing)
Forward-facing receivers for passive defence are housed in the nose as part of the Litton AN/ALR-73 Passive Defence System (PDS). These alert the crew to the presence of electro-magnetic emitters in hostile territory at up to twice the detection range of the radar system, thus significantly expanding Hawkeye's surveillance capability

Catapult launch bar
The nosewheel-mounted catapult launch bar is made of high-tensile steel, with the ability to launch the fully-laden Hawkeye into the air at take-off speed even if the mainwheel brakes are locked on. The launch bar is shown in the carrier deck high-taxi position

Grumman E-2 Hawkeye

Processing of data generated by the radar and other E-2C sub-systems is handled by a pair of Litton L-304 computers, these performing the necessary calculations in real time, thus providing crew members with a continuously updated picture of the developing tactical scene. As already noted, data-link facilities permit information to be rapidly transmitted to friendly interceptors or to ground- or sea-based combat control centres.

As far as the Navy is concerned, the primary tasks of the Hawkeye are those of area and on-station search, and when operating at sea it is usual for the E-2C to launch first so as to be aloft when other carrierborne elements get off the carrier. Since the Navy routinely employs a cyclical pattern of operations, normally launching and recovering waves of aircraft at 105-minute intervals, the E-2C's good endurance characteristics usually result in its performing double- or, on occasion, treble-cycle sorties, thus permitting it to spend a considerable amount of time on station.

Operating at an altitude of around 30,000 ft when employed in the on-station search mode, the E-2C normally flies out to a distance of about 370 km (230 miles) from the parent carrier before initiating a constant orbit, gaining altitude steadily as fuel burns off. In both area and on-station search tasks, the flaps are set at 10° deflection to provide the optimum 3° radar scanning attitude. The on-station Hawkeye maintains constant communication with the parent carrier and other aircraft operating in the area.

Mission variety

Although employed mainly to augment the radar coverage of the aircraft-carrier, the Hawkeye can of course readily undertake a variety of other roles, such as exercising control over strike forces and serving as a communications link between strike aircraft and the combat information centre on the parent carrier. Air traffic control, monitoring of the area around the carrier task group for sea and air threats, and management of inflight-refuelling rendezvous are other missions which are often accomplished, while in

Vietnam it was by no means unknown for the E-2 to observe enemy air space for signs of North Vietnamese MiG interceptors, this aspect extending to control of McDonnell Douglas F-4 Phantoms and Vought F-8 Crusaders engaged in furnishing combat air patrol cover to strike elements, personnel on the E-2 vectoring CAP aircraft into advantageous positions from which to initiate an attack with either Sparrow or Sidewinder air-to-air missiles. Today, of course, the principal Navy fighter is Grumman's Tomcat and the means of control rather more sophisticated, but the same basic task is still undertaken.

The Hawkeye can also be employed on duties of a less militaristic nature. For instance, the excellent resolution of the radar picture over both land and sea readily lends itself to use in the search and rescue task, while the ability to detect small objects (it has been claimed that the radar can observe cruise missile-sized targets at ranges exceeding 185 km; 100 miles) makes it an ideal tool in curtailing drug trafficking. This is a job which it has undertaken with some success in the recent past, Navy Hawkeye squadrons working in close co-operation with narcotics agents in attempting to stem the flow of such illegal substances from Latin American countries. Another mission undertaken by the E-2C has been that of augmenting radar coverage of Space Shuttle launches from Cape Canaveral.

Production of the E-2C is continuing at

Space is always at a premium aboard aircraft carriers, and the Hawkeye, like most naval aircraft, has a wing-fold mechanism which dramatically reduces the area taken up by the aircraft both on deck and in the hangars.

a fairly modest rate, the US Navy having taken delivery of 82 of the planned 102 examples by the end of 1984, whilst the Hawkeye has also enjoyed some success on the world export market in recent years.

Israel's Defence Force/Air Force was the first overseas customer, acquiring four E-2Cs in the late 1970s, while Japan has purchased eight, all of these now being in service. In addition, Egypt has ordered the E-2C and seems certain to obtain at least four, an identical number being due for delivery to Singapore. However, despite expressing considerable interest in Grumman's AEW aircraft at one time, French enthusiasm ran into political troubles and failed to result in any orders.

Glossary
AEW Airborne Early Warning
CAP Combat Air Patrol

With engines wound up to full power and the nosewheel tie-bar securely locked into the deck catapult launch shuttle, a Hawkeye awaits the final 'go' signal from the deck launch officer before being hurtled into the air for another mission.

E-2 Hawkeye in service units and example aircraft

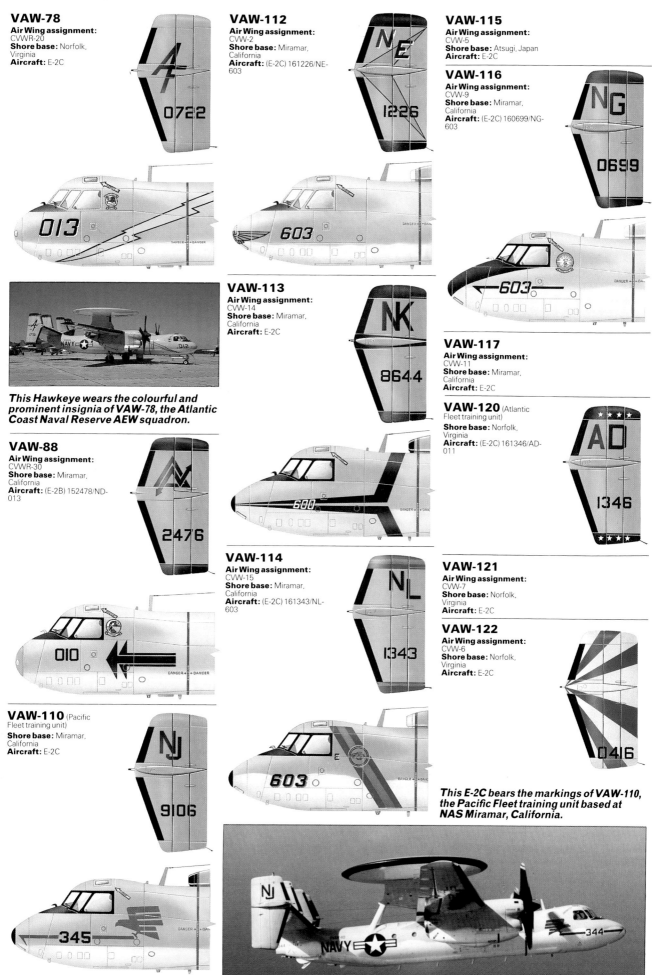

VAW-78
Air Wing assignment: CVWR-20
Shore base: Norfolk, Virginia
Aircraft: E-2C

This Hawkeye wears the colourful and prominent insignia of VAW-78, the Atlantic Coast Naval Reserve AEW squadron.

VAW-88
Air Wing assignment: CVWR-30
Shore base: Miramar, California
Aircraft: (E-2B) 152478/ND-013

VAW-110 (Pacific Fleet training unit)
Shore base: Miramar, California
Aircraft: E-2C

VAW-112
Air Wing assignment: CVW-2
Shore base: Miramar, California
Aircraft: (E-2C) 161226/NE-603

VAW-113
Air Wing assignment: CVW-14
Shore base: Miramar, California
Aircraft: E-2C

VAW-114
Air Wing assignment: CVW-15
Shore base: Miramar, California
Aircraft: (E-2C) 161343/NL-603

VAW-115
Air Wing assignment: CVW-5
Shore base: Atsugi, Japan
Aircraft: E-2C

VAW-116
Air Wing assignment: CVW-9
Shore base: Miramar, California
Aircraft: (E-2C) 160699/NG-603

VAW-117
Air Wing assignment: CVW-11
Shore base: Miramar, California
Aircraft: E-2C

VAW-120 (Atlantic Fleet training unit)
Shore base: Norfolk, Virginia
Aircraft: (E-2C) 161346/AD-011

VAW-121
Air Wing assignment: CVW-7
Shore base: Norfolk, Virginia
Aircraft: E-2C

VAW-122
Air Wing assignment: CVW-6
Shore base: Norfolk, Virginia
Aircraft: E-2C

This E-2C bears the markings of VAW-110, the Pacific Fleet training unit based at NAS Miramar, California.

Wing anchor point
An anchor point is fitted to each outer fin
for the folding jury strut mechanism
inside the underside of the outer wings.
This holds the folded wings firmly
locked, even on a rolling ship

Tail units
The four tailfins and three double-hinged
rudders incorporate an 11° inward cant
while at 90° to the horizontal tailplanes.
Structure above the tailplanes is of
glassfibre, which reduces radar
reflection

PDS receivers (lateral)
Fin-mounted sideways-facing aerial
(antenna) is for the Passive Defence
System (PDS), covering the lateral
sector not 'seen' by the nose and tail-
mounted PDS sensors

Grumman E-2C Hawkeye
VAW-123, USS America
US Navy

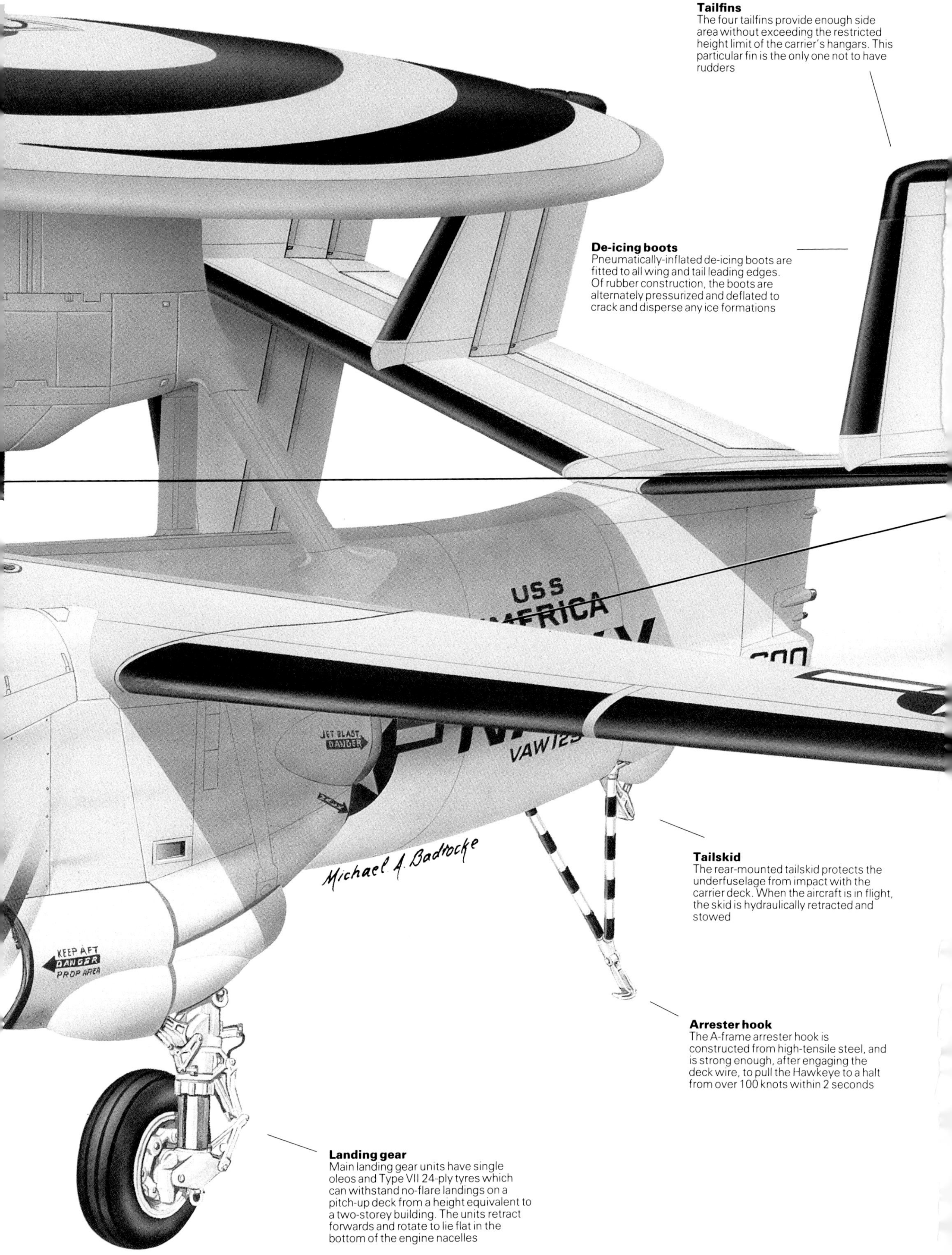

Tailfins
The four tailfins provide enough side area without exceeding the restricted height limit of the carrier's hangars. This particular fin is the only one not to have rudders

De-icing boots
Pneumatically-inflated de-icing boots are fitted to all wing and tail leading edges. Of rubber construction, the boots are alternately pressurized and deflated to crack and disperse any ice formations

USS AMERICA
600
NAVY
VAW125

JET BLAST
DANGER

Michael A. Badrocke

KEEP AFT
DANGER
PROP AREA

Tailskid
The rear-mounted tailskid protects the underfuselage from impact with the carrier deck. When the aircraft is in flight, the skid is hydraulically retracted and stowed

Arrester hook
The A-frame arrester hook is constructed from high-tensile steel, and is strong enough, after engaging the deck wire, to pull the Hawkeye to a halt from over 100 knots within 2 seconds

Landing gear
Main landing gear units have single oleos and Type VII 24-ply tyres which can withstand no-flare landings on a pitch-up deck from a height equivalent to a two-storey building. The units retract forwards and rotate to lie flat in the bottom of the engine nacelles

VAW-123
Air Wing assignment: CVW-1
Shore base: Norfolk, Virginia
Aircraft: (E-2C) 161098/AB-601

VAW-126
Air Wing assignment: CVW-3
Shore base: Norfolk, Virginia
Aircraft: (E-2C) 161701/AC-602

Japanese Air Self-Defence Force
601 Hikotai
Base: Misawa AB
Aircraft: (E-2C) 34-3451, 34-3452, 34-3454

This Hawkeye of VAW-123 carries 'Screwtops', the squadron badge, with the prominent eye seemingly appropriately positioned atop the radar housing.

VAW-127
Air Wing assignment: CVW-13
Shore base: Norfolk, Virginia
Aircraft: (E-2C) 160987/AK-603

Israel Defence Force/Air Force
Four E-2Cs were delivered during 1981, '946' having since been positively identified

VAW-124
Air Wing assignment: CVW-8
Shore base: Norfolk, Virginia
Aircraft: (E-2C) 161552/AJ-600

VAW-125
Air Wing assignment: CVW-17
Shore base: Norfolk, Virginia
Aircraft: (E-2C) 161550/AA-600

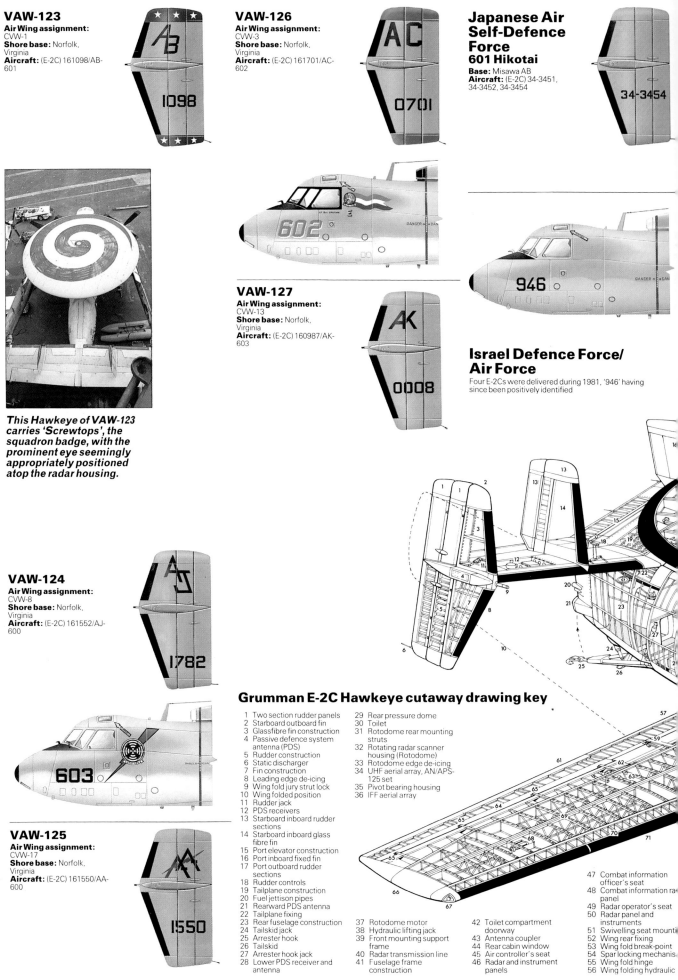

Grumman E-2C Hawkeye cutaway drawing key

1 Two section rudder panels
2 Starboard outboard fin
3 Glassfibre fin construction
4 Passive defence system antenna (PDS)
5 Rudder construction
6 Static discharger
7 Fin construction
8 Leading edge de-icing
9 Wing fold jury strut lock
10 Wing folded position
11 Rudder jack
12 PDS receivers
13 Starboard inboard rudder sections
14 Starboard inboard glass fibre fin
15 Port elevator construction
16 Port inboard fixed fin
17 Port outboard rudder sections
18 Rudder controls
19 Tailplane construction
20 Fuel jettison pipes
21 Rearward PDS antenna
22 Tailplane fixing
23 Rear fuselage construction
24 Tailskid jack
25 Arrester hook
26 Tailskid
27 Arrester hook jack
28 Lower PDS receiver and antenna

29 Rear pressure dome
30 Toilet
31 Rotodome rear mounting struts
32 Rotating radar scanner housing (Rotodome)
33 Rotodome edge de-icing
34 UHF aerial array, AN/APS-125 set
35 Pivot bearing housing
36 IFF aerial array

37 Rotodome motor
38 Hydraulic lifting jack
39 Front mounting support frame
40 Radar transmission line
41 Fuselage frame construction

42 Toilet compartment doorway
43 Antenna coupler
44 Rear cabin window
45 Air controller's seat
46 Radar and instrument panels

47 Combat information officer's seat
48 Combat information radar panel
49 Radar operator's seat
50 Radar panel and instruments
51 Swivelling seat mounti
52 Wing rear fixing
53 Wing fold break-point
54 Spar locking mechanis
55 Wing fold hinge
56 Wing folding hydraulic

Hawkeye of the Japanese Air Self-Defence
ce (JASDF), one of eight examples
rently in service with this nation.

Starboard outboard flap
Flap construction
Flap guide rails
Flap drive motors and shaft
Starboard drooping aileron
Flap to drooping aileron
connection
Aileron jack
Aileron construction
Aileron hinges
Starboard wing tip
Navigation light
ury strut locking
mechanism

69 Outer wing construction
70 Leading edge construction
71 Leading edge de-icing
72 Lattice rib construction
73 Engine exhaust pipe fairing
74 Front spar locking
mechanism
75 Main undercarriage leg
76 Undercarriage leg door
77 Single mainwheel
78 Mainwheel door
79 Engine pylon construction
80 Engine mounting strut
81 Allison T56-A-425 engine
82 Oil cooler
83 Oil cooler intake
84 Engine intake

85 Hamilton Standard four-
bladed propeller
86 Gearbox drive shaft
87 Propeller mechanism
88 Cooling air intake
89 Engine-to-propeller
gearbox
90 Oil tank, usable capacity
9.25 US gal (35 litres) each
nacelle
91 Bleed air supply duct
92 Vapour cycle air
conditioning plant
93 Wing front fixing
94 Computer bank
95 Wing centre rib joint
96 Inboard wing section fuel
tank, capacity 912 US gal
(3452 litres) each wing
97 Lattice rib construction
98 Port inboard flap
99 Wing fold hinge
100 Wing fold joint line
101 Sloping hinge rib
102 Port outboard flap

103 Aileron jack
104 Port aileron
105 Port outer wing panel
106 Port wing tip
107 Navigation light
108 Leading edge de-icing
109 Aileron control cable
mechanism
110 Engine mounting strut
attachment
111 Engine-to-propeller
gearbox
112 Propeller spinner fairing
113 Hamilton Standard four-
bladed propeller
114 Engine intake
115 Gearbox drive shaft
116 Port engine
117 Fuel system piping
118 Cooling air intake
119 Vapour cycle system
radiator
120 Cooling air outlet duct
121 Radar processor
122 IFF processor
123 Radar transmission line
124 Rangefinder amplifier
125 Port side entry doorway
126 Equipment cooling air duct
127 Port side equipment racks

128 Starboard side radio and
electronics racks
129 Radar duplexer
130 Electronics boxes
131 Forward fuselage frame
construction
132 Lower electronics racks
133 Scrambler boxes
134 Navigation equipment
135 Cockpit air conditioning
duct
136 Cockpit doorway
137 Electrical system junction
box
138 Air conditioning diffuser
139 Signal equipment
140 Cockpit floor level
141 Co-pilot's seat
142 Parachute stowage
143 Pilot's seat
144 Headrest
145 Cockpit roof window
146 Cockpit roof construction
147 Instrument panel shroud
148 Windscreen wiper
149 Bulged cockpit side
window

150 Instrument panel
151 Control column
152 Nose undercarriage strut
153 Nose undercarriage door
154 Rudder pedals
155 Nose construction
156 Pitot head
157 Sloping front bulkhead
158 Navigation code box
159 Nose electrical junction
box
160 Rudder pedal linking
mechanism
161 Windscreen heater unit
162 Nose undercarriage leg
163 Steering mechanism
164 Twin nosewheels
165 Catapult strop attachment
arm
166 Nosewheel leg door
167 Nosewheel emergency air
bottle
168 Nose PDS receivers
169 Oxygen tank
170 Landing lamp

171 Landing and taxi light
window
172 Nose PDS antenna array
173 Nose aerial fairing

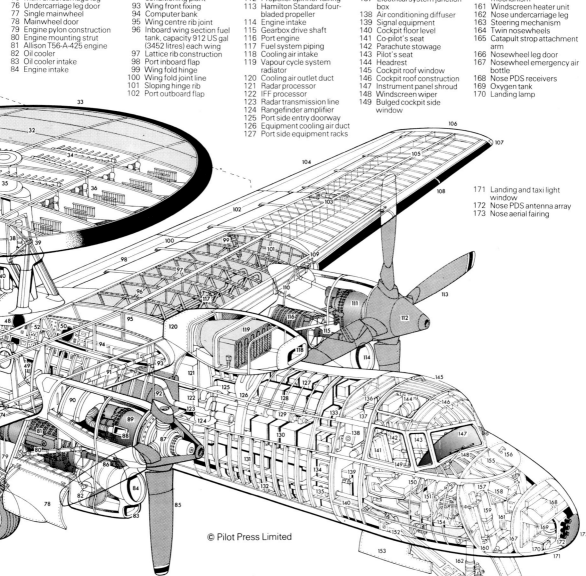

© Pilot Press Limited

Specification: Grumman E-2C Hawkeye

Powerplant

two 3661-kW (4,910 shp) Allison T56-A-425 turboprop engines driving Hamilton Standard four-blade reversible-pitch propellers

Wings

Span, standard	24.56 m	(80 ft 7 in)
with wings folded	8.94 m²	(29 ft 4 in)
Area, standard	65.03 m²	(700 sq ft)

Fuselage and tail unit

Length overall	17.54 m	(57 ft 6.75 in)
Height overall	5.58 m	(18 ft 3.75 in)
Tailplane span	8.53 m	(28 ft 0 in)
Rotodome diameter	7.32 m	(24 ft 0 in)

Weights

Empty	17265 kg	(38,063 lb)
Maximum take-off	23556 kg	(51,933 lb)
Maximum internal fuel	5624 kg	(12,400 lb)
Maximum take-off with auxiliary fuel	27161 kg	(59,880 lb)

E-2 Hawkeye recognition points

Four-fin tail unit with 11° inward cant

Windows above cockpit in addition to main cockpit glazing

Deep engine nacelles tapering towards the front

Slight dihedral on main wing

Wing-split point with hinge unit enabling outer wing section to be folded back

Prominent radiator and ram-air inlet above forward fuselage

Tricycle landing gear, typical of carrier-based aircraft

Four static dischargers on each wing trailing edge

Rotodome supported on four-pylon structure atop rear fuselage

Pylon structure supporting rotodome

Inner tailfins on upper surfaces of tailplane only

Arrester hook under fuselage

Performance

Maximum level speed	323 kts	(599 km/h; 372 mph)
Maximum cruising speed	311 kts	(576 km/h; 358 mph)
Approach speed	103 kts	(192 km/h; 119 mph)
Stalling speed in landing configuration	75 kts	(138 km/h; 86 mph)
Service ceiling	30,800 ft	(9390 m)
Minimum take-off run	610 m	(2,000 ft)
Minimum landing run	439 m	(1,440 ft)
Ferry range	2583 km	(1,605 miles)
Time on station 320 km (200 miles) from base	3-4 hours	
Unrefuelled endurance	6 hours 6 minutes	

Service ceiling

- Il-76 'Mainstay' 45,000 ft E
- Nimrod AEW.Mk 3 42,000 ft
- Tu-126 'Moss' 35,000 ft E
- E-2 Hawkeye 30,800 ft
- E-3 Sentry 29,000+ ft
- Sea King AEW 10,000 ft

Speed

- Nimrod AEW.Mk 3 500 kts
- E-3 Sentry 460 kts
- Il-76 'Mainstay' 459 kts E
- Tu-126 'Moss' 459 kts
- E-2 Hawkeye 323 kts
- Sea King AEW 112 kts

Unrefuelled endurance

- Tu-126 'Moss' 20+ hours E
- E-3 Sentry 11+ hours
- Il-76 'Mainstay' 10+ hours E
- Nimrod AEW.Mk 3 10+ hours
- E-2 Hawkeye 6 hours 6 mins
- Sea King AEW 4 hours

E-2 Hawkeye variants

E-2A: initial production version for the US Navy with APS-96 radar optimized for overwater operation, and T56-A-8/8A engines of 3021 kW (4,050 shp) (total three prototypes and 59 production aircraft)
E-2B: all E-2As were subsequently brought to this improved standard by a series of modifications to improve reliability and by the introduction of a Litton L-304 general-purpose computer giving greater flexibility of operation
E-2C: second production series for the US Navy, with APS-120 radar designed for overland target detection; this became APS-125 with the addition of ARPS (Advanced Radar

Processing System), giving automatic detection and targeting of overland targets and improved resistance to jamming; distinguished from earlier variants by revised avionics cooling, requiring enlarged radiator over front fuselage, and by longer nose for ESM (electronic support measures), increasing length to 17.54 m (57 ft 6.75 in); engines uprated to 3,661 kW (4910 shp) T56-A-422, or Dash-425 when fitted with plastic-blade propellers (at least 83 planned for US Navy, 4 delivered to Israel and 4 on order for Japan)
TE-2C: trainer version of E-2C, externally identical

Layout of the Hawkeye cockpit displays many typical multi-engined operating features; full dual controls are fitted, and basic flight instruments are duplicated in front of each pilot station. Radio transmit and trimming buttons are fitted to each control yoke, and there is a central throttle quadrant incorporating brake levers and reversible-pitch levers. The duplicated engine instruments are placed in front of the captain (left-hand seat).

The LOCKHEED P-3 ORION

Orion: son of Neptune

Rising from the ashes of the ill-starred Electra commercial transport, the Lockheed P-3 Orion has proved a remarkable success story over the last 25 years. Hunting down submarines is its main role, but many other duties are performed by this versatile machine.

The US Navy uses two classes of fixed-wing ASW aircraft. One group are compact enough to operate from carriers as the chief ASW assets of the embarked Carrier Air Wings. The other group operate from shore bases. This frees the second group from restrictions on size and power, and they can if necessary use a long runway for take-off. And well they might, because operating from a shore base there may be a run of 1600 km (1,000 miles) before reaching the scene of action, far out in the ocean.

Until after World War II the shore-based patrol mission was flown chiefly by flying-boats. Gradually the development of better airfields sounded the death-knell of this distinctive species, because landplanes are aerodynamically more efficient, and tend to carry more weapons and fly faster. The Lockheed P-2 Neptune began life with two of the biggest piston engines, for economy, and later received an additional boost, in the form of two turbojets, to give enhanced performance in attack situations and in some circum-

The Orion detects submarines by use of the rear-mounted MAD 'sting' and by dropping sonobuoys. Once detected, the P-3 can sink the vessel with torpedoes or depth-charges. Excellent endurance allows the Orion to track underwater targets for long periods.

stances to fly faster to the scene of action. By the mid-1950s the Neptune was beginning to look rather limited in capability and carrying capacity, and to have a cramped interior.

Rather surprisingly its replacement, the Lockheed P-3 Orion, was derived from a civil airliner (the Lockheed Electra). In fact this had already been done by the Canadians, who turned the turboprop Bristol Britannia into the mighty Canadair Argus, in which the turboprops were replaced by four of the same large piston engines as used in the Neptune. A little later the USSR used the Ilyushin Il-18 'Coot' airliner as the basis of the Il-38 'May' ocean patrol aircraft. The American and Soviet conversions, unlike the Canadian, did not switch to piston engines, but stayed with the original turboprops despite the fact that ASW operations, and most ocean patrol missions, are performed at low level where turboprops tend to burn fuel at a high rate.

Compared with the Neptune, the Orion offered about three times as much space inside the fuselage, and another advantage is that the interior is pressurized for shirtsleeve comfort during high-altitude transit from base to the operating area. The four powerful turboprops enable the

Used by the US Navy maritime patrol community and several other air arms, the Lockheed P-3 Orion has a high degree of responsibility within Western military operations, a challenge to which the type has responded magnificently.

Orion to cruise twice as fast as a Neptune (indeed an Orion holds the world turbo-prop straight-line speed record at 435.256 kts, or 806.1 km/h; 500.89 mph) and compared with the older aircraft there is much less noise and vibration. The Orion also has much greater carrying capacity, though because only an 0.88-m (34.5-in) depth is available under the floor for a weapons bay most of the Orion's weapons are carried externally on pylons under the wings.

But by far the biggest advance in the P-3 Orion is in its avionics and computerized nav/attack systems. These started a generation later than the equipment in the newest Neptune and, such is the pressure to keep abreast of modern submarine development, have been continuously upgraded ever since. Today's P-3s may look almost identical to the earliest examples which entered fleet service in August 1962, but to their crews they are totally different. Hardly a single 'black box' of electronics remains unchanged, and most of today's equipment had not even been thought of in 1962! The rest of this article is concerned with today's P-3, known as the P-3C Update III.

Like all large shore-based maritime patrol and ASW aircraft the Orion needs a substantial crew, despite progressively greater use of automatic features and computer control. As in the Electra the cockpit is arranged for a pilot and (on the right) co-pilot seated side-by-side, with an engineer seat on the centreline behind them. Next comes a compartment occupied by the Tacco (tactical co-ordinator), who in action becomes effectively the aircraft commander, and on the right side the nav/com (navigation and communications) officer; both have a bulged observation window. Amidships is the main tactical compartment, which can be occupied by five Sensos (sensor operators), though only three stations are normally occupied. These comprise a forward-facing non-acoustic sensor station at the front (in a compartment which can be curtained off) and two acoustic sensor stations facing outboard on the left. Farther aft again, above the trailing edge of the wing, are large avionics installations and stores for the two liferafts and racks for 60 Class-A

sonobuoys. Further aft are the sonobuoy launchers in the floor, and at the rear are more observer stations and crew rest and galley areas.

Sonobuoys play a leading role in pinpointing the position and movement of submarines, but first the Orion will probably use its non-acoustic sensors. Biggest of these is the main search radar. The Texas Instruments APS-115 is specially designed for overwater use. Operating in the I-band of frequencies (8 to 10 GHz) and with special electronics to cut down interference from sea 'clutter' (unwanted reflections from waves and spray). It has 360° coverage (like the RAF early-warning BAe Nimrod) from antennas in the nose and tail, each swivelling rapidly to cover a 180° sector. Each of the identical antennas is stabilized so that the picture stays level even when the Orion banks in turns. This radar is designed to spot even the small tip of a submarine periscope in a heavy sea.

Magnetic anomaly detection

A totally different method of sensing, and the only one able to detect a deeply submerged submarine, MAD is able to sense the very small local distortion of the Earth's magnetic field caused by the presence of a large metal mass, such as a submarine. The submarine tends to concentrate the magnetic field through its own hull, in effect pulling down the 'lines of force', and the resultant change in inclination of the field direction (first getting steeper and a few seconds later getting shallower, before returning to normal) is quite characteristic of the presence of a submarine (or, if the water is fairly shallow, it might be an old wreck of a large ship). One US Navy Orion has been rebuilt as the unique RP-3D specifically to conduct super-accurate research into the Earth's magnetic field, to make future MAD systems even more sensitive.

A third kind of sensor is the FLIR. This maps the temperature of every item seen ahead of the aircraft, and it can present the non-acoustic sensor operator with a

black/white video (TV type) picture in which the coldest objects (such as the sea) look black and the hottest items (such as a ship) look white (or the operator can reverse the polarity to make a target look black against a white sea). It has the great advantage in that, unlike the radar, it is passive: it emits no signals itself but merely receives 'heatwaves', and so can be used for covert detection of targets, especially at night, without the enemy being aware of the aircraft's presence. This is rendered easier by the fact that the Orion is one of the quietest aircraft, and at modest power levels can hardly be heard even at close range. The stabilized FLIR receiver is housed in a round turret under the nose. This replaces a KA-74 camera on a pivoted gimbal mount, which formerly looked through glass windows in a small gondola at this location; the camera is now relocated in the bottom of the rear fuselage.

Yet another sensor is the so-called 'sniffer' which continuously analyses the air it sucks in from the atmosphere. Should a diesel-engined submarine be anywhere in the vicinity the traces of perhaps one part in a million of exhaust fumes ring all the alarm bells. This sensor is less important as conventional boats give way to nuclear propulsion, and false

The highly distinctive fairings on this EP-3E contain equipment for electronic eavesdropping, this often taking the form of producing 'fingerprints' of Soviet naval forces. This aircraft is assigned to VQ-2 at Rota, Spain.

alarms from diesel surface ships far outnumber the true contacts.

Thus various forms of sonic sensor, which rely on sound waves travelling through the sea, remain the chief ASW detection and tracking method. Radar cannot be used because electromagnetic waves do not penetrate the ocean. Sound does, however, and the waves travel much faster than through the atmosphere. In one form of sonic detection sharp 'pings' are sent out by hydrophones within the sonobuoy which convert electrical energy into sound waves specially tailored to travel the maximum distance through water and then be reflected clearly from submarine hulls. As in radar in the atmosphere, the received echoes give away the range and bearing of the underwater target. In passive sonar the

An Orion Fleet Readiness Squadron is based on both East and West coasts of the United States; this P-3C belongs to VP-30 at NAS Jacksonville, Florida. Visible on the ramp are some of the many Orions which operate from this East Coast base.

Propellers
The Hamilton Standard propellers have very broad blades with root cuffs, and the spinners have electric de-icing

Engines
Each Allison T566 turboprop is fed with air from an intake above the spinner, the duct curving down behind the propeller gearbox which is carried on struts well in front of the engine

Weapon bay
A shallow but useful weapon bay under the forward fuselage can accommodate torpedoes, mines, depth charges, bombs or other stores

LLTV
Low-light TV can be carried on the right inner wing pylons, the pod containing the AXR-13 set. Today this has been replaced by the AAS-36 FLIR (forward-looking infra-red) under the nose

Body pylons
These pylons can carry torpedoes or mines in the 907 kg (2,000-lb) class

ESM
This large pod is usually carried on the left inner wing pylon and contains the ALQ-78 passive receiver forming the main element in the ESM (electronic surveillance measures) system. Later P-3s have wing-tip ESM installations

Fuel tanks
The entire main wing box is cov with large machine planks abov below, easing the problems of the box to form an integral fuel each side

Main landing gear
Each twin-wheel landing gear retracts forwards into this compartment enclosed by twin doors

WARNING

DANGER ◆ PROPELLOR ◆ DANGER

Aerials
More than 30 separate avionics items are carried by most P-3Cs, but the number of visible aerials is small. These blade aerials serve VHF communications and the Tacan navigation aid

Visual posts
Four observations posts, on each sid front and rear, offer all-round visibility from large bulged windows. The rear stations are screened from the rest o the interior

Cockpit
Most of the crew are mission specialists in the main cabin. In the cockpit is the flight crew of pilot, co-pilot and engineer

Radar (nose)
Specially developed for the P-3, the main radar is the Texas Instruments APS-115. This has two gyro-stabilized aerials (antennas), one in the nose radome and the other in the tail, to give all-round coverage

Camera
Early P-3s were fitted with this chin gondola housing a KA-74A gimbal-mounted surveillance camera. Today this has been replaced by the AAS-36 FLIR (forward-looking infra red) ball turret giving passive day/night 'vision'

Nose landing gear
The steerable twin-wheel nose gear retracts forwards into this bay

APU
A gas-turbine auxiliary power unit drives a 60-kVA electric generator

Oil cooler
Under each engine is a cooler for the engine and propeller gearbox oil. Air enters through a ram inlet and escape via a variable shutter under the nacell

receiver merely listens for the slightest underwater noise, such as is made by a submarine's propeller. Even a quiet submarine can today be detected several miles away.

There are two standard sizes of sonobuoy used in Western aircraft of which Class A is by far the more common: 914 mm (36 in) long and 124 mm (4.9 in) diameter. Another important size is Miniature which is a very short buoy of A diameter. Class B is much larger. Racks in the fuselage store 36 A-size buoys, and these are fired through any available of 48 diagonal launchers under the rear fuselage floor. The 48 tubes are themselves pre-loaded from outside the aircraft before take-off, giving a normal total of 84 sonobuoys. There is also a single tube for B-size stores. The diagonal angle of the launch tubes, from which the buoys are fired by large cartridge devices, helps to cancel out the speed of the aircraft so that buoys can be dropped into the desired spot on the sea surface more readily. Once in the sea, some sonobuoys float on the surface to send back their information by radio. The Australian Barra buoy, used by RAAF Orions and likely to be used by many others, splits into a deep sensing portion and a floating transmitter portion.

Under the wing roots are two of the 10 underwing pylons on which, as an alternative to air-dropped stores, two further permanent sensors may be hung. Under the left wing root is often carried an ALQ-78 ESM pod, which looks rather like a drop tank with two downsloping triangular wings. This normally operates in a search mode, listening to signals from all points of the compass. When a radar signal of interest (i.e. a potentially hostile one) is detected, the ALQ-78 automatically switches to the analysis and direction-finding mode to indicate its precise origin. Under the right wing root can be carried an AXR-13 LLLTV. This can be of value in night target identification, but has been rendered less important by the chin-mounted FLIR. Likewise, the pod-mounted ESM is due to be replaced eventually by the new ALR-77 ESM system which will be housed in wingtip pods.

These wingtip pods will also provide long-range targeting data for anti-ship missiles, detecting signals from target ships and by basic geometric triangulation (working out the different directions of the target as 'seen' by the two wingtips) give its range. The Update II modification gave the Orion this anti-ship capability, the missile being the Harpoon. Originally the only missile carried was the short-range AGM-12 Bullpup, which has to be steered by the aircraft crew to hit its target. In contrast AGM-84 Harpoon is a cruise missile with a range of over 92 km (57 miles) in the current version and considerably more in an upgraded version now in production. This gives Update III Orions, as now in use, great stand-off capability against any sea-surface target.

Up to 10 tonnes of weapons can be carried in the internal bay and on the underwing pylons. The assortment almost always includes AS torpedoes, such as the Mk 44, 46 or 50, as well as bombs, depth charges, mines and rockets.

Numerous auxiliary pyrotechnics such as flares or markers can also be carried.

At all times Orion knows its position with extreme accuracy, without the need for assistance from external sources other than the Omega stations. The latter are a group of eight whose VLF transmitters radiate up to 1000 kW of power initially for communication with the US Navy's own nuclear submarines. Other self-contained navaids carried include the LTN-72 INS and APN-227 Doppler radar, while LORAN and TACAN are radio navaids which do need signals from stations on land. So too do the simpler VOR, ADF and basic radio systems.

From take-off anyone unfamiliar with the Orion could not fail to be impressed by the agility of this large aircraft. From the earliest days of the commercial Electra it was a common party trick to feather three of the giant wide-bladed propellers and then cavort round the sky on one engine. The latter, Allison T56-A-14s of 3661 kW (4,910 ehp), are basically the same as the engines of the Lockheed C-130 'Herky', but they look different because the air inlet is above the propeller spinner instead of below.

All Orion versions have basically the same airframe and systems, though some foreign customers have different mission equipment. This is especially true of the

The sole anti-submarine warfare aircraft within the Netherlands armed forces is the P-3C, 13 of which are in service. In addition to operating from their home base, a permanent detachment is assigned to Keflavik in Iceland for joint operations with the US Navy.

Canadian armed forces, whose CP-140 Aurora version is quite different internally and has avionics and ASW systems similar to those of the Lockheed S-3 Viking.

Glossary
ADF Automatic Direction-Finding
AS Anti-Submarine
ASW Anti-Submarine Warfare
ESM Electronic Surveillance Measures
FLIR Forward-Looking Infra-Red
INS Inertial Navigation System
LLLTV Low-Light-Level TV
LORAN LOng-Range Air Navigation
MAD Magnetic Anomaly Dectector
Senso Sensor operator
TACAN TActical Air Navigation
Tacco Tactical co-ordinator
VLF Very Low Frequency
VOR VHF Omni-Range

Developed to Canadian specifications, the CP-140 Aurora serves with only that nation's armed forces. The Aurora combines the systems of the S-3 Viking with the basic P-3 airframe, and allows effective patrol of the vast Canadian coastal waters.

P-3 Orion in service: units and example aircraft

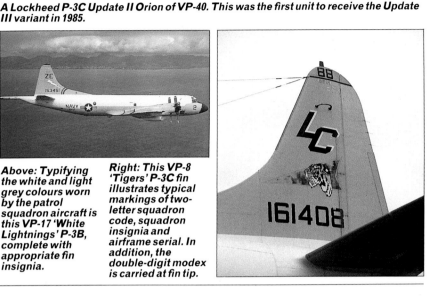

United States

Large numbers of Orions serve in a variety of roles and versions within front-line, Reserve, specialized and testing units. The normal Patrol Squadron complement is nine aircraft, fewer being operated by secondary units. Update III models are entering service, and 30 P-3As are being converted to CP-3A configuration for cargo transport duties.

A Lockheed P-3C Update II Orion of VP-40. This was the first unit to receive the Update III variant in 1985.

Patrol Wings Pacific Fleet

Patrol Wing Two
Base: Barbers Point, Hawaii
Squadrons and example aircraft:
VP-1 (P-3C) 156513/1/'YB'
VP-4 (P-3C) 158914/4/'YD'
VP-6 (P-3B) 154602/2/'PC'
VP-17 (P-3B) 153448/6/'ZE'
VP-22 (P-3B) 154600/9/'QA'

Patrol Wing Ten
Base: Moffett Field, Ca.
Squadrons and example aircraft:
VP-9 (P-3C) 159883/3/'PD'
VP-19 (P-3C) 159507/7/'PE'
VP-31 (P-3A; UP-3A; P-3B;
P-3C) 154587/24/'RP' (P-3B)
VP-40 (P-3C) 161766/1/'QE'
VP-46 (P-3C) 160288/8/'RC'
VP-47 (P-3C) 157331/4/'RD'
VP-48 (P-3C) 158222/2/'SF'
VP-50 (P-3C) 158215/5/'SG'

Patrol Wings Atlantic Fleet

Patrol Wing Five
Base: Brunswick, Maine
Squadrons and example aircraft:
VP-8 (P-3C) 161406/86/'LC'
VP-10 (P-3C) 161129/9/'LD'
VP-11 (P-3C) 161330/8/'LE'
VP-23 (P-3C) 161002/2/'LJ'
VP-26 (P-3C) 161005/5/'LK'
VP-44 (P-3C) 160766/6/'LM'

Patrol Wing Eleven
Base: Jacksonville, Fl.
Squadrons and example aircraft:
VP-5 (P-3C) 158923/9/'LA'
VP-16 (P-3C) 161592/2/'LF'
VP-24 (P-3C) 157312/3/'LR'
VP-30 (P-3A; VP-3A; P-3B;
P-3C) 161411/30/'LL' (P-3C)
VP-45 (P-3C) 156510/40/'LN'
VP-49 (P-3C) 158920/7/'LP'
VP-56 (P-3C) 157322/4/'LQ'

Above: Typifying the white and light grey colours worn by the patrol squadron aircraft is this VP-17 'White Lightnings' P-3B, complete with appropriate fin insignia.

Right: This VP-8 'Tigers' P-3C fin illustrates typical markings of two-letter squadron code, squadron insignia and airframe serial. In addition, the double-digit modex is carried at fin tip.

Miscellaneous Units

Squadron	Base	Example aircraft
VAQ-33	Key West, Florida	150529/130/'GD' (EP-3A)
VC-1	Barbers Point, Hawaii	149675 (VP-3A)
VPU-1	Brunswick, Maine	153450 (P-3B)
VPU-2	Barbers Point, Hawaii	152169 (UP-3A)
VQ-1	Agana, Japan	148887/33/'PR' (EP-3E)
VQ-2	Rota, Spain	150505/24/'JQ' (EP-3E)
VX-1	Patuxent River, Maryland	158206/3/'JA'
VXN-8	Patuxent River, Maryland	150500/'JB' (RP-3A)
US Customs	New Orleans, Louisiana	151391; 152170 (P-3A)
NASA	Wallops Island, Virginia	148276/N428NA (UP-3A)
General Offshore Corp.	Brunswick, Maine	148885; 150604 (UP-3A)
Keflavik NS	Keflavik, Iceland	150495 (UP-3A)
CinC AFSE	Sigonella, Sicily	150511 (VP-/A)

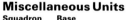

Above: As back-up to the Keflavik Naval Station UP-3A, this P-3A acts as VIP transport for the C-in-C.

Above: Among the most colourful Orions are the RP-3s of VXN-8, this being an RP-3A used in Project Seascan and named 'El Coyote'.

VXN-8's Project Magnet RP-3D is named 'Road Runner', with illustration on the forward fuselage.

US Naval Air Reserve Force

Reserve Patrol Wing Pacific

Squadron	Base	Example aircraft
VP-60	Glenview, Illinois	152732/11/'LS' (P-3B)
VP-65	Point Mugu, California	151383/2/'PG' (P-3A)
VP-67	Memphis, Tennessee	151367/00/'PL' (P-3A)
VP-69	Whidbey Island, Washington	152164/5/'PJ' (P-3A)
VP-90	Glenview, Illinois	153420/6/'LX' (P-3B)
VP-91	Moffett Field, California	152744/3/'PM' (P-3B)

One of the eight widely-dispersed Reserve Force Atlantic patrol units is VP-93, unusual in that its home is an Air National Guard base. The unit currently flies the P-3B variant.

Reserve Patrol Wing Atlantic

Squadron	Base	Example aircraft
VP-62	Jacksonville, Florida	153430/2/'LT' (P-3B)
VP-64	Willow Grove, Pennsylvania	152147/5/'LU' (P-3A)
VP-66	Willow Grove, Pennsylvania	152183/1/'LV' (P-3A)
VP-68	Patuxent River, Maryland	153422/00/'LW' (P-3B)
VP-92	South Weymouth, Massachusetts	153433/12/'LY' (P-3B)
VP-93	Selfridge, Michigan	153415/6/'LH' (P-3B)
VP-94	New Orleans, Louisiana	152727/3/'LZ' (P-3B)
VPMAU	Brunswick, Maine	161014/02/'LB' (P-3C)

Naval Air Systems Command

Unit	Base	Example aircraft
NADC	Warminster, DC	148889 (UP-3A)
NATC	Patuxent River, Maryland	160290 (P-3C)
NRL	Patuxent River, Maryland	153422 (EP-3B)
PMTC	Point Mugu, California	150525/36 (RP-3A)

This distinctively modified Orion is an EP-3A from the Pacific Missile Test Centre (PMTC), the rear fairing housing phased array antennas.

Lockheed P-3C Orion
Patrol Squadron Nineteen (VP-19)
NAS Moffett Field
United States Navy

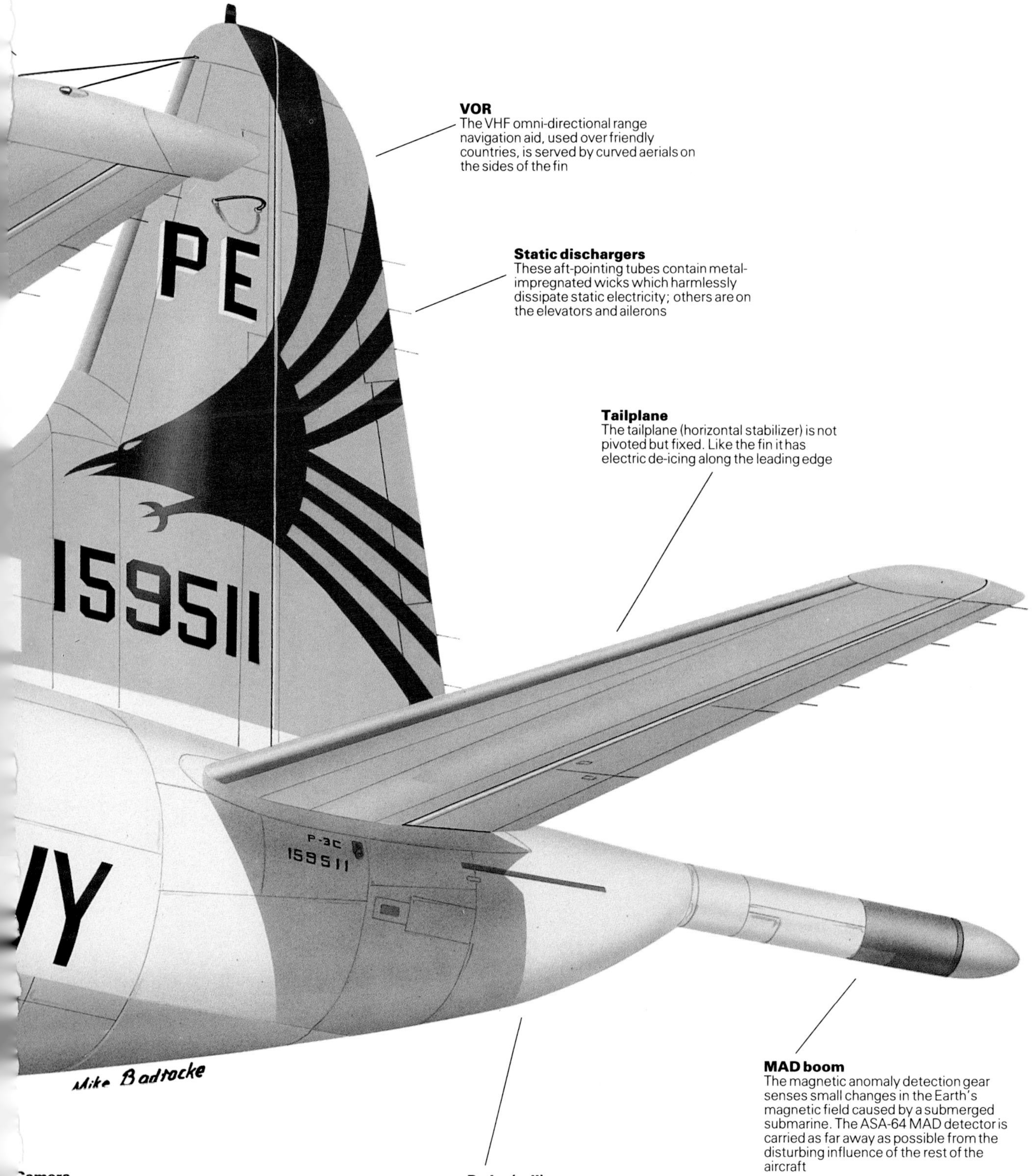

VOR
The VHF omni-directional range navigation aid, used over friendly countries, is served by curved aerials on the sides of the fin

Static dischargers
These aft-pointing tubes contain metal-impregnated wicks which harmlessly dissipate static electricity; others are on the elevators and ailerons

Tailplane
The tailplane (horizontal stabilizer) is not pivoted but fixed. Like the fin it has electric de-icing along the leading edge

PE

159511

P-3C
159511

Mike Badrocke

NY

MAD boom
The magnetic anomaly detection gear senses small changes in the Earth's magnetic field caused by a submerged submarine. The ASA-64 MAD detector is carried as far away as possible from the disturbing influence of the rest of the aircraft

Camera
Among several cameras carried on board is a large KB-18 strike camera to record the results of attacks on submarines and other targets

Radar (tail)
Inside the tailcone the rear scanner (dish aerial) of the APS-115 radar covers the hemisphere behind the aircraft

Wire aerial
The HF (high frequency) radio operates with relatively very long waves needing this long wire aerial. It gives voice contact over very long ranges

Navigation lights
In conformity with all night-flying aircraft the P-3 has a red light on the left wingtip, green on the right and white at the tail facing aft

Pylons
Most of the offensive stores are hung externally, six of the pylons being under the outer wings (rated at 907 kg/2,000 lb inboard, 454 kg/1,000 lb centre and 227 kg/500 lb outboard). Harpoon cruise missiles can be carried

Leading edge
Inside the wing leading edge is a 'piccolo tube' which in icing conditions can blast hot air bled from the engines against the inner skin

Landing light
Powerful landing lights can be hinged down for night landings from their normal stowed position flush with the wing

Beacon
Above and below the fuselage are anti-collision beacons which rotate to give brilliant intermittent red lights visible from many miles

Flaps
Fowler-type flaps can be extended hydraulically from beneath the fixed rear portion of the wing. A feature of this type of flap is that, initially unseen from above, it increases the area of the wing as it slides out to the rear

Main door
The main crew door has a built-in airstair immediately beneath it

Sonobuoys
Sonobuoys can be ejected from 48 inclined launchers. Other launchers can be reloaded from inside the rear fuselage

Australia

The Royal Australian Air Force is currently transitioning from P-3Bs to an all-P-3C force of 20 aircraft, operating with two squadrons, Nos 10 and 11. One P-3B has been sold to New Zealand, and six to Portugal. Example aircraft: A9-751 to A9-760 inclusive; A9-656; A9-657.

Above: The first of Australia's P-3C Orions is assigned to No. 10 Sqn.

Canada

Combining the P-3C airframe with the S-3 Viking avionics and data processing systems, Canada produced the CP-140 Aurora, 18 of which serve within the Canadian Armed Forces. The Greenwood Wing consists of Nos 404, 405 and 415 Squadrons. Example aircraft: 140101; 140109; 140116; 140118; 140102; 140106; 140110; 140115.

Though individual units are assigned to the Greenwood CP-140 Wing, it is the wing emblem that is worn on the fin. This machine serves with No. 404 Sqn.

The relatively spacious flight station in the P-3C Orion has seating for the pilot, co-pilot and (not illustrated) the flight engineer. The main flight instrumentation is in the consoles ahead of and between the forward crew seating. Additional instruments are in an overhead panel, while the flight engineer's avionics bay (A1) is to the left.

Iran

Of the six aircraft purchased in the 1970s, four have either been destroyed or are used for spares. All wore the distinctive three-tone blue camouflage.

All six P-3Fs supplied to Iran (basically P-3C models) have inflight-refuelling capability and a full ASW fitment.

Japan

Current and future procurement plans call for up to 100 P-3C Orions to be operated by the Japanese Maritime Self-Defence Force. This example serves with 3 Kokutai. Example aircraft: 5014; 5016; 5006; 5007; 5010; 5001; 5009; 5013.

Amongst the early deliveries of P-3Cs to Japan, this example now serves with 51 Kokutai.

Netherlands

Thirteen Lockheed P-3Cs were obtained by the navy, all serving with No. 320 Sqn. The aircraft carry a large 'V' on the fin to indicate the home base of Valkenburg. Example aircraft: 300 to 312 inclusive.

New Zealand

The sole air force Orion squadron, No. 5, operates six P-3Bs from Whenupai. The last (NZ4206) is an ex-RAAF machine which is currently being modernized before entering service. Example aircraft: NZ4201 to NZ4206 inclusive.

Duplicating the US Navy patrol squadron colour scheme, the RNZAF P-3B Orions wear the last two digits of the serial on the nose.

Norway

Seven P-3Bs are based at Andoya in western Norway with No. 333 Squadron, fulfilling a vital NATO maritime patrol role. All seven wear a dark grey colour scheme with small codes. Example aircraft: 576; 583; 599 to 603.

Spain

The Spanish air force (EdA) currently operates a single squadron, Escuadron 221, of seven P-3A Orions, three of which were bought and four leased. Example aircraft: P.3-1/221-20; P.3-6/220-25.

Lockheed P-3C Orion cutaway drawing key

1 Static dischargers
2 MAD detection head
3 MAD boom
4 Tail cone
5 APS-115 radar
6 Elevator trim tab
7 Starboard elevator
8 Elevator torque tube
9 Tailplane structure
10 Leading-edge hot air anti-icing
11 Elevator (starboard) and rudder (port) hydraulic booster units
12 Rudder linkage
13 Elevator tube universal joint
14 Rudder lower hinge
15 Rudder structure
16 Rudder trim tab
17 Rudder post
18 Antenna
19 Rudder upper hinge
20 Fin tip
21 Aerial attachment
22 Fin leading-edge
23 Port elevator
24 Port tailplane
25 Fin root fairing
26 Integral fin/rear fuselage
27 Aft pressure bulkhead
28 Tail unit anti-icing timer
29 Bunk (hinged: in-flight maintenance work bench beneath)
30 Elevator trim tab servo
31 Avionics bay (K2)
32 Avionics bay (K1)
33 Refuse bins (2)
34 KB-18 ventral camera (strike assessment)
35 Avionics bay (J2)
36 Avionics bay (J1)
37 Galley
38 Bunk (hinged)
39 Four-place dinette
40 Window ports
41 Lavatory
42 Avionics bay (H3)
43 Coat closet
44 Avionics bay (H2)
45 Avionics bay (H1)
46 Port observation static (screened compartme
47 Starboard observation station (screened compartment)
48 Observation window
49 'A'-stores angle of rele
50 'B'-store launchers (1)
51 'A'-store launchers (3)
52 Guard rail
53 Under-deck 'A'-store launchers (48)
54 Entry ladder (stowed i flight position)
55 Main entrance door
56 Avionics bay (G2)
57 Avionics bay (G1)
58 Life-raft stowage (port
59 Avionics bay (F2)
60 'A'-store stowage rack (36 stores)
61 Under-deck hydraulics service centre
62 Wingroot fairing
63 Ventral KA-74 camera
64 Avionics bay (F1)
65 Emergency exit (port)
66 Avionics bay (E2)

Lockheed P-3 Orion variants

Avionics bay (E1)
Life-raft stowage starboard)
Emergency exit (starboard)
Main electrical load centre starboard)
Operators' seats
Sensor station 2 (acoustic)
Sensor station 1 (acoustic)
No. 2 fuel tank
Engine aft nacelles
Jet-pipe cooling-air inlets
Jet-pipe exhausts
HF aerial
Fowler-type flaps
Aileron trim tab
Static dischargers
Port aileron
Wingtip fairing
Port navigation light
Formation/identification light
No. 1 fuel tank
Integrally stiffened machined skin panels
Hot-air tapered ejector tubes ('piccolo' tubes)
Engine bleed air shut-off valve
Engine firewall
Nacelle cowling
Engine air intakes
Four-blade propellers
Spinners
Propeller cuffs
Oil cooler intake
ESM pod and pylon mounted under port wingroot)
Oil cooler system
Engine oil cooling augmentor (jet pump)
control valve
Starter control valve
Engine 14th stage bleed air taps
Engine bleed air shut-off valve
Fuselage bleed air shut-off valve (port and starboard)

Avionics bay (D3)
Sensor compartment
Centre-aisle curtain

ress Limited

106 Operator's seat
107 Window port
108 Sensor station 3 (non-acoustic)
109 Avionics bay (D2) (computer)
110 Avionics bay (D1)
111 Ditching station (13 places)
112 Avionics bay (B3)
113 Avionics bay (B2)
114 Avionics bay (B1)
115 Avionics bay (C3)
116 Avionics bay (C2)
117 Avionics bay (C1)
118 Observation window
119 Nav/com station
120 Nav/com console
121 Taco seat
122 Taco station
123 Antenna
124 Curtains/doorway to flight-deck
125 Flight crew emergency exit
126 Avionics bay (A1)
127 Pilot's seat
128 Flight engineer's seat
129 Overhead instrument console
130 Windshield
131 Instrument panel shroud
132 Control column
133 Forward pressure bulkhead
134 Radar support
135 Nose cone
136 APS-115 radar
137 Retractable FLIR
138 Pitot head
139 Nosewheel well beams
140 Rudder pedal
141 Nosewheel retraction jack
142 Nosewheel doors
143 Forward-retracting twin nosewheels
144 Nosewheel leg torque link
145 Nosewheel leg pivot
146 Co-pilot's seat
147 Forward electrical load centre
148 Under-deck APU compartment
149 Under-deck weapons bay
150 Weapons bay doors
151 Bomb load (eight bombs)
152 Spinners
153 Four-blade propellers
154 Engine air intake

155 Intake trunking
156 Engine bearers ('V'-frame)
157 Oil tank
158 Inboard leading-edge section
159 Wingroot fillet
160 Fuselage fuel cell (no. 5 bag)
161 Water-alcohol tank
162 Wing centre-section front beam
163 Centre-section integral fuel tank (No. 5)
164 Centre-section end rib
165 No. 3 fuel tank
166 Flap structure
167 Jet-pipe exhausts
168 Flap profile
169 Bonded double skin
170 No. 4 fuel tank

171 Mainwheel well aft doors
172 Twin mainwheels
173 Mainwheel leg pivot
174 Retraction jack

185 Stainless-steel heat-resistant trough
186 Aileron control linkage
187 Twin (fail-safe) trim actuators
188 Aileron trim tab
189 Static dischargers
190 Starboard aileron
191 Starboard navigation light

YP-3A: following an aerodynamic test aircraft flown in 1958, this prototype with full avionics flew in 1959; subsequently converted to NP-3 (see below)

P-3A: first production version, small numbers still in use with US Navy and Navy Reserve and other countries
CP-3A: up to 30 P-3As are being rebuilt as ABSA (Advanced Base Support Aircraft) cargo/passenger transports for the US Navy
EP-3A: US Naval Air Test Center electronic research aircraft (BuNo. 149673)
NP-3A: special P-3 systems development aircraft
RP-3A: cartographic reconnaissance version operated by VXN-8 on major survey projects
VP-3A: three conversions from WP-3A as VIP executive transports
WP-3A: four initially converted, and one aircraft (BuNo. 149674) used for special tests by US Naval Research Laboratory
P-3A (149670): rebuild for electronic reconnaissance, operated by US Naval Research Laboratory
P-3A (150499): major rebuild with giant phased-array aerial ahead of fin, used for over-the-horizon telemetry in weapon trials from Point Mugu
P-3A(CS): six rebuilds for US Customs Service with Hughes APG-63 (F-15 type) nose radar and infra-red detection system
P-3A SMILS: rebuilds for Peacekeeper and Trident missile programmes, using Sonobuoy Missile Impact Location System
P-3B: second major production version with T56-A-14 engines, Bullpup missile guidance and other updates

EP-3B: two rebuilds for electronic surveillance, later becoming EP-3E (see below)
P-3 (AEW&C): rebuild of RAAF P-3B with General Electric APS-138 radar and APA-171 rotodome revolving above fuselage
P-3C: third major production version, with A-NEW sensor/control installation; entered production 1968; from 1975 upgraded to **Update** standard with new avionics and software; from 1977 **Update II** added infra-red detection system, sonobuoy reference system and underwing Harpoon missiles; from 1984 **Update III** added new acoustic processor, new sonobuoy receiver, new APU (auxiliary power unit) and environmental-control systems
RP-3D: special aircraft used by VXN-8 to map Earth's magnetic field to support MAD (magnetic anomaly detection) submarine location systems; on 4 November 1972 it set a closed-circuit distance record of 10085.25 km (6,266.68 miles)
WP-3D: extensive rebuild of two P-3Cs for atmospheric research and weather modification

EP-3E: 10 P-3A and two EP-3B rebuilt as Elint (electronic intelligence) and surveillance aircraft with VQ-1 and -2 squadrons

P-3F: six similar to P-3C but with inflight-refuelling capability for Iran; at least three still operating
CP-140 Aurora: totally different ASW/patrol version for Canadian Armed Forces, with ASW sensor/processing/display systems similar to those of Lockheed S-3A Viking

175 Mainwheel well forward doors
176 Engine air intake
177 Propeller reduction gear box
178 Oil cooler intake
179 Engine support struts

180 Drive shaft housing
181 Allison T56-A-10 turboprop engine compressor section
182 Combustion section
183 Turbine section
184 Jet pipe

192 Formation/identification light
193 Rear spar
194 Integrally stiffened wing planks
195 Wing rib construction
196 Front spar
197 Leading-edge structure
198 Underwing stores pylons (three outboard, two inboard)

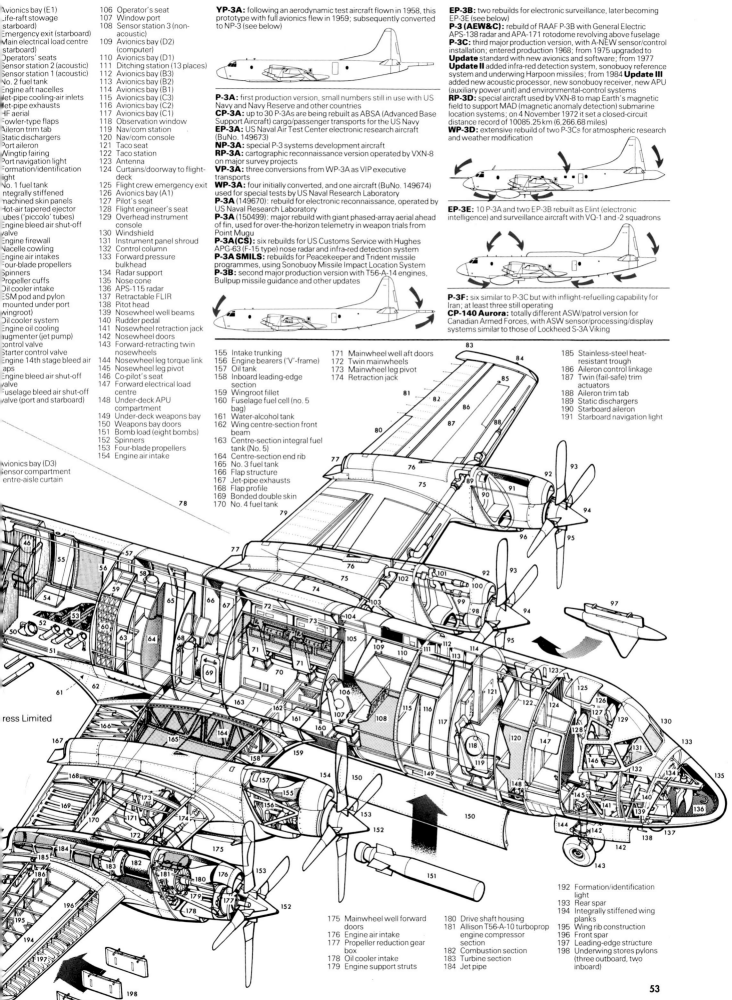

Lockheed P-3C Orion warload

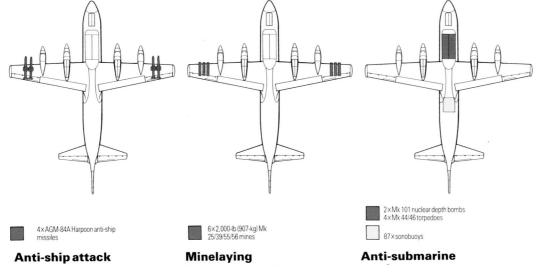

■ 4 × AGM-84A Harpoon anti-ship missiles

Anti-ship attack
The P-3C Update II and P-3C Update III can fire Harpoon anti-ship missiles against hostile surface vessels from a range of 60 miles (97 km). Provided the approximate position of the target is known, and that no friendly vessel is in its vicinity, the Harpoon can be left to navigate itself before homing with its own radar.

■ 6 × 2,000-lb (907-kg) Mk 25/39/55/56 mines

Minelaying
Minelaying is routinely practised by US Navy Orion squadrons. The mines are hung on six of the underwing pylons and are released from a low altitude. Over relatively short ranges this load can be augmented by three 1,000-lb (454-kg) Mk 36/52 mines in the internal bay.

■ 2 × Mk 101 nuclear depth bombs
■ 4 × Mk 44/46 torpedoes
□ 87 × sonobuoys

Anti-submarine warfare
The basic anti-submarine warfare mission was central to the design of the P-3. Sonobuoys are stored in diagonal tubes at the rear of the fuselage, while weapons are carried in the internal bay. Torpedoes can be carried externally on pylons for ferry purposes only.

Specification:

Lockheed P-3C Update III Orion

Wings
Span	30.38 m	(99 ft 8 in)
Area	120.77 m^2	(1,300 sq ft)

Fuselage and tail unit
Length overall	35.61 m	(116 ft 10 in)
Height overall	10.27 m	(33 ft 8.5 in)
Fuselage diameter	3.45 m	(11 ft 4 in)
Tailplane span	13.06 m	(42 ft 10 in)

Landing gear
Wheelbase	9.07 m	(29 ft 9 in)
Wheel track	9.50 m	(31 ft 2 in)

Weights
Empty typically	28089 kg	(61,925 lb)
Expendable ordnance (maximum)	9072 kg	(20,000 lb)
Maximum take-off	61235 kg	(135,000 lb)

P-3 Orion recognition features

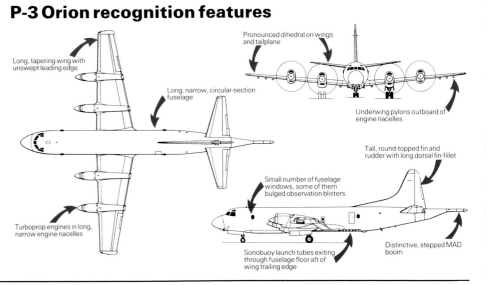

Long, tapering wing with unswept leading edge

Pronounced dihedral on wings and tailplane

Long, narrow, circular-section fuselage

Underwing pylons outboard of engine nacelles

Turboprop engines in long, narrow engine nacelles

Small number of fuselage windows, some of them bulged observation blisters

Tall, round-topped fin and rudder with long dorsal fin-fillet

Sonobuoy launch tubes exiting through fuselage floor aft of wing trailing edge

Distinctive, stepped MAD boom

Performance:

Maximum speed at 15,000 ft (4575 m)	411 kts	761 km/h (473 mph)
Patrol speed at 1,500 ft (457 m)	206 kts	381 km/h (237 mph)
Service ceiling	28,300 ft	(8625 m)
Maximum range with max normal take-off weight; no time on station	3835 km	(2,383 miles)
Combat radius with 3 hours on station at 1,500 ft (457 m)	2494 km	(1,550 miles)
Take-off distance	1673 m	(5,490 ft)

Weapon load
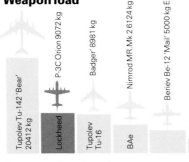

Tupolev Tu-142 'Bear' 20412 kg
P-3C Orion 9072 kg
Badger' 8981 kg
Nimrod MR.Mk 2 6124 kg
Beriev Be-12 'Mail' 5000 kg E
Breguet Atlantic 1 3000 kg E
Lockheed
Tupolev Tu-16
BAe

Service ceiling

BAe Nimrod MR.Mk 2 42,000 ft
Tupolev Tu-16 'Badger' 40,350ft E
Tupolev Tu-142 'Bear' 40,000 ft E
Beriev Be-12 'Mail' 37,000 ft
32,800 ft
Breguet Atlantic 1
28,300 ft
Lockheed P-3C Orion

Maximum speed

Tupolev Tu-16 'Badger' 535 kts E
Tupolev Tu-142 'Bear' 500 kts
BAe Nimrod MR.Mk 2 500 kts
Lockheed P-3C Orion 411 kts
Breguet Atlantic 1 355 kts
Beriev Be-12 'Mail' 328 kts

Speed at low level

Tupolev Tu-16 'Badger' 500 kts E
BAe Nimrod MR.Mk 2 475 kts
Tupolev Tu-142 'Bear' 450 kts E
Lockheed P-3C Orion 400 kts E
Breguet Atlantic 1 300 kts
Beriev Be-12 'Mail' 300 kts E

Operational range (internal fuel)

Tupolev Tu-142 'Bear' 12550 km
BAe Nimrod MR.Mk 2 9265 km
Breguet Atlantic 1 9000 km
Lockheed P-3C Orion   7670 km
Tupolev Tu-16   'Badger' 4800 km E
Beriev Be-12   'Mail' 4000 km

The BOEING
E-3 SENTRY

Boeing E-3: Skyborne Sentinel

Since its introduction into operational service, the distinctive E-3 Sentry has proved itself time and again to be an invaluable component in the USAF and NATO air defence systems, tracking enemy intruders and directing friendly interceptors to their quarry.

At the end of World War II aircraft began to carry large surveillance radars. Unlike previous airborne radars, these are designed to search vast volumes of sky and detect every aircraft present. The most widely used of the early generation of AEW 'picket' aircraft was the Lockheed EC-121 Warning Star, a series of versions based on the Super Constellation airliner. These did a great job and served from the early 1950s until after the Vietnam War, but they had several limitations.

One limitation was that, being, a piston-engined aircraft, the EC-121 had quite modest performance, and it could not climb very high. The higher an observer is, the farther he can see. Walking on the beach, the horizon at sea is about 3.2 km (2 miles) away. From a tall seaside hotel one might see 16 km (10 miles). An EC-121 might 'see' 240 km (150 miles). In the 1960s the US Air Force calculated that a radar in a big jet aircraft at 30,000 ft (9145 m) would 'see' 395 km (245 miles). Obviously, the farther one can see the better: it brings in a greater number of targets, and it increases the warning time of an enemy attack.

The other big problem with the EC-121s was that their old-technology radars could not see aircraft flying at low level. In the 1950s this was not very important, because supersonic jets have to fly at high altitude. The idea of an enemy aircraft making an attack at much lower speed at low altitude would have been thought not

worth considering. But the development of SAMs gradually made flight at high altitude so perilous that the only way to penetrate hostile airspace has ever since been at the lowest height possible, to stay down out of the line of sight of enemy radars. Nobody can stay out of sight of a high-altitude airborne radar, but the older radars could not see low-flying aircraft. This is because the tiny picture of the enemy aircraft on the radar screen was swamped by the giant reflection of the radar signals from the ground, just beneath the aircraft.

Radar design

In 1965 the US Air Force began its ORT programme to try to find out how to make a radar that could look down over land and see small jets speeding across the ground at so-called treetop height. The answer proved to be 'pulse-Doppler' radar, a kind of radar that uses not only successive pulses of energy but also the Doppler phase shift of the echoes received back from the target. The best-known example of the Doppler effect is when we stand near a moving source of a fixed-frequency sound, such as a whistling train or a car sounding its horn. As the source goes past, the note goes from high to low in pitch. If we could accurately measure the difference between the high pitch of the oncoming sound and the low pitch of the receding sound we could work out the speed of the vehicle.

Though somewhat odd in appearance with the massive rotodome incorporating the radar antenna, the E-3 Sentry is a highly effective surveillance platform, offering high- or low-level detection, tracking and identification of air vehicles over land and sea.

This is how pulse-Doppler radar works: it compares the pitch (or PRF) of the radar signal sent out with the PRF of the echoes received back. Most signals will be received back from the ground, and here the difference in PRF is due to the speed of one's own aircraft. All other PRFs come from targets moving relative to the ground, and they show up clearly. Even so there are plenty of problems. There are certain target angles and ranges where either the target cannot be seen or the apparent range may be half or twice (or four times) the true value. A lot of research was needed to get an overland downlook radar that really worked. Even then it suffered from such problems as the false 'velocities' of leaves agitated by wind, or waves and spray blown across the sea.

Of course it needed more than just a new pulse-Doppler high-PRF radar, able

For such a highly complex system, the E-3 has proved a most useful aircraft in front-line operational use. Deployments by USAF aircraft include Arctic conditions at Keflavik and the heat of Saudi Arabia and Egypt, but the Sentry has proved up to the job again and again.

U.S. AIR FORCE

70351

to send out signals at high and low PRFs together, in order to sort out the true target ranges from the false ones. It also needed a very powerful and fast computer, to check each one of the billions of radar pulses and echoes and to display on the operator screens only the real targets and the real target speeds and distances. Even then there are still problems. How can the radar tell whether a target at very low level moving at 87 kts (160 km/h; 100 mph) relative to the ground is a Soviet helicopter bristling with weapons or a harmless BMW on the autobahn?

Taking shape

The winner of the overland downlook radar was Westinghouse. There was study of purpose-designed carrier aircraft, but these could not do much better than the existing Boeing 707-320C airliner. To increase endurance on station it was planned in 1968 to fit the AWACS aircraft with eight TF34 engines (as used in the Fairchild-Republic A-10), in twin pods, but to save money this was dropped and the E-3 went into production with four regular TF33 engines (special KE-3As for the Royal Saudi air force have bigger CFM56 engines giving higher performance, much longer endurance and less noise). Almost all parts of the E-3 are the same as those of the commercial transport except for the windowless fuselage and the giant 'rotodome' mounted on a braced pylon above the rear fuselage.

The APY-1 radar fills a large part of the fuelage just aft of the wing, both below and above the floor. Radar signals, and received echoes, travel up or down the two sloping struts above the fuselage on which the rotodome is mounted. The main radar antenna (aerial) is a beam 9.14 m (30 ft) long and about 1.83 m (6 ft) high, formed from 53 slotted waveguides one above the other. The top and bottom waveguides get progressively shorter so that, seen square-on, the antenna looks roughly oval. From the whole of this enormous flat face the radar energy is emitted under precise computer control from the thousands of fine slits, in such a way that it forms a fine flat beam (with very little energy sent out as unwanted 'sidelobes') which can be pointed down

to the Earth's surface and take in the sky above up to the greatest height at which aircraft can fly.

On the back of this vast antenna is mounted a mass of auxiliary equipment inside a large structural beam giving ample strength to resist distortion that would harm accuracy. On the back of this beam is a communications and digital data-link antenna which is used for IFF purposes and for secure communications with perhaps hundreds of other friendly stations such as ground headquarters, ships at sea, other aircraft and possibly even the President of the United States. The rotodome is completed by adding a liquid cooling system and then streamlining everything inside front and rear radomes of glassfibre sandwich to form a shape like a giant flattened egg. This has only a minor effect on aircraft speed and handling.

Internal systems

In operation the radar is extremely complex, but basic principles are straightforward. The antennas are mounted on large bearing pivots, and these rotate at 0.25 rpm (1.5° per second) to keep the bearings lubricated. When the radar is in operation the rotodome speeds up to 6 rpm (36° per second) to keep the colossal radar beam sweeping round to all points of the compass. In the first 24 E-3s, designated Core E-3As, an IBM CC-1 computer processes the incoming radar echoes at the rate of 740,000 per second and feeds the results to nine SDCs and

US Air Force E-3 Sentries carry a dual responsibility: as part of Tactical Air Command they act as command and control centres during quick-reaction deployments, and within the North American Air Defense system the force tracks enemy air forces over the USA.

two ADUs. The consoles are arranged in rows of three across the cabin above the leading edge of the wing. Immediately behind them is the station for the Duty Officer. Up front are the flight crew, masses of electronics (concerned mainly with navigation and communications) and the station for the computer operator. Further aft is the console for the radar maintenance officer, and right at the tail end is a large galley and crew rest area.

The E-3A has an unrefuelled endurance of more than 11 hours, and this can be extended by inflight-refuelling via a boom receptacle above the cockpit. Once on station the radar is brought to full power and operated in any of six modes. Simplest is Passive, in which no signals are emitted; instead the mighty rotating antennas receive every kind of electronic signal (from air, sea and land sources) and the on-board equipment can pinpoint their position and analyse their characteristics to identify the sources. In the BTH

The ubiquitous Boeing 707 airframe now flying as the E-3 Sentry is crammed full with state-of-the-art surveillance systems, and progressive updates from E-3A to E-3B and E-3C configurations have greatly increased operational flexibility, including maritime surveillance.

(WF)

IFF
Six groups of blade aerials (antennas) serve the IFF (identification friend or foe) system based on the Eaton A/L APX-103 interrogator. This is the first IFF system able to interrogate automatically every aerial target simultaneously in commercial (Mk X selective ident facility) and military (Mk XII) modes, giving instantaneous range, azimuth, elevation, coded identification and IFF status of all targets seen

SDC
The main cabin contains nine (in E-3B and E-3C, 14) Hazeltine high-resolution colour situation display consoles at which every feature and target within radar radius (typically 370 km/230 miles) is clearly displayed. An operator from one of the NATO air forces sits at each SDC. All nine men could come from different nations

Radar
The Westinghouse APY-1 radar most powerful and versatile fitte Western aircraft. All signals are through a flat plate electronically scanned aerial (antenna) 7.32 m across, with liquid cooling

Radomes
Two D-shaped radomes are attached at front and rear of the 9.14-m (30-ft) central beam. They are transparent to the radar and IFF signals and serve as aerodynamic fairings. Radar vision is adversely affected by the presence of the aircraft under the rotodome

Emergency exits
Emergency escape doors are located above the wing on each side. There are main doors at front and rear on the left and an aft door on the right

Vortex generators
Rows of small vortex generators turbulators, stir up and re-energi airflow over the wings, giving im airflow over the high-speed ailer high speeds and altitudes

Core jets
The hot gas jet from each engine is expelled through a plain nozzle, fitted with a reverser to give braking after landing

Spoilers
Recessed into the upper surface of each wing are two pairs of spoilers, which can be forced open hydraulically on hinges along the forward edge. When all eight sections are opened symmetrically they act as airbrakes. When opened on one side only they serve as powerful lateral control surfaces

HF radios
Three separate high-frequency radio sets provide worldwide voice communications. Each is served by a separate long 'probe' aerial (antenna), either projecting aft from a wingtip or forwards from the fin

Boeing E-3A Sentry
NATO Airborne Early Warning Force (NAE
Geilenkirchen, West Germany

Receptable
In the top of the forward fuselage is the receptacle for the refuelling boom of USAF tanker aircraft. The responsibility for making the connection rests with the tanker boom operator, who guides the boom to the receptacle with the aid of red lines painted on the E-3A

Communications
The E-3A has an exceptional array of communications radio systems. Most of the equipment is grouped above the floor just behind the flight deck

Computers
Very powerful electronic data-processing equipment is installed. In the NATO E-3A the standard mainframe computer is the IBM 4-Pi CC-2, with main storage of 665,360 words and over 1.2 million words of mass memory. Boeing interface adapters link all the avionics and processing systems

Nose radar
A Bendix colour radar display is fed from a stabilized scanner in the nose. This is used to warn of storm clouds, and can also serve a navigation mapping function and assist rendezvous with tankers

ECM
Comprehensive electronic countermeasures are installed in the E-3A, but additional jammer pods can be hung on pylons under the inboard wings. In theory these hardpoints could receive different pylons for self-defence missiles, but this is not at present a requirement

Pylon strut
Each engine hangs from the spars of a pylon which holds it in the correct position below and ahead of the wing. Along the top is a duct fairing which in the first E-3 housed a turbocompressor with an inlet at the front

Engines
The Pratt & Whitney TF33-100 or -100A engines are turbofans derived from the original J57 which powered the first B-52 and 707 aircraft well over 30 years ago. They are fitted with exceptionally large electric generators to supply the electrical loads needed by the E-3A

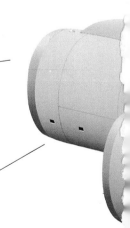

Fan jets
The fan section at the front of each engine discharges plain compress at about the speed of sound throug three 'banana ducts', so called beca of their cross-section shape. The ou ring cowl can slide aft to block off ar reverse the flow after landing

mode, all radar power is put into achieving range, without elevation data, for full-range detection to beyond the visual horizon (limits are classified). The commonest mode is PDES, in which the main beam is electronically swept up and down to cover the whole surveillance airspace. The received signals, of which there may be many hundreds, are analysed to determine the exact time of peak signal (echo) strength, which in turn gives target elevation. At all times, of course, target direction is read off by applying a small time-of-flight correction to the direction in which the antenna is pointing.

PDES provides the maximum information and suffers the greatest loss in range. Where detection of distant targets is more important than knowing their height it is possible to switch to PDNES, in which the vertical scanning is eliminated. When over the sea, it is possible in E-3As nos 25 to 34 to switch to a Maritime mode in which surface ships can be detected in various sea states. The sixth operating mode is Interleaved, in which various high-PRF and low-PRF modes are sent out together to give the best combination of signals for long-range detection of both aircraft and ship targets.

Progressive updates

USAF aircraft nos 25-34 are designated Standard E-3As, but these have since 1984 been upgraded to E-3C configuration with five extra SDCs, five more UHF radio installations and the Have Quick anti-jamming improvements. Meanwhile the 24 original Core E-3As have been progressively updated to E-3B standard. These have the CC-2 computer (faster and with roughly quadrupled main storage capacity), five extra SDCs, the five more UHF radios and an an extra long-range HF set, ECM-resistant voice communications, radio teletypewriter, Have Quick anti-jamming and an 'austere' maritime capability for overwater use (though not as good as that of the Standard E-3A).

The USAF establishment of 34 aircraft will eventually all be brought to the E-3C standard. They operate all over the world with the 552nd AWAC Wing, whose home base and training squadron is at Tinker AFB, Oklahoma. Permanent overseas detachments are the 960th AWAC Support Squadron at NAS Keflavik, Iceland, and the 961st at Kadena AB, Okinawa, in the western Pacific. They operate in partnership with EC-135 and WC-135 support aircraft of the 8th Tactical Deployment Control Squadron, and with various tanker forces.

In addition, for use in the European theatre the European NATO nations, except the UK, have purchased 18 aircraft of USAF/NATO Standard E-3A type. These closely resemble the USAF Standard but have minor variations in equipment. These 18 aircraft were flown to Dornier's factory at Oberpfaffenhofen, West Germany, where they were completed to the NATO standard. Among their special features are a third HF radio for overwater use, as well as a radio-teletype for hard-copy communication with maritime forces. They also have a new data analysis and programming group, and hardpoints under the inner wings where pylons could be added if

needed. Like USAF Sentries the NATO aircraft normally fly extremely accurate 'racetrack' patterns in the sky whilst on station. Unlike all other aircraft they have multi-national crews drawn from many nations, and it is said that even the most trivial decision on the NATO-AWACS bases at Geilenkirchen, Germany, and in Norway, have to be reached after careful deliberation by representatives of the 15 countries! The aircraft themselves are registered in Luxembourg (they bear the arms of the Grand Duchy on the tail) as being the fairest way to proclaim their multi-national status.

The one question never answered is how a Sentry would survive in wartime. To fly 150 tons of metal at low speed round and round in the sky whilst pumping out powerful signals is today the quickest possible way to be shot down, especially at a height of around 30,000 ft near a hostile frontier. Thirty years ago there were SAMs such as Nike Hercules with a range of over 87 miles (140 km) and effective ceiling of 150,000 ft (45720 m). Since then the USSR has developed SAMs with vastly greater capability. And there is no reason to suppose that a Sentry has some secret weapon it can use against interceptors. The underwing pylons that late models can carry could be used to mount ECM pods or even small self-defence missiles such as the AIM-9 Sidewinder, but these would not be useful against SAMs and to a modern fighter an E-3 would be an ideal 'sitting duck' target. The answer is awaited with interest.

Though home-based at Geilenkirchen in West Germany, the 18-strong NATO E-3A force regularly deploys to several forward airfields throughout Europe. Ironically, these include RAF Waddington in Great Britain, a potential late customer for the E-3's capabilities.

Glossary

AB Air Base
ADU Auxiliary Display Unit
AEW Airborne Early Warning
AFB Air Force Base
AWACS Airborne Warning And Control System
BTH Beyond The Horizon
ECM Electronic CounterMeasures
HF High Frequency
IFF Identification Friend or Foe
NAS Naval Air Station
ORT Overland Radar Technology
PDES Pulse-Doppler Elevation Scan
PDNES Pulse-Doppler Non-Elevation Scan
PRF Pulse Repetition Frequency
SAM Surface-to-Air Missile
SDC Situation Display Console
TDCS Tactical Deployment Control Squadron
UHF Ultra High Frequency

Inside the E-3 fuselage, a variety of multi-purpose display consoles and equipment bays cover tasks such as target identification and tracking, communications and data processing. The number of AWACS specialists for each flight varies with each mission profile.

Boeing E-3 Sentry in service units and example aircraft

Tactical Air Command, US Air Force
552nd Airborne Warning & Control Wing
Bases: Tinker AFB, Oklahoma; Keflavik AB, Iceland; and Kadena AB, Japan
Squadrons: 960th Airborne Warning & Control Squadron (Temporary Duty from Keflavik AB)
961st Airborne Warning & Control Squadron (Temporary Duty from Kadena AB)
963rd Airborne Warning & Control Squadron
964th Airborne Warning & Control Squadron
965th Airborne Warning & Control Squadron
966th Airborne Warning & Control Training Squadron
Aircraft: The six squadrons forming the 552nd Airborne Warning & Control Wing draw aircraft from a wing pool of 34 E-3A/B/C Sentries; E-3B aircraft include 31675, 50559, 61605 and 80577; examples of the E-3C include 00138, 10005, 20006 and 30009

552nd Airborne Warning & Control Wing

960th Airborne Warning & Control Squadron
Base: Detached to Keflavik AB, Iceland

961st Airborne Warning & Control Squadron
Base: Detached to Kadena AB, Okinawa

963rd Airborne Warning & Control Squadron
Base: Tinker AFB, Oklahoma
Fin-band colours: Black

964th Airborne Warning & Control Squadron
Base: Tinker AFB, Oklahoma
Fin-band colours: Red

965th Airborne Warning & Control Squadron
Base: Tinker AFB, Oklahoma
Fin-band colours: Yellow

966th Airborne Warning & Control Training Squadron
Base: Tinker AFB, Oklahoma
Fin-band colours: Blue

NATO Airborne Early Warning Force (NAEWF)
Base: Geilenkirchen AB, West Germany
Aircraft: 18 E-3As are operated by the NAEWF, comprising LX-N90442 to LX-N90459 inclusive; the Luxembourg civil aircraft prefix is followed by the US Air Force fiscal year and unit serial, the aircraft having been procured by the USAF on behalf of NATO in 1979

In addition to the highly prominent markings on the forward fuselage, NATO E-3As carry two other crests. Immediately below the cockpit is the NATO Airborne Early Warning Force (NAEWF) crest, while on the tailfin the Grand Duchy of Luxembourg's coat of arms is prominent. The latter crest is worn to acknowledge the country of registration for the NATO E-3A force.

NATO Airborne Early Warning Force

Grand Duchy of Luxembourg coat of arms

Loran aerials
The flush internal aerials for the Loran (long-range air navigation) system are in the tip of the fin. Loran is a hyperbolic navaid based upon groups of ground stations

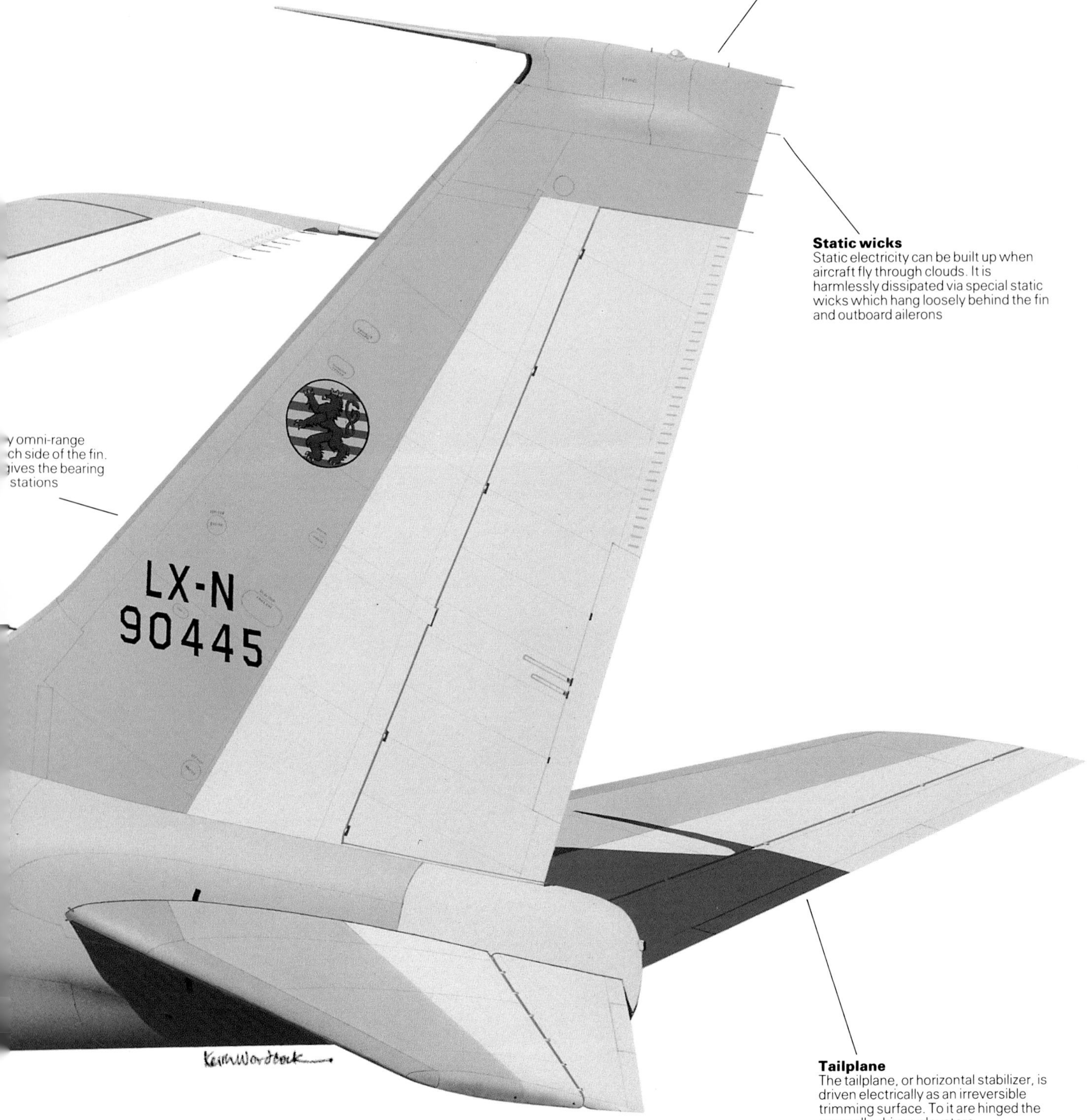

Static wicks
Static electricity can be built up when aircraft fly through clouds. It is harmlessly dissipated via special static wicks which hang loosely behind the fin and outboard ailerons

y omni-range
ch side of the fin.
gives the bearing
stations

LX-N
90445

Keith Woodcock

Tailplane
The tailplane, or horizontal stabilizer, is driven electrically as an irreversible trimming surface. To it are hinged the manually-driven elevators

Main beam
The structural heart of the rotodome is a light-alloy beam 9.14 m (30 ft) long and 1.82 m (6 ft) deep, to which the aerials and radomes are attached. It rotates on sliprings and microwave guides feeding the current and radar signals. Speed is 6 rpm in operation; on other flights speed is 0.25 rpm to keep the bearings lubricated

IFF
A giant high-power IFF system works through an aerial on the reverse side of the rotodome central beam. This 'looks' through a special window moulded in the reverse half of the rotodome

VOR
The very high frequen⟨c⟩ uses flush aerials on e⟨a⟩ VOR is a navaid which ⟨ ⟩ of friendly ground radi⟨o⟩

Pylon
The rotodome is carried on twin pylon struts faired into the structure of the rear fuselage. Electric power, microwave waveguide ducts and cooling pipes fill the interior of each strut

Flaps
Track-mounted flaps, often incorrectly called Fowler flaps, are fitted in two sections to the wings wherever the jets from the engines do not make this impossible. When fully extended the flaps increase wing lift to enable the aircraft to land relatively slowly. Krueger flaps hinge down from under the wing leading edge

Inlet
Under the rear fuselage are the main high-power electrical systems associated with the giant APY-1 radar, together with the signal generators and main radar transmitter. These units have liquid cooling, this ram-air inlet being used to pass cooling air through the main liquid cooling radiator. Total electric power is 600,000 watts

Ailerons
Lateral control is provided by two all-speed ailerons hinged between the flaps on each wing and two longer-span outboard ailerons, supplemented by the spoilers. The ailerons and flap circuits are interconnected, so that when the flaps are up the outboard ailerons are disconnected

Performance:

Maximum speed	460 kts	853 km/h (530 mph)
Service ceiling	29,000 ft+	(8850 m+)
Maximum unrefuelled endurance	11 hours+	
Endurance on station (6 hours from base)	1610 km	(1,000 miles)

Service ceiling

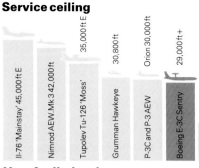

Il-76 'Mainstay' 45,000 ft E	Nimrod AEW.Mk 3 42,000 ft	Tupolev Tu-126 'Moss' 35,000 ft E	Grumman Hawkeye 30,800 ft	P-3C and P-3 AEW Orion 30,000 ft	Boeing E-3C Sentry 29,000 ft+	Westland / Sea King AEW 10,000 ft

Maximum level speed

Nimrod AEW.Mk 3 500 kts	
Boeing E-3C Sentry 460 kts	
Il-76 'Mainstay' 459 kts E	
Tupolev Tu-126 'Moss' 459 kts	
P-3C and P-3 AEW Orion 411 kts	
Grumman E-2C Hawkeye	323 kts
Westland	Sea King AEW 112 kts

Unrefuelled endurance

Tupolev Tu-126 'Moss' 20 hours+ E	
P-3C and P-3 AEW Orion 14 hours+	
Boeing E-3C Sentry	11 hours+
Il-76 'Mainstay'	10 hours+ E
Nimrod AEW.Mk 3	10 hours+
Grumman E-2C	Hawkeye 6 hours 6 mins
Westland	Sea King AEW 4 hours

Recent additions to the overall light grey colour scheme worn by USAF E-3s have been coloured fin bands, these identifying the E-3 squadrons. The blue fin band is worn by the 966th AW&CTS. The nose illustration shows a non-standard application of TAC, 28th Air Division and 552nd AW&CW crests.

The basic cockpit of the Boeing 707 airliner, with equipment changes and modifications, forms the 'front office' of the Boeing E-3 Sentry. Pilot and co-pilot exterior view is excellent via the six-piece glazing and two overhead viewpoints. Behind the pilots' seats are the flight engineer's station (right) and an observer's jump-seat (left).

Boeing E-3A Sentry cutaway drawing key

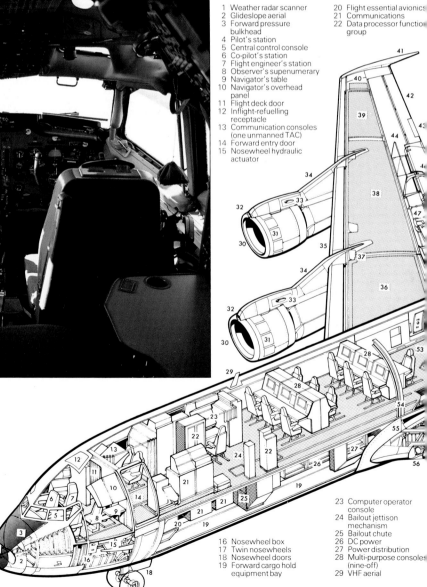

1 Weather radar scanner
2 Glideslope aerial
3 Forward pressure bulkhead
4 Pilot's station
5 Central control console
6 Co-pilot's station
7 Flight engineer's station
8 Observer's supenumerary
9 Navigator's table
10 Navigator's overhead panel
11 Flight deck door
12 Inflight-refuelling receptacle
13 Communication consoles (one unmanned TAC)
14 Forward entry door
15 Nosewheel hydraulic actuator

16 Nosewheel box
17 Twin nosewheels
18 Nosewheel doors
19 Forward cargo hold equipment bay

20 Flight essential avionics
21 Communications
22 Data processor function group

23 Computer operator console
24 Bailout jettison mechanism
25 Bailout chute
26 DC power
27 Power distribution
28 Multi-purpose consoles (nine-off)
29 VHF aerial

E-3 recognition features

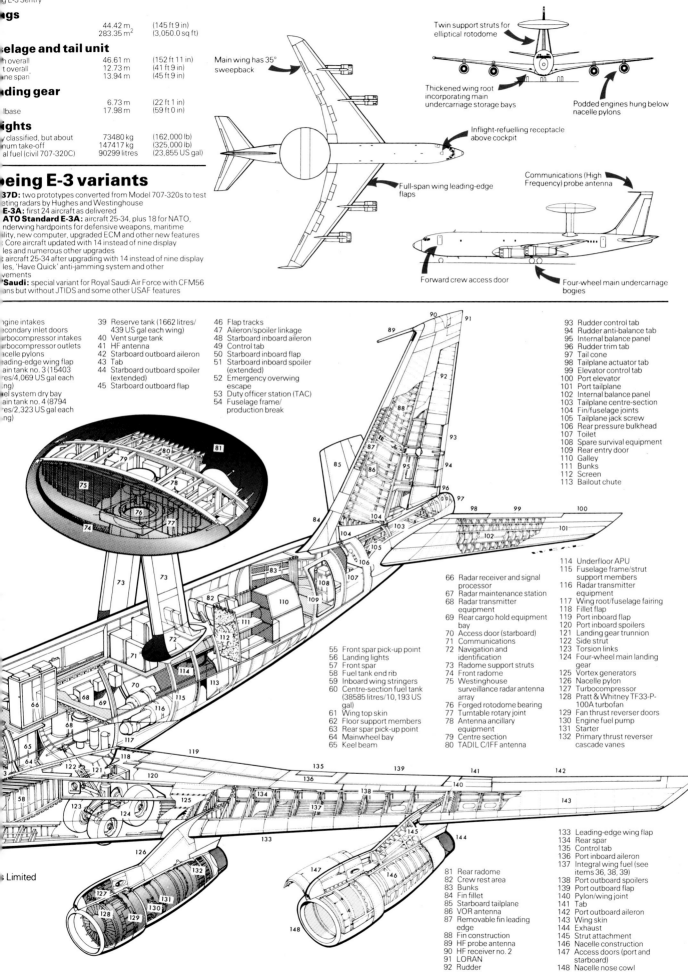

ecification:

g E-3 Sentry

gs

	44.42 m²	(145 ft 9 in)
	283.35 m²	(3,050.0 sq ft)

selage and tail unit

h overall	46.61 m	(152 ft 11 in)
t overall	12.73 m	(41 ft 9 in)
ne span	13.94 m	(45 ft 9 in)

ding gear

lbase	6.73 m	(22 ft 1 in)
	17.98 m	(59 ft 0 in)

ights

y classified, but about	73480 kg	(162,000 lb)
num take-off	147417 kg	(325,000 lb)
al fuel (civil 707-320C)	90299 litres	(23,855 US gal)

eing E-3 variants

37D: two prototypes converted from Model 707-320s to test eting radars by Hughes and Westinghouse
E-3A: first 24 aircraft as delivered
ATO Standard E-3A: aircraft 25-34, plus 18 for NATO, nderwing hardpoints for defensive weapons, maritime ility, new computer, upgraded ECM and other new features Core aircraft updated with 14 instead of nine display les and numerous other upgrades
: aircraft 25-34 after upgrading with 14 instead of nine display les, 'Have Quick' anti-jamming system and other vements
Saudi: special variant for Royal Saudi Air Force with CFM56 ans but without JTIDS and some other USAF features

Twin support struts for elliptical rotodome

Main wing has 35° sweepback

Thickened wing root incorporating main undercarriage storage bays

Podded engines hung below nacelle pylons

Inflight-refuelling receptacle above cockpit

Full-span wing leading-edge flaps

Communications (High Frequency) probe antenna

Forward crew access door

Four-wheel main undercarriage bogies

engine intakes
econdary inlet doors
urbocompressor intakes
urbocompressor outlets
acelle pylons
eading-edge wing flap
ain tank no. 3 (15403 res/4,069 US gal each ng)
el system dry bay
ain tank no. 4 (8794 res/2,323 US gal each ng)

39 Reserve tank (1662 litres/ 439 US gal each wing)
40 Vent surge tank
41 HF antenna
42 Starboard outboard aileron
43 Tab
44 Starboard outboard spoiler (extended)
45 Starboard outboard flap

46 Flap tracks
47 Aileron/spoiler linkage
48 Starboard inboard aileron
49 Control tab
50 Starboard inboard flap
51 Starboard inboard spoiler (extended)
52 Emergency overwing escape
53 Duty officer station (TAC)
54 Fuselage frame/ production break

55 Front spar pick-up point
56 Landing lights
57 Front spar
58 Fuel tank end rib
59 Inboard wing stringers
60 Centre-section fuel tank (38585 litres/10,193 US gal)
61 Wing top skin
62 Floor support members
63 Rear spar pick-up point
64 Mainwheel bay
65 Keel beam

66 Radar receiver and signal processor
67 Radar maintenance station
68 Radar transmitter equipment
69 Rear cargo hold equipment bay
70 Access door (starboard)
71 Communications
72 Navigation and identification
73 Radome support struts
74 Front radome
75 Westinghouse surveillance radar antenna array
76 Forged rotodome bearing
77 Turntable rotary joint
78 Antenna ancillary equipment
79 Centre section
80 TADIL C/IFF antenna

81 Rear radome
82 Crew rest area
83 Bunks
84 Fin fillet
85 Starboard tailplane
86 VOR antenna
87 Removable fin leading edge
88 Fin construction
89 HF probe antenna
90 HF receiver no. 2
91 LORAN
92 Rudder

93 Rudder control tab
94 Rudder anti-balance tab
95 Internal balance panel
96 Rudder trim tab
97 Tail cone
98 Tailplane actuator tab
99 Elevator control tab
100 Port elevator
101 Port tailplane
102 Internal balance panel
103 Tailplane centre-section
104 Fin/fuselage joints
105 Tailplane jack screw
106 Rear pressure bulkhead
107 Toilet
108 Spare survival equipment
109 Rear entry door
110 Galley
111 Bunks
112 Screen
113 Bailout chute

114 Underfloor APU
115 Fuselage frame/strut support members
116 Radar transmitter equipment
117 Wing root/fuselage fairing
118 Fillet flap
119 Port inboard flap
120 Port inboard spoilers
121 Landing gear trunnion
122 Side strut
123 Torsion links
124 Four-wheel main landing gear
125 Vortex generators
126 Nacelle pylon
127 Turbocompressor
128 Pratt & Whitney TF33-P-100A turbofan
129 Fan thrust reverser doors
130 Engine fuel pump
131 Starter
132 Primary thrust reverser cascade vanes

133 Leading-edge wing flap
134 Rear spar
135 Control tab
136 Port inboard aileron
137 Integral wing fuel (see items 36, 38, 39)
138 Port outboard spoilers
139 Port outboard flap
140 Pylon/wing joint
141 Tab
142 Port outboard aileron
143 Wing skin
144 Exhaust
145 Strut attachment
146 Nacelle construction
147 Access doors (port and starboard)
148 Nacelle nose cowl

Limited

The LOCKHEED S-3 VIKING

Lockheed Viking: Sub Stalker

The Lockheed S-3A Viking forms a vital part of the contemporary US Navy carrier air wing, employing a vast array of sensor and tracking systems against enemy submarine forces lurking beneath the vast oceans of the world.

Making its operational debut aboard the USS *John F. Kennedy* (CV-67) during the latter half of 1975 when VS-21 conducted a tour of overseas duty with the 6th Fleet in the Mediterranean, the Lockheed S-3 Viking is one of two dedicated anti-submarine warfare elements which routinely deploy on the US Navy's large aircraft-carriers, the other being the Sikorsky SH-3H Sea King helicopter.

Considerably more sophisticated and certainly rather more youthful than Sikorsky's veteran helicopter, the Viking can trace its origins back to the late 1960s, when serious consideration was first given to the question of replacing the Grumman S-2 Tracker which at that time was the mainstay of US Navy fixed-wing carrierborne ASW capability. Five companies were initially involved in the competition. Early Navy evaluation of the various proposals soon eliminated three candidates, leaving Lockheed and General Dynamics continuing to slug it out for the potentially lucrative contract.

Subsequently, in early 1969, Lockheed emerged victorious, being rewarded with a $461 million contract on 4 August of that year, although it should be noted that the company was essentially just the prime contractor responsible for building the fuselage, for integration of the avionics system and for final assembly. Other elements of the team were Vought, with responsibility for the wings, tail unit, landing gear and engine nacelles, and Univac, which produced the highly advanced digital computer which tied together all of the onboard sensor systems employed in submarine detection and tracking.

The S-3 was flown for the first time in prototype form on 21 January 1972, and, as considerable urgency was attached to this programme, within a year no less than seven more R&D examples had entered flight status, these pursuing various aspects of the test effort in vigorous fashion. Indeed, despite its undoubted sophistication in comparison with the Tracker which it would eventually replace, the Viking progressed rapidly through all of the many test objectives, and deliveries to the Navy actually got under way in late February 1974, training unit VS-41 at North Island, California receiving the first production examples.

Not surprisingly, in view of the quantum leap in ASW state-of-the-art that the S-3A represented, it took some time to work the new type to deployable status,

With its deep fuselage, large nose and short, stubby landing gear, the S-3 Viking is hardly the most appealing of naval aircraft; but in front-line operation it is second to none, keeping the navy fleets free from the submarine attack threat.

and it was not until just before the end of June 1975 that VS-21 finally took 10 aircraft aboard the *Kennedy* for the first fully-fledged tour of overseas duty. This was undeniably a highly successful debut, the Viking performing well throughout the six-month cruise which cleared the way for further deployments. The original plan called for procurement of sufficient S-3As to equip 12 fully-operational squadrons as well as a permanently shore-based training unit.

Squadron deployment

Ultimately, the nonavailability of sufficient large-deck carriers (at the time the S-3A acquired its sea-legs only 10 of the so-called 'super carriers' existed) resulted in just 11 squadrons forming for duty at sea. However, subsequent additions to the fleet may eventually prompt the commissioning of further units in due course. At present, though, the Viking serves with just 11 deployable squadrons (VS-21/22/24/28/29/30/31/32/33/37/38) plus VS-41 which is still primarily responsible for the majority of Viking crew training in association with a rather smaller training-orientated element known as the VSSU. In line with normal US Navy practice, separate shore bases exist for Atlantic and Pacific Fleet elements, those west coast squadrons that are now active with ComNavAirPac being concentrated at North Island, California whilst their east coast ComNavAirLant counterparts may be found at Cecil Field, Florida.

As far as the basic airframe is concerned, the S-3 Viking is essentially quite simple and surprisingly small in view of its undoubted capability. A high-wing design, with a fuselage which can only be described as portly in appearance, the Viking is powered by a pair of podded General Electric TF34-GE-400 high-bypass-ratio turbofan engines, these bestowing the dual advantages of economy of operation with superior 'dash' speed so that the Viking can reach the designated area of operation with the minimum delay. Once there, the Viking normally loiters at a

Once a target has been detected, a wide range of weapons can be utilized, these being carried in the internal weapons bays and on underwing pylons. This aircraft is dropping a torpedo.

speed of around 160 kts (296 km/h; 184 mph), which enables it to remain on station for prolonged periods. Since it can be refuelled in flight the Viking is, or course, not range-limited, crew fatigue being a far more influential factor as far as mission duration is concerned.

In for the kill

Armament options are many and varied, it being possible to carry offensive stores both internally in the weapons bay or externally on two underwing hard-points located outboard of the TF34 engine pods. In the primary ASW role, the Viking can employ torpedoes or depth bombs, but it can also be used for mine-laying or even, in certain circumstances, conventional bombing, the external stores stations being able to accept triple ejector racks. Rockets, cluster bomb units and flares may also be delivered and the forthcoming S-3B is compatible with the McDonnell Douglas Harpoon stand-off anti-ship missile, thus permitting the Viking to be employed against hostile warships.

So far as mission-related sensor systems are concerned, the Viking truly represents a classic instance of cramming the proverbial quart into a pint pot, virtually every spare cubic inch of space being occupied. Yet the necessary miniaturization does not appear to have been achieved at the cost of degraded performance. Indeed, clear and incontrovertible evidence of the efficacy of the Viking suite can be gleaned from the fact that the original ASW avionics and data-processing package was specified by the Canadians for installation in the CP-140 Aurora derivative of Lockheed's bigger ASW stablemate, the P-3 Orion.

At the heart of the Viking's complex system is the Univac 1832A general-purpose digital computer, for it is this which performs the myriad calculations that are so much a part of the art of submarine hunting. Data generated by the

various sensors (including radar, FLIR, passive ESM, MAD and up to 60 pre-loaded sonobuoys in a cluster of launch tubes located in the belly) are relayed automatically to the computer for processing and display to crew members via CRT. In addition to presenting mission-related data in a comprehensible format, the computer also performs a number of other tasks such as the storage of information for post-mission analysis, the calculation of weapons trajectories and management of offensive stores. A data-link facility enables information to be transferred and received whilst the aircraft is in flight, thus enabling a relieving aircraft (either another S-3A or a P-3C Orion) to continue to 'prosecute' a contact or, alternatively, to pick up the hunt where the departing machine left off.

Crew duties

Despite this ambitious array of equipment, the S-3A carries a crew of just four, all housed in a pressurized and air-conditioned compartment in the forward fuselage section. Two of the crew (the pilot and co-pilot) are actually more concerned with the physical act of flying the aircraft, whilst responsibility for sub-hunting rests with the Tacco and Senso who occupy the centre portion of the

In addition to a fuselage crammed full of detection systems, external features include a long magnetic anomaly detection (MAD) boom which extends from the rear fuselage.

cabin directly ahead of the avionics compartment. All four crew members have McDonnell Douglas Escapac 1-E zero/zero ejector seats.

As far as routine operations are concerned, it is usual for the Viking and Sea King to be considered as a team, both being responsible for the protection of the attack carrier striking force and, by definition, other elements of the fleet. In practice, this normally means that the Sea King helicopter is tasked with close-in protection, seldom operating much more than 10 miles (16 km) from the parent aircraft-carrier.

Surface combatants also form part of the defensive screen, whilst it is more usual for the Viking to operate at extreme range, essentially endeavouring to estab-

Anti-submarine warfare is a round-the-clock responsibility for the 10-aircraft S-3A squadrons aboard US Navy aircraft carriers. Despite its complexity, the Viking is popular with crews and easy to maintain, thanks to complete deck-level servicing access.

UHF/IFF
Projecting blade aerials (antennas) not
associated with the ARS-2 are either
UHF (ultra high frequency) radio and IFF
(identification friend or foe) or concerned
with alternative radio systems

VHF
Very high frequency radio sets use
dorsal (upper surface blade aerials). One
at the rear, hidden by the wing, serves
the Tacan (tactical air navigation) system

Senso station
Behind the pilots are the sensor operator
and tactical co-ordinator, side-by-side.
The senso looks out of this window
during visual searches

TF34 turbofans
The General Electric TF34 high-bypass
ration turbofan was specially designed
for this aircraft. Later a version of the
same engine was chosen for the A-10A
of the USAF. The engine is specially
designed for full power through the
steam of catapults, and the inlet is de-
iced by hot bleed air

Hinge
The long-span wings can be folded
hydraulically to reduce space on d
The hinges are skewed so that the
folded wings overlap

Pylon
The S-3 has always been able to carry
weapons, tanks or cargo pods on these
deep underwing pylons. After
conversion to S-3B it can fire Harpoon
missiles

JET
DANGER
INTAKE

APU
The Williams gas turbine auxiliary power
unit provides emergency electric power
in flight, or power for test purposes on
the ground

Weapon bay
The internal weapon bay is arranged in
left and right halves, each of which can
accommodate two torpedoes or various
other loads (see loads panel)

Main landing gears
The main landing gears were based on
those of the Vought F-8 Crusader fighter,
but strengthened. They were among
many large parts (including the wings,
tail and engine pods) made by Vought

Lockheed S-3A Viking
VS-32 `Norsemen', CVW-1
USS America
US Navy Atlantic Fleet

Pilot
All four crew members occupy
McDonnell Douglas Escapac IE-1
ejection seats. The co-pilot sits on the
right

Inflight-refuelling probe
An inflight-refuelling probe can be
extended ahead of the cockpit. When
retracted it occupies a fuel-filled tube
extending aft to the wing tankage

Radar
The Texas Instruments APS-116 is a
high-resolution radar specially designed
for overwater operation in the S-3. The
same radar goes into the Canadian
CP-140 version of the P-3 Orion

Nose gear
The steerable twin-wheel nose gear is
made extremely strong. The catapult
towbar at the bottom of the leg could
fling the Viking off the deck at flying
speed even if its brakes were locked on!

FLIR
The forward-looking infra-red is one of
the chief attack sensors. The OR-89 AA
is made by Texas Instruments and gives
a clear monochrome picture of
everything ahead on a basis of
temperature, no matter what the
weather or darkness of the night

Doppler radar
The Ryan APN-200 Doppler radar
provides the DGVS (Doppler groun
velocity system) which gives a
continuous exact read-out of spee
direction over the ground. From th
wind and drift angle can be obtaine

lish a 'sanitized' area in which the parent carrier may operate secure in the knowledge that it is unlikely to be threatened by sub-surface forces. Consequently, missions frequently employ the 'double-cycle' pattern, Vikings often remaining aloft for 210 minutes rather than the more normal 105-minute cycle adopted by fighter and attack types. Surveillance is generally accomplished from medium to high altitude, but once a submarine has been detected it is usual to descend for a vigorous prosecution of the contact. Employing this mode of operation significantly reduces the risk of the watching aircraft betraying its position and, as a consequence, alerting a potential sub-surface enemy that it is indeed being hunted.

B-model features

Lockheed has held discussions with several potential customers, most notably West Germany, but no overseas orders were ever received for the Viking, and production eventually terminated during the summer of 1978 when the 187th example to roll from the Burbank assembly line was delivered to the US Navy. Since then, a number of other variants have appeared, of which the most significant is the S-3B.

Studies into the possibility of updating mission-related subsystems began during the summer of 1980 although it was not until 1981 that Lockheed received a $14.5 million contract to proceed with full-scale engineering development of a new version to be known as the S-3B. Essentially, this benefits from the provision of much-improved avionics systems, this work including increasing acoustic-processing capacity, expanding the capability of ESM equipment, enhancing radar processing and installing a new sonobuoy telemetry receiver system. Weapons capability is also updated in that the S-3B is compatible with the Harpoon ASM.

Thus far, the S-3B programme anticipates conversion rather than procurement of new aircraft, although it should be noted that tooling still exists and Lockheed has actually prepared figures for the Navy based on the manufacture of 82 or 103 brand new aircraft.

Future service

Initially, though, it was decided to modify a couple of existing S-3As to S-3B standard and the first of these duly got airborne in modified form during 1984. Assuming that test objectives are met satisfactorily, it seems likely that approximately 160 existing S-3As will ultimately be modernized to S-3B standard in a programme beginning in 1987. Whether or not this will be sufficient aircraft to satisfy Navy plans, which now call for a 15-carrier fleet, remains to be settled. Certainly, 160 S-3Bs would not be enough to permit allocation of a 10-aircraft squadron to each of the 15 proposed air wings, and thus reinstatement in production must be a very real possi-

A Weapons System Improvement Program (WSIP) and avionics upgrading distinguish the new S-3B model, initial examples of which are currently undergoing naval evaluation. Up to 160 S-3As could be converted.

bility. The Navy may well get round the problem by limiting the number of squadrons or, alternatively, by cutting the number of aircraft assigned to a squadron.

As far as other variants are concerned, the most interesting is probably the US-3A, a handful of RDT&E examples having been converted to this configuration for use in the COD mission. In essence, the conversion entailed removal of specialized mission avionics in order to permit the carriage of cargo and/or mail in the Pacific and Indian Oceans, all of the US-3A conversions being assigned to VRC-50 squadron.

Another derivative, and one which failed to meet with any success, was the KS-3A inflight-refuelling tanker which was extensively tested by the Navy in 1980 before eventually being reconfigured as a US-3A during 1983. Although this failed to progress further, the Navy is still showing some signs of interest in a tanker Viking but the latest proposal is rather simpler, a 'buddy' refuelling pack capable of transferring fuel from the aircraft's own tanks having been the subject of a test programme conducted in 1984. This approach, however, means that the Viking's basic ASW mission is retained.

One US Navy squadron (VRC-50) is equipped with the US-3A, a carrier on-board delivery (COD) derivative which can carry cargo and up to six passengers. Weapons, ASW systems and associated equipment is deleted, with cargo also carried in two underwing pods.

Yet another, much older, proposal envisaged employing a suitably configured variant of the Viking in the Elint and Sigint roles, but this also failed to meet with approval, the Navy electing to continue with the truly-vintage Douglas EA-3B Skywarrior for the time being.

Glossary

ASM Air-to-Surface Missile
ASW Anti-Submarine Warfare
COD Carrier Onboard Delivery
ComNavAirLant Commander Naval Air Forces Atlantic Fleet
ComNavAirPac Commander Naval Air Forces Pacific Fleet
CRT Cathode Ray Tube
Elint Electronic intelligence
ESM Electronic Support Measures
FLIR Forward-Looking Infra-Red
MAD Magnetic Anomaly Detector
R&D Research & Development
RDT&E Research, Development, Test & Evaluation
Senso Sensor operator
Sigint Signals intelligence
Tacco Tactical co-ordinator
VSSU ASW Support Unit

Lockheed S-3 Viking in service units and example aircraft

US Navy

VS-31
Shore base: NAS Cecil
Field, Florida
Task: Anti-submarine
warfare
Tail code: 'AG'
Example aircraft: (S-3A)
158863 AG-710, 159733 AG-
700, 160142 AG-705

VS-22
Shore base: NAS Cecil
Field, Florida
Task: Anti-submarine
warfare
Tail code: 'AC'
Example aircraft: (S-3A)
158861 AC-704, 159752 AC-
705, 160141 AC-703

VS-24
Shore base: NAS Cecil
Field, Florida
Task: Anti-submarine
warfare
Tail code: 'AJ'
Example aircraft: (S-3A)
159729 AJ-703, 159761 AJ-
707, 160604 AJ-702

VS-28
Shore base: NAS Cecil
Field, Florida
Task: Anti-submarine
warfare
Tail code: 'AE'
Example aircraft: (S-3A)
158873 AE-702, 159764 AE-
700, 160602 AE-704

VS-30
Shore base: NAS Cecil
Field, Florida
Task: Anti-submarine
warfare
Tail code: 'AA'
Example aircraft: (S-3A)
159732 AA-701, 159758 AA-
702, 160125 AA-703

VS-32
Shore base: NAS Cecil
Field, Florida
Task: Anti-submarine
warfare
Tail code: 'AB'
Example aircraft: (S-3A)
158866 AB-705, 159753 AB-
702, 160121 AB-706

VSSU
Base: NAS Cecil Field,
Florida
Task: ASW Support Unit
Tail code: 'AR'
Example aircraft: (S-3A)
160122 AR-11, 160153 AR-16

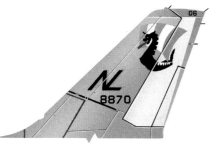

VRC-50
Base: NAS Cubi Point,
Philippines
Task: Fleet tactical support
(COD)
Tail code: 'RG'
Example aircraft: (US-3A)
157994 RG-715, 158868 RG-
713

VS-21
Shore base: NAS North
Island, California
Task: Anti-submarine
warfare
Tail code: 'NH'
Example aircraft: (S-3A)
160124 NH-701, 160157 NH-
700, 160567 NH-706

VS-29
Shore base: NAS North
Island, California
Task: Anti-submarine
warfare
Tail code: 'NL'
Example aircraft: (S-3A)
158870 NL-706, 160136 NL-
703, 160754 NL-700

VS-33
Shore base: NAS North
Island, California
Task: Anti-submarine
warfare
Tail code: 'NG'
Example aircraft: (S-3A)
160130 NG-704, 160135 NG-
711, 160581 NG-701

VS-37
Shore base: NAS North
Island, California
Task: Anti-submarine
warfare
Tail code: 'NK'
Example aircraft: (S-3A)
158862 NK-700, 159738 NK-
702, 160571 NK-705

VS-38
Shore base: NAS North
Island, California
Task: Anti-submarine
warfare
Tail code: 'NE'
Example aircraft: (S-3A)
159414 NF-7120, 160159 NE-
700, 160579 NE-707

VS-41
Shore base: NAS North
Island, California
Task: Anti-submarine
warfare
Tail code: 'NJ'
Example aircraft: (S-3A)
158865 NJ-721, 159409 NJ-
725, 159745 NJ-736, 160161
NJ-734, 160598 NJ-746

Lockheed S-3 Viking warload

4 x Mk 54 depth charges in split
weapon bay

2 x 300-US gal (1136-litre) fuel
tanks on underwing pylons

60 sonobuoys in belly tubes

4 x Mk 46 torpedoes in split
weapon bay
6 x LAU-69/A rocket pods (each
containing 19 2.75-in/69.85-mm
FFARs) on TER-7 triple ejector
racks on underwing pylons

4 x Mk 46 torpedoes in split
weapon bay
2 x AGM-84 Harpoon stand-off
air-to-surface missiles on
underwing pylons

4 x Mk 53 mines in split weapon
bay

1 x 'buddy' refuelling store under
port wing
1 x 300-US gal (1136-litre) fuel
tank under starboard wing

Anti-submarine
The Viking's weapon bay can
accommodate a wide variety of
stores, including torpedoes,
bombs, depth charges or mines.
This offensive armament can be
augmented by bombs, mines
and rocket pods carried on the
two underwing pylons.
Sonobuoys are loaded on the
ground.

Anti-shipping (S-3A)
The Viking can carry a wide
range of anti-shipping weapons,
and gives carrier air groups a
versatile strike tool which can
pack a mighty punch. The
Viking's impressive weapon
load is backed up by a
comprehensive range of
sensors and communications
equipment.

Anti-shipping (S-3B)
S-3A Vikings modified under the
Weapons System Improvement
Program will be redesignated
S-3B. Improvements include
increased data-processing
capacity, better ESM and ECM,
a new sonobuoy telemetry
system, and provision for the
Harpoon ASM.

Buddy-tanking
During 1980 a demonstrator of a
proposed tanker version of the
Viking, the KS-3A, was
evaluated by the US Navy. It
seems more likely that any
Viking refuelling tankers will be
standard S-3As which will retain
full multi-mission capability.

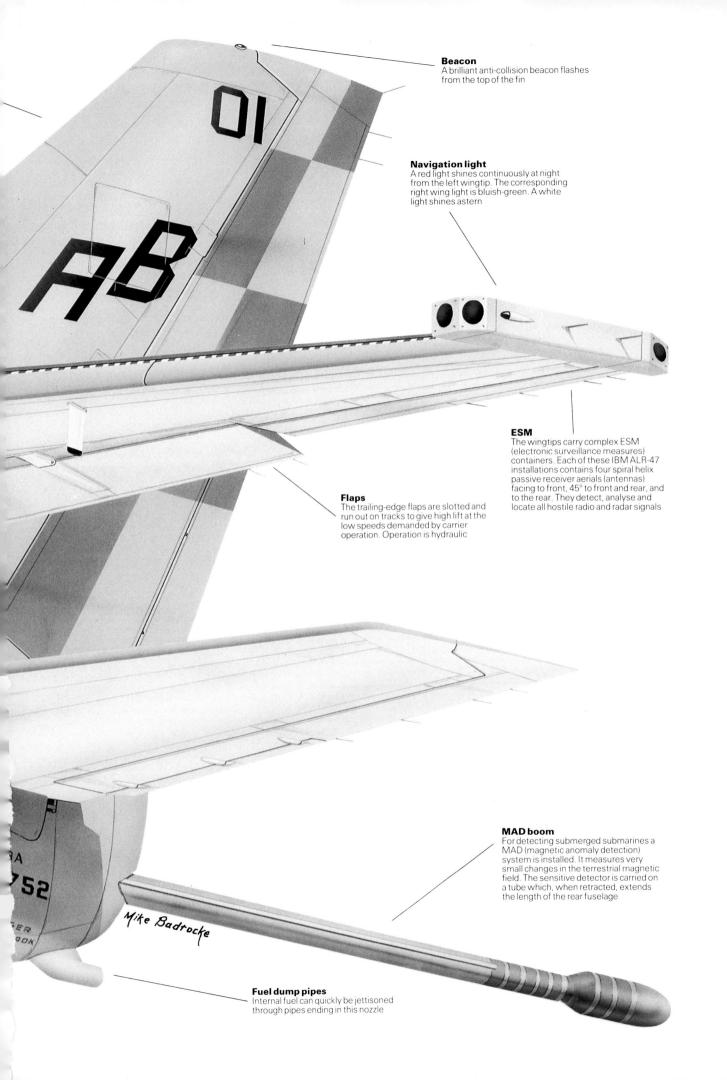

Beacon
A brilliant anti-collision beacon flashes from the top of the fin

Navigation light
A red light shines continuously at night from the left wingtip. The corresponding right wing light is bluish-green. A white light shines astern

ESM
The wingtips carry complex ESM (electronic surveillance measures) containers. Each of these IBM ALR-47 installations contains four spiral helix passive receiver aerials (antennas) facing to front, 45° to front and rear, and to the rear. They detect, analyse and locate all hostile radio and radar signals

Flaps
The trailing-edge flaps are slotted and run out on tracks to give high lift at the low speeds demanded by carrier operation. Operation is hydraulic

MAD boom
For detecting submerged submarines a MAD (magnetic anomaly detection) system is installed. It measures very small changes in the terrestrial magnetic field. The sensitive detector is carried on a tube which, when retracted, extends the length of the rear fuselage

Mike Badrocke

Fuel dump pipes
Internal fuel can quickly be jettisoned through pipes ending in this nozzle

Fin
The fin, which incorporates the inlet to the ram-air cooling duct for the ECS (environmental control system) folds over to the left to reduce height in aircraft-carrier hangars

Receiver
Two of the ARS-2 sonobuoy reference system receiver aerials are recessed into the top of the fin, one facing to each side

ARS-2 system
The Cubic Corporation ARS-2 sonobuoy reference system uses a cross formed by 10 receiver aerials (antennas) grouped in pairs along the fuselage and along the wings. Even from 30,000 ft (9144 m) this system can detect and locate sonobuoys and the position of submarines, but from low level the system can fix the position of a submarine in real time in three dimensions

Leading edge flap
The entire leading edge of the wing outboard of the engines is hinged. At take-off or landing it is pivoted down to increase lift to meet the severe demands of carrier operation. Actuation is electric

Harpoon missile
The AGM-84 Harpoon gives the S-3B a long stand-off attack capability against surface ships. The turbojet-propelled missile weighs 517 kg (1,145 lb) and has a range exceeding 92 km (57 miles)

Sonobuoys
In the rear fuselage are inclined launch tubes for 60 sonobuoys of five different types. Any one can be selected and released individually. A red line surrounds the sonobuoy bay

Arrester hook
The steel carrier arrester hook is normally retracted into the rear fuselage

ECS
Much of the rear fuselage is filled by the environmental control system which provides cooling for the powerful avionics and all other heat-generating on-board systems. This is the hot-air exhaust

Performance:

Maximum speed	450 kts	834 km/h (518 mph)
Loiter speed	160 kts	296 km/h (184 mph)
Service ceiling more than	35,000 ft	(10670 m)
Ferry range more than	5558 km	(3,454 miles)
Combat range more than	3706 km	(2,303 miles)
Initial rate of climb more than	4,200 ft (1280 m)	per minute
Take-off distance	670 m	(2,200 ft)

Weapon load

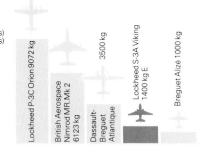

Lockheed P-3C Orion 9072 kg
British Aerospace Nimrod MR.Mk 2 6123 kg
Dassault-Breguet Atlantique 3500 kg
Lockheed S-3A Viking 1400 kg E
Breguet Alizé 1000 kg
Grumman E-2C Hawkeye none

Maximum endurance

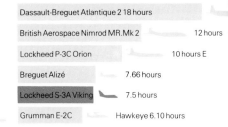

Dassault-Breguet Atlantique 2 18 hours	
British Aerospace Nimrod MR.Mk 2	12 hours
Lockheed P-3C Orion	10 hours E
Breguet Alizé	7.66 hours
Lockheed S-3A Viking	7.5 hours
Grumman E-2C	Hawkeye 6.10 hours

Maximum speed at optimum altitude

British Aerospace Nimrod MR.Mk 2 500 kts	
Lockheed S-3A Viking 450 kts	
Lockheed P-3C Orion 411 kts	
Dassault-Breguet Atlantique 2	350 kts
Grumman E-2C Hawkeye	323 kts
Breguet Alizé 280 kts	

Cruising speed at optimum altitude

British Aerospace Nimrod MR.Mk 2 475 kts	
Lockheed S-3A Viking 370 kts	
Lockheed P-3C Orion 328 kts	
Dassault-Breguet Atlantique 2	320 kts
Grumman E-2C Hawkeye 311 kts	
Breguet Alizé 247 kts	

Maximum range

British Aerospace Nimrod MR.Mk 2 9265 km	
Lockheed P-3C Orion 7670 km	
Dassault-Breguet Atlantique 2 7300 km	
Lockheed S-3A Viking 5550 km	
Grumman	E-2C Hawkeye 2580 km
Breguet Alizé	2500 km

*An inflight refuelling capability is availab[le]
the S-3 fleet via a pack under the port wing
which transfers fuel from internal reserve[s]
and a tank under the starboard wing.*

VX-1
Base: NAS Patuxent River,
Maryland
Task: Air test and evaluation
Tail code: 'JA'
Example aircraft: (S-3A)
160591 JA-167, 160592 JA-
17

NATC
Base: NAS Patuxent River,
Maryland
Task: Test
Tail code: none
Example aircraft: (S-3A)
159736, 159770

Lockheed S-3 Viking variants

S-3A: initial production model, currently in service with fixed-wing carrierborne ASW squadrons of the US Navy; 187 manufactured between 1971 and 1978; first flown on 21 January 1972 in prototype form (BuNo. 157992) and entered Navy service with VS-41 at North Island in February 1974; maiden operational deployment began 28 June 1975 and has since seen operational service in most areas where US Navy maintains a presence
S-3B: projected improved variant intended for carrierborne ASW task; two S-3As initially modified to this standard as prototypes, first flying in 1984; will incorporate much-enhanced avionics package as well as revised armament capability; present planning anticipates conversion of approximately 160 S-3As from 1987 on
ES-3A: proposed electronic surveillance platform for use by US Navy; not proceeded with
KS-3A: proposed dedicated tanker model, evaluated by US Navy during 1980; not proceeded with, sole conversion (BuNo. 157996) being later brought to US-3A standard
US-3A: utility variant for use in COD task with VRC-50 in Western Pacific area; handful of aircraft modified following successful evaluation of 'prototype' in late 1970s; specialized ASW avionics and crew positions deleted to permit carriage of cargo and mail

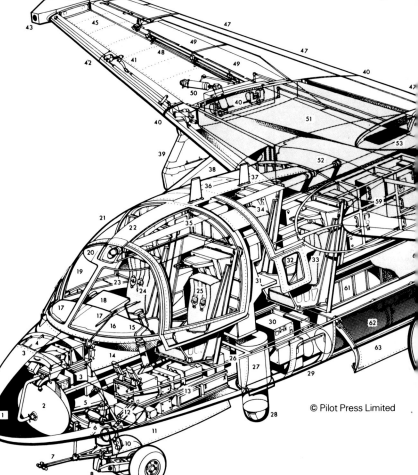

© Pilot Press Limited

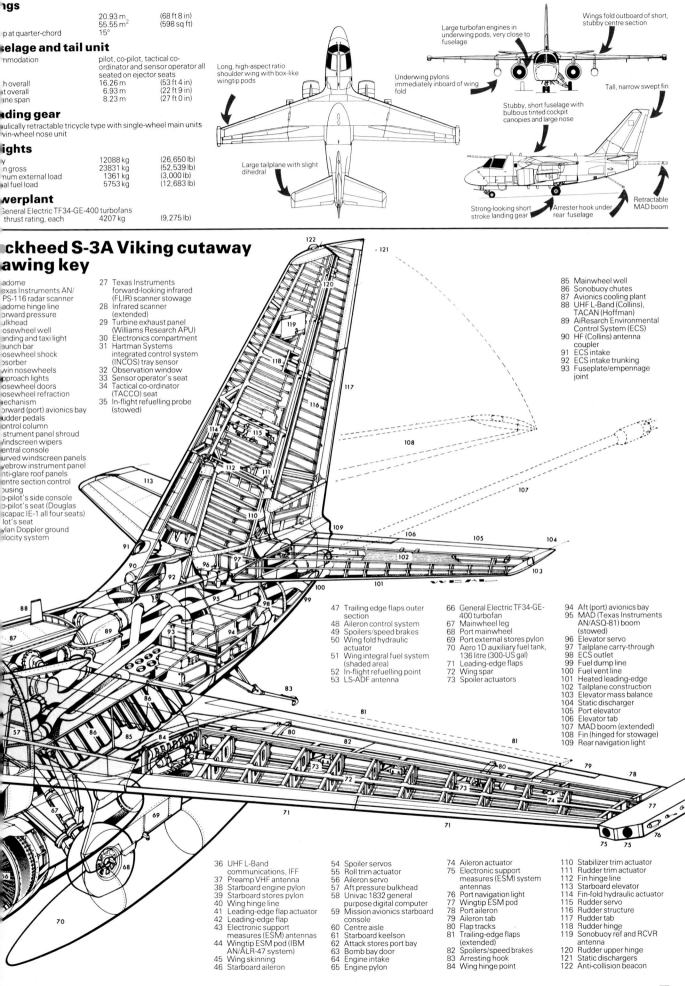

ecification: Lockheed S-3A Viking

S-3 Viking recognition features

ngs

	20.93 m	(68 ft 8 in)
	55.55 m²	(598 sq ft)
p at quarter-chord	15°	

selage and tail unit

mmodation	pilot, co-pilot, tactical co-ordinator and sensor operator all seated on ejector seats	
h overall	16.26 m	(53 ft 4 in)
t overall	6.93 m	(22 ft 9 in)
ne span	8.23 m	(27 ft 0 in)

ding gear

ulically retractable tricycle type with single-wheel main units
win-wheel nose unit

ights

y	12088 kg	(26,650 lb)
gross	23831 kg	(52,539 lb)
num external load	1361 kg	(3,000 lb)
al fuel load	5753 kg	(12,683 lb)

werplant

General Electric TF34-GE-400 turbofans
thrust rating, each   4207 kg   (9,275 lb)

Long, high-aspect ratio shoulder wing with box-like wingtip pods

Large tailplane with slight dihedral

Large turbofan engines in underwing pods, very close to fuselage

Wings fold outboard of short, stubby centre section

Underwing pylons immediately inboard of wing fold

Tall, narrow swept fin

Stubby, short fuselage with bulbous tinted cockpit canopies and large nose

Strong-looking short stroke landing gear

Arrester hook under rear fuselage

Retractable MAD boom

ckheed S-3A Viking cutaway awing key

adome
exas Instruments AN/
PS-116 radar scanner
adome hinge line
orward pressure
bulkhead
osewheel well
anding and taxi light
aunch bar
osewheel shock
bsorber
win nosewheels
pproach lights
osewheel doors
osewheel refraction
echanism
orward (port) avionics bay
udder pedals
ontrol column
strument panel shroud
Vindscreen wipers
entral console
urved windscreen panels
yebrow instrument panel
nti-glare roof panels
entre section control
ousing
p-pilot's side console
o-pilot's seat (Douglas
scapac IE-1 all four seats)
lot's seat
ylan Doppler ground
elocity system

27 Texas Instruments forward-looking infrared (FLIR) scanner stowage
28 Infrared scanner (extended)
29 Turbine exhaust panel (Williams Research APU)
30 Electronics compartment
31 Hartman Systems integrated control system (INCOS) tray sensor
32 Observation window
33 Sensor operator's seat
34 Tactical co-ordinator (TACCO) seat
35 In-flight refuelling probe (stowed)

47 Trailing edge flaps outer section
48 Aileron control system
49 Spoilers/speed brakes
50 Wing fold hydraulic actuator
51 Wing integral fuel system (shaded area)
52 In-flight refuelling point
53 LS-ADF antenna

66 General Electric TF34-GE-400 turbofan
67 Mainwheel leg
68 Port mainwheel
69 Port external stores pylon
70 Aero 1D auxiliary fuel tank, 136 litre (300-US gal)
71 Leading-edge flaps
72 Wing spar
73 Spoiler actuators

85 Mainwheel well
86 Sonobuoy chutes
87 Avionics cooling plant
88 UHF L-Band (Collins), TACAN (Hoffman)
89 AiResearch Environmental Control System (ECS)
90 HF (Collins) antenna coupler
91 ECS intake
92 ECS intake trunking
93 Fuseplate/empennage joint

94 Aft (port) avionics bay
95 MAD (Texas Instruments AN/ASQ-81) boom (stowed)
96 Elevator servo
97 Tailplane carry-through
98 ECS outlet
99 Fuel dump line
100 Fuel vent line
101 Heated leading-edge
102 Tailplane construction
103 Elevator mass balance
104 Static discharger
105 Port elevator
106 Elevator tab
107 MAD boom (extended)
108 Fin (hinged for stowage)
109 Rear navigation light

36 UHF L-Band communications, IFF
37 Preamp VHF antenna
38 Starboard engine pylon
39 Starboard stores pylon
40 Wing hinge line
41 Leading-edge flap actuator
42 Leading-edge flap
43 Electronic support measures (ESM) antennas
44 Wingtip ESM pod (IBM AN/ALR-47 system)
45 Wing skinning
46 Starboard aileron

54 Spoiler servos
55 Roll trim actuator
56 Aileron servo
57 Aft pressure bulkhead
58 Univac 1832 general purpose digital computer
59 Mission avionics starboard console
60 Centre aisle
61 Starboard keelson
62 Attack stores port bay
63 Bomb bay door
64 Engine intake
65 Engine pylon

74 Aileron actuator
75 Electronic support measures (ESM) system antennas
76 Port navigation light
77 Wingtip ESM pod
78 Port aileron
79 Aileron tab
80 Flap tracks
81 Trailing-edge flaps (extended)
82 Spoilers/speed brakes
83 Arresting hook
84 Wing hinge point

110 Stabilizer trim actuator
111 Rudder trim actuator
112 Fin hinge line
113 Starboard elevator
114 Fin-fold hydraulic actuator
115 Rudder servo
116 Rudder structure
117 Rudder tab
118 Rudder hinge
119 Sonobuoy ref and RCVR antenna
120 Rudder upper hinge
121 Static dischargers
122 Anti-collision beacon

The BOEING RC-135

Boeing RC-135 Super Snooper

Although small in numbers, the RC-135 family is vitally important to the West's security. Packed with the wildest electronics, these aircraft patrol around any country that may pose a threat, consuming and collecting vast amounts of electromagnetic signals and sifting, storing and analysing them. The family has been performing this top-priority task for years.

The most characteristic features of the RC-135 fleet are the thimble nose and the cheek SLAR fairings. The refuelling receptacle and open cargo door are visible on this RC-135V.

In September 1983, a high-ranking Soviet official, Chief-of-Staff Nikolai Ogarkov, stood before the world and solemnly pointed out the track of a USAF aircraft operating near the Sea of Okhotsk. Other aircraft were on the chart, among them a Korean Air Lines Boeing 747, which had tragically ended its flight in the Sea of Japan, having been shot down by Sukhoi Su-21 (originally known in the West as Su-15 'Flagon-F') fighters scrambled to intercept it from Sakhalin Island. Ogarkov explained that the USAF aircraft, identified as a Boeing RC-135, had been confused with the 747, and in the dark the Soviet fighters shot down the wrong aircraft. During the heated arguments that followed the tragedy, the designation RC-135 was often heard, bringing this shy and secretive aircraft into the limelight of public scrutiny, as had happened with the Lockheed U-2 and Boeing RB-47 following earlier tragic events. After years of operating beneath a cloak of secrecy, the RC-135 was now the focus of attention. Such is the lot of the spyplane.

The story of the RC-135 reaches back into the 1950s, when the Cold War was at its peak. Strategic Air Command crews flew long, uncomfortable missions, delving into and around the peripheries of communist countries. After the elderly Boeing RB-29s and RB-50s had been phased out, the signals intelligence gathering effort was entrusted largely to the Boeing RB-47H, which offered better performance than its predecessors, but only at considerable loss of comfort for

the crew. The electronics operators ('Crows') were sealed into what had been the bomb bay, surrounded almost totally by the electronic wizardry needed to perform their tasks. Cold, wet and often soaked in fuel, the 'Crows' spent long hours staring at dials. A replacement was desperately needed.

Welcome replacement

SAC's Boeing KC-135 and C-135 tanker/transport family seemed an obvious choice for a larger, longer-ranged and more comfortable Sigint platform in which the crew could work to best effect. Possessing great range, stability and internal volume, the basic type had all the attributes needed for the job. The 55th Strategic Reconnaissance Wing at Forbes AFB, Kansas, looked forward to receiving reconnaissance-configured variants of the C-135, and took its RB-47s to Offutt AFB, Nebraska to await the first aircraft. The first reconnaissance C-135 was 55-3121, a converted KC-135A which had been used for various test purposes. This aircraft came to the 55th SRW just before the move from Forbes, and was configured for the CIA 'Iron Lung' and 'Briar Patch' projects. This carried three or four 'Crows' and trailed a capsule packed with listening gear on a 12,000-ft (3658-m) wire. During its early life this aircraft saw many changes in configuration and many special missions. For a while it had a row of five fence aerials along its spine, giving rise to the nickname 'Porcupine'. The special missions flown by this machine built up in importance dramatically, so a

second aircraft (59-1465) was also acquired. This pair, designated KC-135R, underwent many transformations until 59-1465 was written off. By this time the aircraft featured a single fence aerial, thimble nose and teardrop fairings on the sides of the rear fuselage, just forward of the tail. The inflight refuelling boom was retained and small camera ports were cut into the cargo door. Three further KC-135Rs were delivered, and after several years service with the 55th SRW these returned to tanker units, albeit with some of their reconnaissance equipment still installed.

The first operational variant to bear the RC-135 designation was the RC-135D. Several tests had been undertaken with C-135s investigating side-looking airborne radars (notably NKC-135A 55-3132). The RC-135D 'Cotton Candy' was a converted KC-135A featuring a thimble nose and a cylindrical SLAR fairing forward of the wing root. These aircraft operated with the 6th SW out of Alaska, where the lack of range resulting from use of the J57 turbojet was not critical. One of the four aircraft became the first RC-135S, while the other three returned to tanker status. Further SLAR tests led to the single RC-135E 'Lisa Ann'. This aircraft was easily distinguishable by the two pods slung underneath the

The most radically modified of the variants are the RC-135Us. This aircraft sports a non-standard nose artwork (Soviet unit badge of excellence), bringing some playful humour into the deadly serious world of strategic reconnaissance.

wing inboard of the engines and a giant wrap-round fibreglass fairing hiding a Hughes SLAR in the forward fuselage. This aircraft operated out of Alaska with the 6th SW too, but its service life was short, ending in the Bering Strait following a massive structural failure of the wrap-round radome.

The successor to the RC-135D and RC-135E is the RC-135S 'Rivet Ball'/'Cobra Ball' which first appeared in 1968. The first aircraft (59-1491) had been converted from an RC-135D and was specifically configured for telemetry intelligence gathering, a role in which the RC-135S continues today. This aircraft was lost in 1969, but another two of the same basic type have been operating since the early 1970s (one being lost and quickly replaced). These have seen a bewildering variety of configurations, involving large circular camera ports for photographing re-entry vehicles, 'towel rail' antennas for intercepting guidance commands and blister fairings hiding special radars and listening devices. Constant features have been a thimble nose and teardrop fairings on the rear fuselage. The starboard wing is usually painted black to reduce glare for photography. Now under conversion at E-Systems in Texas to supplement the 6th SW's Telint fleet is the single RC-135X 'Cobra Eye', although little is known of its eventual configuration.

The 55th SRW at Offutt meanwhile awaited its RB-47 replacements, which eventually arrived from 1967 onwards. These had been delivered to the Air Force in 1964-5, and sent straight to Martin at Baltimore for fitting out with Sigint gear and a camera bay in the original boomer's position. Designated RC-135B, the aircraft were soon back in the workshops being fitted with the now familiar cheek SLAR fairings and wingtip HF probes. Under the codename 'Big Team' and with the designation RC-135C, these sounded the death knell for the RB-47H, and 55th SRW crews took to the new aircraft quickly. At the heart of the RC-135C's Sigint equipment lay the ASD-1 automatic reconnaissance unit and the QRC-259 unit:

The RC-135V is the most numerous of the variants, numbering some eight examples. The massive blade aerials under the fuselage are prominent in this landing pose, as are the small aerials under the nose.

the ASD-1 can collect all signals in the operating area, locate, analyse and record them, and assign abnormalities to specialist units and operators for further analysis; the QRC-259 is a fast-sweep analyser, one of the most capable 'black boxes' ever carried aloft. With the RC-135C, not only did comfort increase out of all recognition, but the intelligence-gathering capability was infinitely greater.

Further developments

The RC-135C spent some time in the South East Asia combat zone and became configured at times for special projects. These led to the RC-135U 'Combat Sent' and 'Combat Pink'. Three RC-135C aircraft were modified in 1971, retaining the basic layout but adding more and larger fairings. Wingtips, cheek SLARs, fin tip, tailcone and boom position have all gained new fairings hiding ever more capable receivers. Two aircraft are currently in use, easily identified by the giant SLARs and 'rabbit's ear' antennas mounted above them. After five or six years' service, the remaining seven RC-135Cs were converted in 1973-6 to RC-135V standard, followed in 1977 by one of the RC-135Us. These are the mainstay aircraft of the 55th SRW's Sigint fleet and have additionally received a thimble nose, along with giant plate aerials under the centre-section. Other blade and hook aerials also serve the sophisticated analysis gear within.

The final major family of RC-135s began with the RC-135M, a fairly simple conversion of the C-135B transport with thimble nose and teardrop fairings. Flying with the 4252nd SW out of Yokota AB

Seen in one of the numerous configurations for the variant, one of the RC-135S Telint specialist aircraft departs on a mission. There are currently two examples serving with the 24th SRS, 6th SW in Alaska, where they operate in close concert with the 'Cobra Dane' missile surveillance radar on Shemya island. The RC-135s also use this forward base.

in Japan under the codename 'Burning Candy', the 'Hog Nose' was initially assigned to ChiCom and eastern Soviet missions, but soon found itself flying increasingly over South East Asia. Constant 24-hour 'Combat Apple' operations over the war zone were maintained for several years, with a transfer to Kadena AB in Okinawa bringing the aircraft to a base nearer Vietnam. A unit change introduced the 376th SW, and operations continued until the fall of Saigon. The RC-135Ms moved to Offutt and the 55th SRW, where they adopted global missions. During the early 1980s, the six aircraft were modified to RC-135W standard, similar to the RC-135V, and all are current today.

Specialist training

Since the early 1970s, aircraft have been specially configured for Sigint training. The first aircraft so used was 55-3121, which was relieved of its special missions by the new RC-135Us. Under the designation RC-135T, it flew first with the 55th SRW, then the 376th SW at Kadena and finally the 6th SW at Eielson AFB before being lost in Alaska in 1985. To replace it, a surplus EC-135B has been converted to Telint trainer standard, designated TC-135S. Other KC-135R aircraft were used for training.

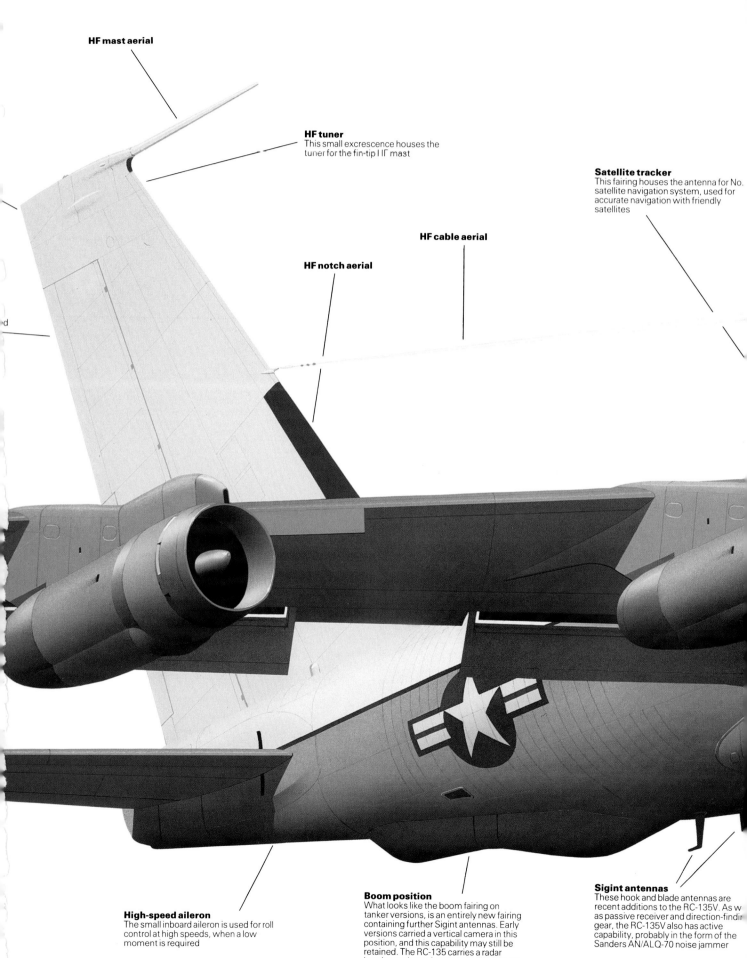

HF mast aerial

HF tuner
This small excrescence houses the
tuner for the fin-tip HF mast

Satellite tracker
This fairing houses the antenna for No.
satellite navigation system, used for
accurate navigation with friendly
satellites

HF cable aerial

HF notch aerial

High-speed aileron
The small inboard aileron is used for roll
control at high speeds, when a low
moment is required

Boom position
What looks like the boom fairing on
tanker versions, is an entirely new fairing
containing further Sigint antennas. Early
versions carried a vertical camera in this
position, and this capability may still be
retained. The RC-135 carries a radar
homing and warning system, likely to be
the Loral AN/APR-17 intercept receiver

Sigint antennas
These hook and blade antennas are
recent additions to the RC-135V. As w
as passive receiver and direction-findir
gear, the RC-135V also has active
capability, probably in the form of the
Sanders AN/ALQ-70 noise jammer

Boeing RC-135V
55th Strategic Reconnaissance Wing
Strategic Air Command
US Air Force

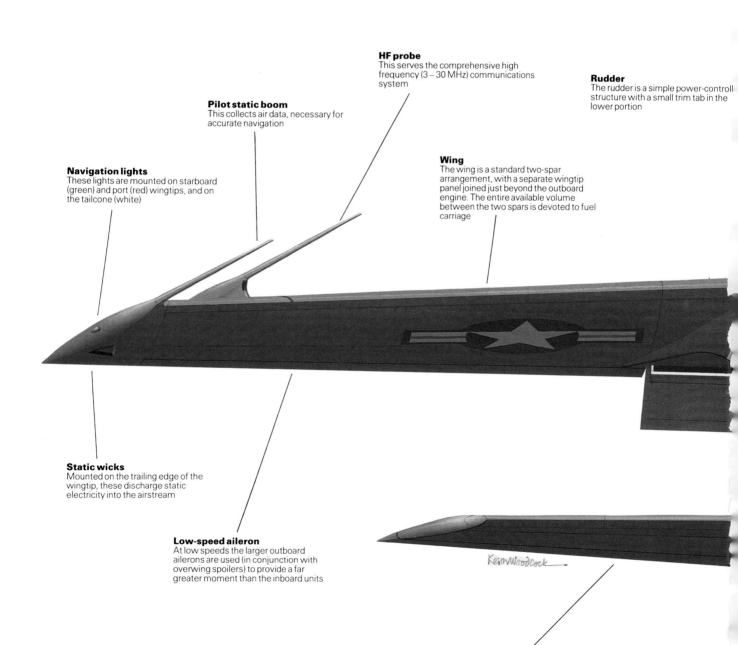

Loran
Mounted on the trailing edge of the fin tip is the aerial for the LOng Range Aid to Navigation system, utilizing ground stations

HF probe
This serves the comprehensive high frequency (3 – 30 MHz) communications system

Rudder
The rudder is a simple power-controll structure with a small trim tab in the lower portion

Pilot static boom
This collects air data, necessary for accurate navigation

Wing
The wing is a standard two-spar arrangement, with a separate wingtip panel joined just beyond the outboard engine. The entire available volume between the two spars is devoted to fuel carriage

Navigation lights
These lights are mounted on starboard (green) and port (red) wingtips, and on the tailcone (white)

Static wicks
Mounted on the trailing edge of the wingtip, these discharge static electricity into the airstream

Low-speed aileron
At low speeds the larger outboard ailerons are used (in conjunction with overwing spoilers) to provide a far greater moment than the inboard units

Elevator
The tailplane is trimmed by varying the incidence of the whole unit at the roots. Trailing edge elevators work in a conventional fashion

Aircraft 55-3121 was the first recon-configured C-135, and was still in use as a trainer in 1985, before its untimely demise in Alaska. By this time it had lost the refuelling boom and gained TF33 turbofan engines, and was designated RC-135T. Its replacement is the TC-135S.

One final subclass of aircraft to carry the RC-135 designation was the RC-135A. The four aircraft bearing this designation were the last C-135s delivered to the Air Force, and were used by the 1370th Photo Mapping Wing, a MATS unit. Flying from Turner AFB, Georgia, the quartet performed cartographic and geodetic survey missions, armed with a battery of cameras hidden behind a sliding door in the space occupied by the forward fuel tank in other versions. In 1972 these aircraft passed to the 55th SRW, where they operated on SAC support duties before being released for tanking in 1979 under the designation KC-135D.

Internal layout

The RC-135s are similar structurally to the other members of the C-135 family. Most have been based on the C-135B transport and consequently have TF33 turbofans. Fuel dump pipes have been installed in the boomer's position, and most have air refuelling receptacles mounted above the cockpit. The ARR allows almost unlimited endurance, most important for the type of operations these specialist aircraft undertake. The basic flight crew is four, comprising two pilots and two navigators, the latter being vitally necessary because of the proximity of operations to hostile airspace. Astro-inertial systems and constant vigilance

ensure that no unintentional overflights of such hostile territory occur. On long flights relief crews are carried, bunks and a rest area being situated to the rear of the cabin. The forward part of the cabin is filled with electronics racking, while the rear has the operator stations. In the general Sigint variants, the starboard side has seven fixed positions, two for the ASD, four for special analysis and one for the QRC. The port side is for the special equipment carried. The RC-135 family is regularly reconfigured for specific missions, resulting in different internal layouts. The inherited cargo door makes for comparatively trouble-free alterations. Comint-configured aircraft carry foreign language specialists who can not only eavesdrop on enemy transmissions, but also broadcast spurious messages. Increasingly aircraft are configured for Rint, the analysis of non-emitted signals such as dormant radar stations, ignition motors and power lines. Active jamming is also possible as a means of goading the target into using different frequencies.

RC-135 operations are global, but fall into five main areas. Eastern Europe and the western borders of the USSR are the domain of RC-135Us and Vs operating from RAF Mildenhall in England, while in the Far East aircraft operate from Kadena. The Mediterranean, Middle East, North Africa (especially Libya) and southern USSR are largely watched by RC-135Ws from Hellenikon in Greece, while the 38th SRS at Patrick AFB in Florida is very active over Central America, in particular Nicaragua. The 6th SW Telint specialists from Alaska watch the Sea of Okhotsk, where Soviet re-entry vehicles are targeted during test launches

from the Urals. Eighteen aircraft (two S-, two U-, eight V- and six W-models) are current, and these are used intensively to maintain the USAF's national security commitment, alongside the 9th SRW's Lockheed U-2s and SR-71s. The missions are obviously highly classified, but involve flying close to enemy airspace for long periods, recording and analysing all the signals intercepted. Various methods may be employed to stir up a reaction, such as jamming and the spurious broadcasts mentioned above, but these are strictly controlled: the potential results are highly dangerous. In common with the Soviet snoopers around NATO airspace, the RC-135s expect to spend long periods shadowed by fighters sent up by the target nation.

Israel operates several similar aircraft but these are based on the slightly larger Boeing 707 airframe, and most retain their windows. Featuring SLARs and plate aerials similar to those of the RC-135V, these aircraft are highly active against Israel's Arab neighbours and were instrumental in recent military successes against Syria.

The RC-135 has been snooping around communist territory for over 20 years, handling much intelligence of supreme national importance. The constant updates, modifications and fitments enable the RC-135 to hold its unchallenged position as king of the Sigint gatherers.

Glossary
AB Air Base
AFB Air Force Base
ARR Air-Refuelling Receptacle
ChiCom Chinese Communists
CIA Central Intelligence Agency
Comint Communications Intelligence
HF High Frequency
MATS Military Air Transport Service
Rint Radiation Intelligence
SAC Strategic Air Command
Sigint Signals Intelligence
SLAR Side-Looking Airborne Radar
SRS Strategic Reconnaissance Squadron
SRW Strategic Reconnaissance Wing
SW Strategic Wing
Telint Telemetry Intelligence

Taxiing out of the mist for an early morning departure from Mildenhall, this RC-135W displays the slightly longer SLAR fairings which characterize this variant. The W-models usually use Mildenhall as a stopover on their way to Hellenikon, from where they conduct missions in the Med and Europe.

RC-135 in service

The following list describes individual aircraft and their histories. Several individual aircraft were modified to several different standards throughout their lives. Most aircraft have served with the 55th SRW based at Offutt AFB, Nebraska, with the exception of the RC-135D, E, S, T and X, which have all flown with the 6th SW at Eielson, AFB, Alaska

55-3121: originally a JKC-135A, this machine moved to 55th SRW in 1963 for the CIA projects 'Iron Lung' and 'Briar Patch'; became KC-135R at this time and used for many special projects; later used as a trainer under designation RC-135T; lost 26 February 1985 at Valdez, Alaska

55-3132: NKC-135A used for testing SLARs and other Sigint equipment

55-3133: KC-135A rumoured as converted to semi-RC-135S standard; lost in 1968

58-0124 and 58-0126: KC-135As converted to KC-135R standard; back to tanker by 1980

59-1465: KC-135A converted to KC-135R; later used as a trainer airframe by the 55th SRW; lost 17 July 1967

59-1491: KC-135A converted to RC-135D; later converted to RC-135S before lost at Eielson AFB on 10 March 1969

59-1514: KC-135A converted to KC-135R for 'Iron Lung' and 'Briar Patch'; back to tanker by September 1975; still flown by the 55th SRW as a KC-135E

60-0356, 60-0357 and 60-0362: C-135As converted to RC-135D standard, to tanker by 1976

61-2662 and 61-2663: C-135Bs converted to RC-135S standard; current'

61-2664: C-135B converted to RC-135S; lost 16 March 1981

62-4128: C-135B under conversion to RC-135X; current

62-4131 and 62-4132: C-135Bs converted to RC-135Ms; later converted to RC-135Ws; current

62-4133: EC-135B converted to TC-135S; current

62-4134 and 62-4135: C-135Bs converted to RC-135Ms; later converted to RC-135Ws; current

62-4137: one C-135B became the sole RC-135E; lost over Bering Strait 5 June 1969

62-4138 and 62-4139: C-135Bs converted to RC-135Ms; later converted to RC-135Ws; current

63-8058, 63-8059, 63-8060 and 63-8061: built as RC-135As, all were converted to tanker (as KC-135D) by 1978

63-8062, 63-8063, 63-8064, 63-8065 and 63-8066: RC-135As cancelled

63-9792: KC-135B converted to RC-135B; subsequently became RC-135C, RC-135U and RC-135V; current

64-14841, 64-14842, 64-14843, 64-14844, 64-14845 and 64-14846: KC-135Bs converted to RC-135Bs; subsequently modified as RC-135Cs and RC-135Vs; current

64-14847: KC-135B converted to RC-135B; subsequently became RC-135C and RC-135U; current

64-14848: KC-135B converted to RC-135B; subsequently became RC-135C and RC-135V; current

64-14849: KC-135B converted to RC-135B; subsequently became RC-135C and RC-135U; current

Seen at Offutt AFB in the late 1960s, this is one of the 'Big Team' RC-135Cs. The addition of the SLAR fairings led to the nickname 'Chipmunk'. Aircraft no. 9792 received the most conversions of any, being a U-model before refit to its current RC-135V configuration.

Above: KC-135R in definitive configuration, with camera ports cut into the cargo door. Used for various special purposes, this aircraft (58-0126) is now a tanker serving with the 305th ARW at Grissom, albeit with some of the reconnaissance gear still installed.

The fated RC-135E lifts off from an Alaskan air base. As well as the prominent fuselage radome, the RC-135E carries an Elint pod under the wings, and has a camera port for re-entry vehicle photography. The Douglas C-124s, C-133s and Boeing C-135 in the background are supporting an early warning radar project.

Below: The first RC-135S aircraft is seen in Alaska; these Telint aircraft have been noted in many different configurations. The large circular windows are for missile re-entry photography, for which the wings are blacked to reduce glare.

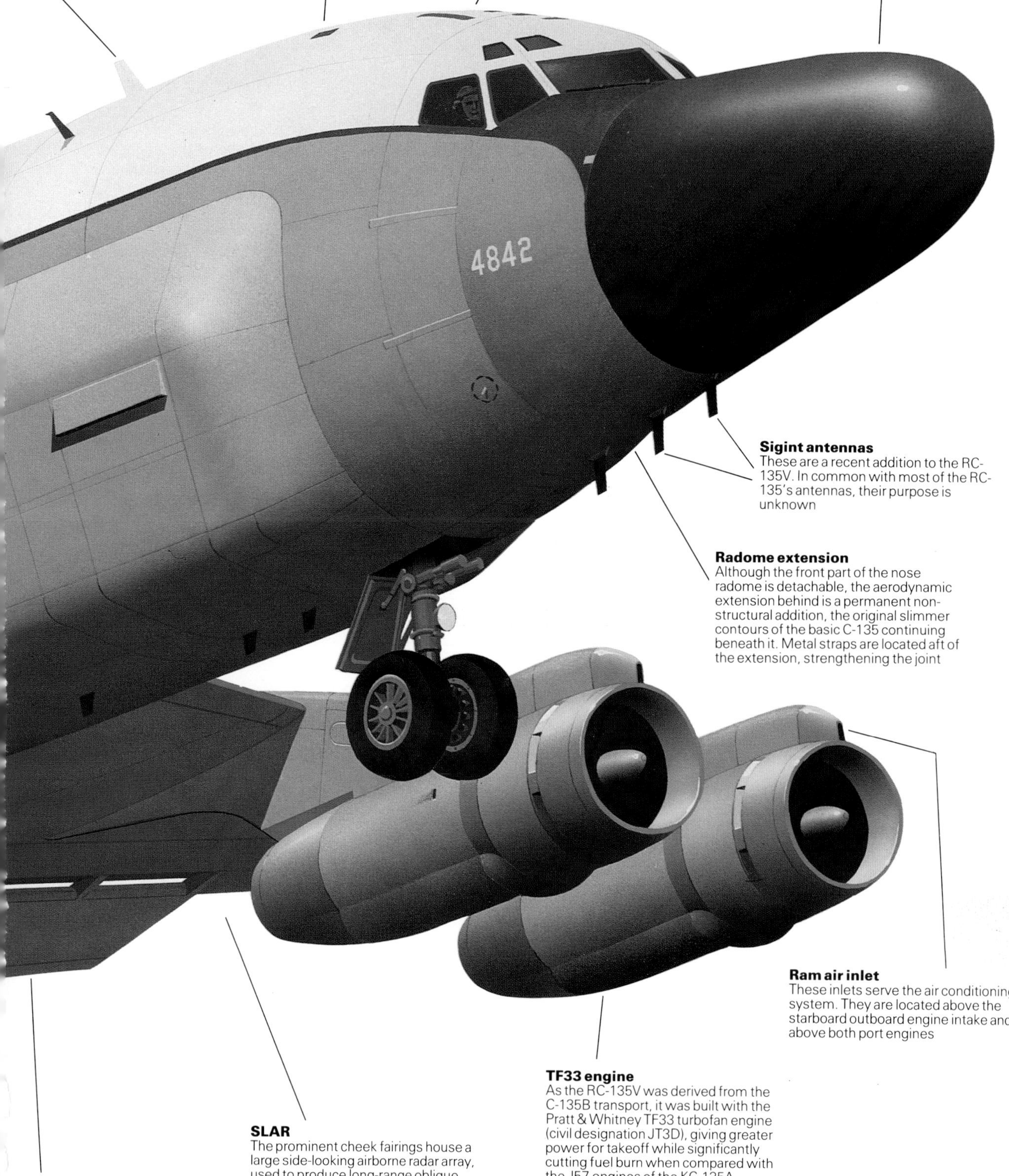

Stellar navigation system
Two small windows in the cockpit ceiling serve the astro-inertial navigation system

ARR
The air-refuelling receptacle allows the RC-135 to refuel in flight, so vastly increasing endurance or distance covered in a single sortie

Nose radome
This strap-on radome, commonly known as the 'Hog Nose', contains an advanced radar array for surveillance duties. The radome is not hinged but is easily removed on a trolley for access to the radar

1 UHF/VHF aerial

4842

Sigint antennas
These are a recent addition to the RC-135V. In common with most of the RC-135's antennas, their purpose is unknown

Radome extension
Although the front part of the nose radome is detachable, the aerodynamic extension behind is a permanent non-structural addition, the original slimmer contours of the basic C-135 continuing beneath it. Metal straps are located aft of the extension, strengthening the joint

Ram air inlet
These inlets serve the air conditioning system. They are located above the starboard outboard engine intake and above both port engines

TF33 engine
As the RC-135V was derived from the C-135B transport, it was built with the Pratt & Whitney TF33 turbofan engine (civil designation JT3D), giving greater power for takeoff while significantly cutting fuel burn when compared with the J57 engines of the KC-135A

SLAR
The prominent cheek fairings house a large side-looking airborne radar array, used to produce long-range oblique radar imagery from friendly airspace

ps
RC-135 has two sets of flaps, one ard and one outboard. Both are of double-slotted type, seen here in eoff configuration

No. 2 UHF/VHF aerial
This is part of the extensive communications suite carried by the RC-135. Secure wide-frequency datalinks are also available for real- or near real-time information

Crew escape hatch
This is used for emergency egress, providing access to the wing area (port side also). A further hatch is mounted in the rear cabin on the starboard side only

Landing lights
Two powerful landing/taxi lights are mounted in each wing root, with a further unit mounted on the nosewheel oleo strut

ADF aerials
The automatic direction finder further augments the highly sophisticated navigation suite

Sigint antennas
The large blade and plate aerials under the fuselage are used for intercepting hostile emissions. Many of these signals are probably collected by the AN/APR-34 system, for receipt by the Watkins-Johnson QRC-259 solid-state superheterodyne receiver system. This super-sensitive system allows the collected radiation to be broken down into constituent signals and passed on for further analysis. Other known equipment consists of the AN/ASD-1 Elint system, the AN/ASR-5 automatic reconnaissance system and the AN/ALA-6 pulse analyser

Cheek fairing
As well as containing the SLAR, the cheek fairing holds other Sigint equipment. The fairing itself is non-structural. On the port side the large cargo door juts into the fairing

Fl
Th
in
th
tak

RC-135 variants

KC-135R: five aircraft converted from tankers, and not to be confused with later KC-135R tankers (KC-135As refitted with turbofan engines etc); the first two aircraft were initially configured for the 'Iron Lung' and 'Briar Patch' projects, and had five fence aerials along their spines, which gave them the nickname 'Porcupine'; reconfigured many times for special projects, all five aircraft ended up with thimble nose, one fence array and a teardrop shaped radome on the rear fuselage; J57 engines and refuelling boom retained, served with 55th SRW until 1976

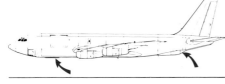

RC-135A: photographic reconnaissance and mapping variant with cameras mounted in lower fuselage; J57 engines and refuelling probe retained; served with 55th SRW until 1978

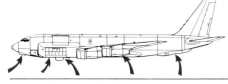

RC-135B: 10 aircraft converted on line from C-135B transports (Sigint equipment installed) and delivered during 1964-5 with TF33 engines; served with 55th SRW until 1967

RC-135C: 10 RC-135Bs modified in 1967 to 'Big Team' configuration; cheek fairings for SLARs and wingtip HF probe added; small radome under chin and larger radome under forward fuselage appeared; camera mounted in what was the boomer's position; some aircraft configured for classified 'Blue Bird' programme in Vietnam; TF33 engines; served with 55th SRW until 1974

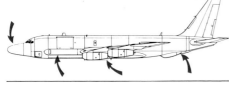

RC-135D: at least four conversions from C/KC-135As; thimble nose and cylindrical SLAR fairings leading forward from the wing root, and small fence LORAN aerial under centre section; used in Vietnam when RC-135M was away on maintenance; associated with 'Rivet Brass' programme; J57 engines

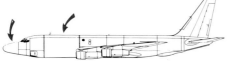

RC-135E: single C-135B fitted with giant Hughes SLAR in forward fuselage with a wrap-round fibreglass radome replacing the metal structure of the aircraft; also two Sigint pods carried on the wings between the landing gear and fuselage; operating with the 6th SW from Shemya, this aircraft was lost over the Bering Strait as a result of massive structural failure of the radome; codenamed 'Lisa Ann' and associated with the 'Rivet Amber' programme; TF33 engines

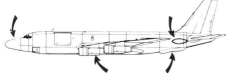

RC-135M: six aircraft produced from C-135Bs; features included thimble nose and teardrop fairings on the rear fuselage; associated programmes include 'Rivet Card' and 'Rivet Quick'; codenamed 'Combat Apple', these aircraft saw extensive service during the Vietnam War, flying from Kadena AB; TF33 engines; served with 55th SRW until 1982

RC-135S: at least four conversions; associated programmes are 'Rivet Ball' and 'Cobra Ball'; used extensively in the Pacific, these aircraft have always featured the thimble nose, but have appeared in many major configurations with various numbers of large circular windows, one, two or three 'towel rail' aerials on the forward fuselage, blister fairings on the forward fuselage and teardrop fairings on the rear fuselage, together with numerous blade aerials; concerned primarily with Telint, these have black-painted wings to reduce glare during photography of re-entry vehicles (this was also found on various KC-135R, RC-135D and RC-135E aircraft); 59-1491 had J57 engines while others have TF33; current with the 6th SW

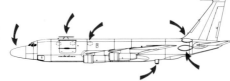

RC-135T: on the arrival of the RC-135U, the KC-135R 55-3121 was released of its special programmes and became a Sigint trainer with the 376th SW at Kadena AB and then the 6th SW at Eielson AFB; it eventually lost its fence aerial and refuelling probe and gained TF33 engines late in life.

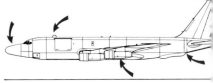

RC-135U: three RC-135Cs converted in 1971; the first U-mo_ had only a fin extension and tailcone extension in its first guise the definitive RC-135U has these antennas in addition to much larger SLAR aerials, 'rabbit's ear' aerials on the forward fuselage above the SLARs, extended wingtip fairings, a large radome ur the forward fuselage, large chin radar and a more angular fairin_ the old boomer's position; used over Vietnam, the RC-135U ha_ been associated with the 'Combat Sent' and 'Combat Pink' programmes; TF33 engines; two active with the 55th SRW

Boeing RC-135W cutaway drawing key

1 Radome
2 Forward radar antenna
3 Front pressure bulkhead
4 Ventral antennas
5 Extended nose radome fairing
6 Nose compartment framing
7 Cockpit floor level
8 Pilot's side console panel
9 Rudder pedals
10 Control column
11 Instrument panel
12 Windscreen wipers
13 Windscreen panels
14 Cockpit eyebrow windows
15 Overhead systems switch panels
16 Co-pilot's seat
17 Direct vision opening side window panel
18 Pilot's seat
19 Safety equipment stowage
20 Chart/plotting table
21 Navigator's instrument console
22 Boom type inflight-refuelling receptacle, open
23 Dual navigators' seats
24 Retractable escape spoiler, stowed position
25 Entry hatch floor grille
26 Nose landing gear wheel bay
27 Crew entry hatch, open
28 Retractable boarding ladder
29 Twin nosewheels, forward retracting
30 Nose landing gear pivot fixing
31 Underfloor avionics equipment racks
32 Electrical equipment racking
33 Supernumerary crew seat
34 Star tracking windows, celestial navigation system
35 Cockpit doorway
36 Circuit breaker panels
37 Overhead air distribution ducting
38 No. 1 UHF/VHF aerial
39 Starboard side avionics equipment racks
40 Toilet compartment
41 Water heater
42 Wash basin
43 Water storage tanks
44 Toilet
45 Side-Looking Airborne Radar (SLAR) antenna panels
46 SLAR equipment fairing

47 Cargo doorway, electronic equipment loading
48 Main cabin flooring
49 Modular equipment package
50 Cargo door hydraulic jacks and hinges
51 Cargo door, open
52 ADF aerials
53 Electronics equipment racks
54 Air conditioning ducting
55 Aerial lead-in
56 Front spar attachment fuselage main frame
57 Centre section fuel tanks, capacity 27656 litres (7,306 US gal)
58 Overwing emergency exit hatch, port only
59 Floor beam construction
60 AN/ASD-1 avionics equipment racks
61 Tacan aerial
62 No. 1 satellite navigation system aerial
63 Inboard wing fuel tank, capacity 8612 litres (2,275 US gal)
64 Fuel filler cap
65 Detachable engine cowling panels
66 No. 3 starboard inboard engine nacelle
67 Intake cowling
68 Nacelle pylon
69 Pylon strut access panels
70 Wing centre main fuel tank, capacity 7805 litres (2,062 US gal)
71 Fuel venting channels
72 Leading edge flap hydraulic jacks
73 Krueger-type leading edge flap, down position
74 No. 4 starboard outboard engine nacelle
75 Outboard nacelle pylon
76 Outer wing panel joint rib
77 Wing outboard fuel tank, capacity 1643 litres (434 US gal)
78 HF antenna tuner
79 Lightning arrester panel
80 HF aerial mast
81 Pitot static boom
82 Starboard navigation light
83 Static dischargers
84 Outboard, low speed, aileron

85 Aileron internal balance panels
86 Spoiler interconnection linkage
87 Aileron hinge control mechanism
88 Aileron tab
89 Outboard double-slotted Fowler-type flap, down position

90 Outboard spoilers, ope
91 Spoiler hydraulic jacks
92 Flap guide rails
93 Flap screw jacks
94 Aileron control and trir

5V: seven RC-135Cs and one RC-135U converted with
airings and thimble nose; large blade aerials under the centre
hold horizontal, oval plates while three smaller blade aerials
uated under the rear fuselage; these have recently adopted
erials as detailed under RC-135W; TF33 engines; active with
h SRW

RC-135W: six RC-135Ms recently converted to similar standard to
RC-135V; extra antennas are three small blade aerials under the
nose, plus four blades and a hook aerial under the rear fuselage;
distinguishable from the RC-135V by having slightly larger SLAR
(projects into crew access hatch) and by having no air inlets on the
engine pylons; TF33 engines; active with the 55th SRW

RC-135X: new conversion of C-135B still under fitment at E-
Systems; Telint aircraft for 6th SW likely to be similar to RC-
135S; codenamed 'Cobra Eye'; TF33 engines

TC-135S: conversion of EC-135B to Sigint trainer, to replace the
lost RC-135T; current with the 6th SW

NKC-135A: various equipment test aircraft, including 55-3132
SLAR testbed shown below

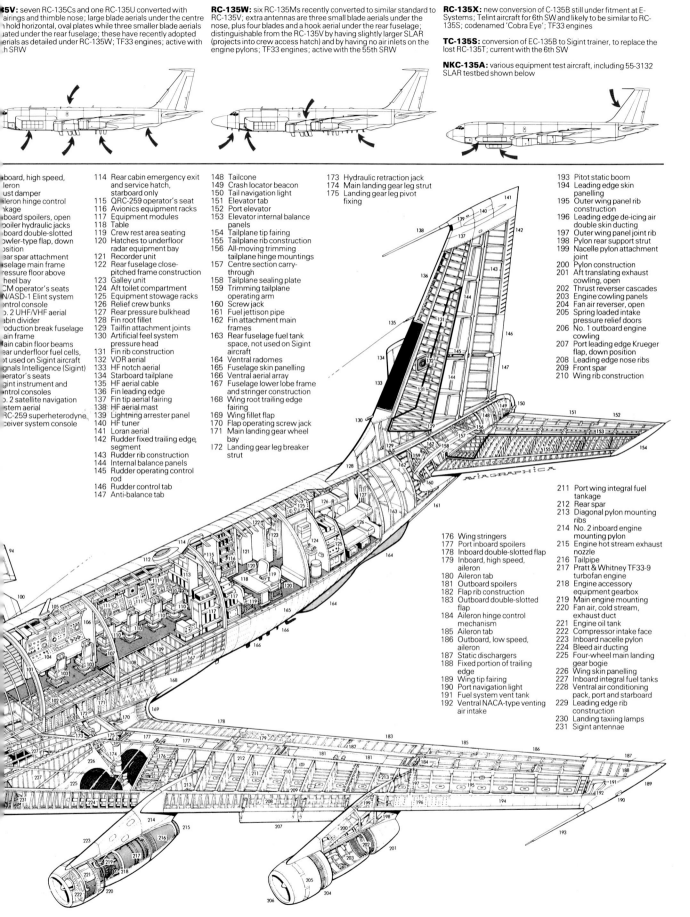

board, high speed,
leron
ust damper
ileron hinge control
nkage
board spoilers, open
poiler hydraulic jacks
board double-slotted
owler-type flap, down
osition
ear spar attachment
iselage main frame
ressure floor above
heel bay
CM operator's seats
N/ASD-1 Elint system
ontrol console
o. 2 UHF/VHF aerial
abin divider
oduction break fuselage
ain frame
ain cabin floor beams
ear underfloor fuel cells,
ot used on Sigint aircraft
gnals Intelligence (Sigint)
erator's seats
gint instrument and
ontrol consoles
o. 2 satellite navigation
stem aerial
RC-259 superheterodyne
ceiver system console

114 Rear cabin emergency exit
    and service hatch,
    starboard only
115 QRC-259 operator's seat
116 Avionics equipment racks
117 Equipment modules
118 Table
119 Crew rest area seating
120 Hatches to underfloor
    radar equipment bay
121 Recorder unit
122 Rear fuselage close-
    pitched frame construction
123 Galley unit
124 Aft toilet compartment
125 Equipment stowage racks
126 Relief crew bunks
127 Rear pressure bulkhead
128 Fin root fillet
129 Tailfin attachment joints
130 Artificial feel system
    pressure head
131 Fin rib construction
132 VOR aerial
133 HF notch aerial
134 Starboard tailplane
135 HF aerial cable
136 Fin leading edge
137 Fin tip aerial fairing
138 HF aerial mast
139 Lightning arrester panel
140 HF tuner
141 Loran aerial
142 Rudder fixed trailing edge
    segment
143 Rudder rib construction
144 Internal balance panels
145 Rudder operating control
    rod
146 Rudder control tab
147 Anti-balance tab

148 Tailcone
149 Crash locator beacon
150 Tail navigation light
151 Elevator tab
152 Port elevator
153 Elevator internal balance
    panels
154 Tailplane tip fairing
155 Tailplane rib construction
156 All-moving trimming
    tailplane hinge mountings
157 Centre section carry-
    through
158 Tailplane sealing plate
159 Trimming tailplane
    operating arm
160 Screw jack
161 Fuel jettison pipe
162 Fin attachment main
    frames
163 Rear fuselage fuel tank
    space, not used on Sigint
    aircraft
164 Ventral radomes
165 Fuselage skin panelling
166 Ventral aerial array
167 Fuselage lower lobe frame
    and stringer construction
168 Wing root trailing edge
    fairing
169 Wing fillet flap
170 Flap operating screw jack
171 Main landing gear wheel
    bay
172 Landing gear leg breaker
    strut

173 Hydraulic retraction jack
174 Main landing gear leg strut
175 Landing gear leg pivot
    fixing

176 Wing stringers
177 Port inboard spoilers
178 Inboard double-slotted flap
179 Inboard, high speed,
    aileron
180 Aileron tab
181 Outboard spoilers
182 Flap rib construction
183 Outboard double-slotted
    flap
184 Aileron hinge control
    mechanism
185 Aileron tab
186 Outboard, low speed,
    aileron
187 Static dischargers
188 Fixed portion of trailing
    edge
189 Wing tip fairing
190 Port navigation light
191 Fuel system vent tank
192 Ventral NACA-type venting
    air intake

193 Pitot static boom
194 Leading edge skin
    panelling
195 Outer wing panel rib
    construction
196 Leading edge de-icing air
    double skin ducting
197 Outer wing panel joint rib
198 Pylon rear support strut
199 Nacelle pylon attachment
    joint
200 Pylon construction
201 Aft translating exhaust
    cowling, open
202 Thrust reverser cascades
203 Engine cowling panels
204 Fan air reverser, open
205 Spring loaded intake
    pressure relief doors
206 No. 1 outboard engine
    cowling
207 Port leading edge Krueger
    flap, down position
208 Leading edge nose ribs
209 Front spar
210 Wing rib construction

211 Port wing integral fuel
    tankage
212 Rear spar
213 Diagonal pylon mounting
    ribs
214 No. 2 inboard engine
    mounting pylon
215 Engine hot stream exhaust
    nozzle
216 Tailpipe
217 Pratt & Whitney TF33-9
    turbofan engine
218 Engine accessory
    equipment gearbox
219 Main engine mounting
220 Fan air, cold stream,
    exhaust duct
221 Engine oil tank
222 Compressor intake face
223 Inboard nacelle pylon
224 Bleed air ducting
225 Four-wheel main landing
    gear bogie
226 Wing skin panelling
227 Inboard integral fuel tanks
228 Ventral air conditioning
    pack, port and starboard
229 Leading edge rib
    construction
230 Landing taxiing lamps
231 Sigint antennae

© Pilot Press Ltd

An RC-135D lifts off in a cloud of smoke from the J57 engines. When operating in South East Asia, the lack of power and range was a problem for these aircraft, as was the steamy weather after prolonged exposure to the freezing Alaskan cold.

Least conspicuous of the Sigint C-135s was the RC-135M. Following their sterling service in the South East Asia war, they adopted more global responsibilities before finally being fitted out as RC-135Ws. Note the teardrop fairing on the rear fuselage.

Specification: Boeing RC-135V

Wings
Span	39.88 mm	(130 ft 10 in)
Area	226.03 m²	(2,433.0 sq ft)
Sweep at quarter-chord	35°	

Fuselage and tail unit
Accommodation	flight crew of four plus a variable number of equipment operators	
Length overall	42.82 m	(140 ft 6 in)
Height overall	12.70 m	(41 ft 8 in)
Tailplane span	13.85 m	(45 ft 3 in)

Landing gear
Hydraulically retractable tricycle landing gear each with single-bogie main units, each with four wheels, and a twin-wheel nose unit
Wheelbase	13.92 m	(45 ft 8 in)
Wheel track	6.73 m	(22 ft 1 in)

Weights
Empty	46403 kg	(102,300 lb)
Maximum take-off	135624 kg	(299,000 lb)

Powerplant
Four Pratt & Whitney TF33-P-9 non-afterburning turbofans
Static thrust, each	8165 kg	(18,000 lb)

Performance
Maximum speed, at altitude	521 kts 966 km/h	(600 mph)
Service ceiling	40,600 ft	(12375 m)
Maximum range with reserves	9100 km	(5,655 miles)
Combat radius (aircraft usually inflight-refuelled on a mission)	4305 km	(2,675 km)

Boeing RC-135 recognition features

all current versions have turbofan engines, characterized by the larger diameter annular cowling on the front

cheek fairings are prominent from the front (RC-135U, V, and W)

the four large blade aerials under the centre-section of the RC-135V and W hold oval shaped plates on the end

RC-135S, V and W have a highly distinctive thimble nose

two small blister fairings are situated in tandem on the spine

large flat-sided cheek fairings (RC-135U, V, and W)

swept-back wing, often mounting HF probes near the tips

RC-135V and W have many prominent blade aerials under fuselage

fairing covering original boom position

The internal layout of the RC-135 family has largely remained a mystery, and each aircraft is differently configured for specific missions. Equipment is for intercepting hostile communications (Comint) and for analysing hostile radars (Elint). This shows an Elint console in an RC-135M, and is typical of the type. The main functions of Elint are to locate hostile radars by direction-finding and analyse the pulse, both individual pulses and the repetition frequency. Individual returns are 'sifted out' from the overall electromagnetic 'catch' and passed to other consoles for inspection. This console has oscilloscopes to display radar wave patterns, and these may be able to break up the pulse for deeper analysis. Data is recorded on magnetic tape, and some may be transmitted by secure datalink to ground stations. Further intelligence can be gleaned from analysing the radiation given off by a dormant radar station when it is not emitting. This specialized but increasingly important operation is known as Rint. In such a way, the RC-135 helps keep the USAF up to date with changes in hostile radars and to enable countermeasures to be formulated.

The GRUMMAN EA-6B PROWLER

EA-6B Prowler: `Q-Birds` are go!

Though the aircraft of the strike force squadrons may take all the credit when the US Navy swings into action, those in the know appreciate the vital role played by several less glamorous types. Notable among these is the Grumman EA-6B Prowler, which causes havoc among enemy air defence operations.

Attaining full operational status in the summer of 1972 when VAQ-132 deployed to the South East Asia war zone aboard USS *America* (CVA-66), Grumman's EA-6B Prowler has for the past 15 years or so been the US Navy's primary carrierborne electronic warfare platform. Today, it is active with about a dozen squadrons in all, but despite the fact that it has been in production for more than 15 years the quantity built has only just passed the 100 mark.

Sheer cost is one important factor when seeking explanations for this low production rate, for the Prowler (or, to be more specific, its sophisticated electronics suite) is horrendously expensive. Probably no less significant, though, is the fact that a mere handful of EA-6Bs can satisfy a typical carrier air wing's needs in the EW arena, it being usual for Navy aircraft-carriers to include one tactical EW squadron (VAQ) with only four examples of the EA-6B amongst the 80 or more warplanes normally embarked for the operational deployment.

A cursory glance at the Prowler quickly

With 'everything down' and the characteristic wing tip speed brakes split open, a Prowler approaches the deck. Four examples of this big and sturdy aircraft are assigned to the Electronic Warfare Squadron (VAQ) within each US Navy Carrier Air Wing for ECM and EW tasks.

betrays its heritage in the A-6 Intruder all-weather medium attack aircraft and, indeed, its designation as the EA-6B provides further confirmation of the fact that it is closely allied to that type. It would be wrong, however, to dismiss the Prowler as merely a four-seater Intruder, for it is a 'bird of a very different feather'.

Although both types can be said to be packed with electronic 'goodies', those of the A-6 Intruder are optimized for offensive operations, their principal function being to assist in the accurate delivery of ordnance on a specific target in all weather conditions. The Prowler, on the other hand, embodies an entirely different fit, aimed at permitting it to detect and classify hostile radars and take whatever countermeasures are necessary to disrupt an enemy's ability to detect and localize an incoming strike force.

Since sheer performance was not a key consideration in design, Grumman not unnaturally elected to use the Intruder as a starting point rather than 'a clean sheet of paper' when it came to developing a dedicated EW type for service with the Navy, a decision which must have helped to cut down the time taken to move from the project definition stage to entry into service. Nevertheless, the Prowler was still a long time in development, the first prototype making a successful maiden flight on 25 May 1968. This prototype was

With its impressive electronics suite, based around the AN/ALQ-99 tactical jamming system, the EA-6B Prowler in its various improved configurations is an essential and highly effective force multiplier within the US Navy and Marine Corps front-line air operations.

one of three conversions employing A-6A test airframes used in bringing the Prowler to fruition.

Of this trio of aircraft only two were assigned to flight test duties, the third machine being ground-based following modification, and this actually spent most of its time out of public view in Grumman's own anechoic chamber where its extensive array of electronic equipment was comprehensively wrung-out.

The first new-build Prowlers were five pre-production test specimens which were assigned to formal Navy evaluation with the Naval Air Test Center at Patuxent River in Maryland. With that hurdle safely negotiated delivery of production-configured aircraft began in January 1971 when training squadron VAQ-129 accepted its first EA-6B at NAS Whidbey Island in Washington.

In the same month the unit which would have the distinction of introducing the Prowler to fleet service and combat also received its first aircraft, this being VAQ-132, also at Whidbey Island. There-

after, the Prowler force expanded fairly rapidly, VAQ-131 and VAQ-134 acquiring the type later in 1971, VAQ-133 in 1972, VAQ-136 and VAQ-137 in 1973, VAQ-135 in 1974, VAQ-130 in 1975, and VAQ-138 in 1976.

Attention then switched to the US Marine Corps, which received about 15 aircraft for service with VMAQ-2 at MCAS Cherry Point in North Carolina, deliveries to this unit getting under way in the autumn of 1978. There was then a long interval before VAQ-139 joined the Navy Prowler community in 1983, the most recent addition being VAQ-140 which stood up in 1985. Thus by 1986 the Navy had almost reached its long-established goal of 12 Prowler squadrons, an objective it should attain during 1987 when VAQ-141 forms.

Intruder heritage

With regard to the Prowler's basic structure, the airframe is essentially similar to that of the A-6 Intruder although a cursory glance quickly reveals one or two major differences. For a start, the fuselage is rather longer, being stretched by some 1.37 m (4 ft 6 in) in order to accommodate a second cockpit for two of the three ECMOs that the Prowler usually carries. And because of the heavy warload there has been a certain amount of structural strengthening in the vicinity of the landing gear and arrester hook.

Initially the Prowler was powered by two Pratt & Whitney J52-P-8A turbojet engines, each rated at 4218-kg (9,300-lb) thrust but, following production of 23 standard or 'Basic' aircraft, a switch was made to the J52-P-408 which puts out 5080-kg (11,200-lb) thrust when operating at full bore. This engine model has been fitted as standard to all subsequent Prowlers as well as retrofitted to the 21

Easily distinguished by the AN/ALQ-41 spear antenna protruding forward from each outer wing pylon, this EXCAP EA-6B Prowler carries the current maximum of five TJS pods on the underwing and underfuselage stations.

'Basic' aircraft which were modified to 'ICAP 1' configuration.

Apart from the extra cockpit, perhaps the most visible external difference concerns the fin, which is crowned by a bulbous fairing containing antennas associated with the Eaton Corporation (AIL Division) ALQ-99 TJS. Signal data picked up by these antennas are fed to an AYA-6 (AYK-14 in 'ICAP 2' aircraft) solid state digital computer for processing and display, the computer being able to analyse, arrange in order of priority and counter threats entirely automatically.

Alternatively, system control may be accomplished wholly manually by the three ECMOs or in conjunction with the computer, the latter analysing threats and the crew initiating necessary countermeasures action. All in all, it is a flexible and capable piece of kit, jamming signals generated by the EA-6B emanating from the distinctive slab-sided external pods, each of which contains two high-powered smart noise jamming units. Power for each pod is provided by a built-in ram air turbine capable of producing 27 kVA at speeds of 220 kts (407 km/h; 253 mph) and above, and a maximum of five pods may be carried on hardpoints beneath the wings (four) and centre fuselage (one).

In practice, however, it is rare to see this configuration during routine peace-

The most obvious feature of the EA-6B design other than the fin-tip 'football' is the double cockpit, which houses the four-man aircrew in tandem paired seating. The forward cockpit is occupied by the pilot (port seat) and the ECMO 1 on Martin-Baker GRU.7A ejector seats.

time sea-going operations, EA-6Bs generally toting a mix of TJS pods and 1136-litre (300-US gal) auxiliary fuel tanks. Typical configurations can include three fuel tanks on the centreline and inboard stations with two TJS pods outboard, or three TJS pods on the centreline and outboard stations with two fuel tanks inboard.

As had occurred with the A-6 Intruder, so the Prowler has been progressively improved since it first joined the fleet way back in 1971. Whilst it represented a vast improvement over the Douglas EKA-3B Skywarrior, the original 'Basic' Prowler was in many respects something of a compromise in terms of capability since it was able to counter threats in only four frequency bands rather than the 10 originally envisaged for the ALQ-99 TJS.

Basically, this situation arose from the desire to limit the risk factor involved in what was clearly an ambitious undertaking. In consequence, it was decided to move fairly cautiously at the outset, relying on continuing development to maximize the Prowler's ultimate potential.

Fuselage extension
The fuselage extension adds 1.32 m
(4 ft 4 in) to the length of the EA-6B when
compared with the EA-6A

ECMO 2 and 3
The two ECM officers in the rear cabin
control the tactical jamming system. The
three ECMOs sometimes swap
positions

Anti-collision light
These are mounted under the nose, on
the spine and on each wingtip

UHF/Tacan
This blade aerial serves both UHF and
Tacan systems. Inter-Prowler datalink is
handled by the Tacan system

ADF
The automatic direction finder on the
EA-6B is the ARA-48 unit

GDY 021   GDY 017   DNM 014   PJL 127

Access steps
Entry to the aft cockpit is gained via
steps which pull down from the engine
intake

Refuelling boom
For long periods on station, and accompanying long carrier strikes, the EA-6B is inflight-refuellable, usually by KA-6D Intruders

ECMO 1
The ECM officer is primarily concerned with navigation, radar operation and control of the ALQ-92 communications jamming system

Ejector seats
The pilot and ECMOs sit on Martin-Baker GRUEA-7 ejector seats

DECM
The excrescence at the base of the refuelling boom houses a receiver for the AN/ALQ-126 DECM unit

Radar
The search and navigation radar is the APS-130 unit, capable of multi-mode operation. Impressive terrain portrayal gives excellent adverse conditions capability.

Onboard computer
The ICAP 2 version has the AN/AYK-14 computer, which controls the tactical jamming and other systems. It can operate in full or semi-automatic modes, or in manual. This computer is faster and more reliable than the AYA-6 fitted to earlier Prowlers

IFF
Operating in L-band, this small aerial is for the IFF (identification friend or foe) system

Ram-air turbine
To provide power for each pod, it is provided with a ram-air turbine. Once the minimum required airspeed of 220 knots (407.6 km/h) has been reached, the RAT provides 27 kVA of power

VHF
The large blade aerial serves VHF communications

Taxi light
The taxi and approach lights are mounted in the nosewheel door, which swings forward when the nosewheel is lowered

Splitter plate
The small intake ramp allows only cle airflow into the Pratt & Whitney J52 engine

605

With the benefit of hindsight this proved to be a wise move, for today's EA-6B is infinitely superior to the original model, whilst the upcoming 'ADVCAP' subtype will be even better still, satisfying virtually all of the objectives laid down back in the 1960s and exceeding some.

Constant improvements

As already noted, production kicked off with 23 examples of the 'Basic' aircraft, this subtype remaining in the front-line inventory until late 1976 and, incidentally, being the only Prowler variant to see combat in South East Asia. 'EXCAP' came next, some 25 aircraft being produced to this standard with deliveries beginning in January 1973. Improvements to the system enabled it to counter threats in eight frequency bands whilst associated computer memory capacity was doubled, and this model remained in front-line use until at least late 1984, the surviving examples now being likely candidates for modernization and upgrading to 'ICAP 2' configuration.

The next variant to make its debut was 'ICAP 1' which featured much more modern electronic equipment including digitally-tuned receivers, computer-controlled EW systems and enhanced display units, all of which made life a little easier for the harassed ECMOs. Making its sea-going debut with VAQ-135 aboard USS Nimitz (CVN-68) in late 1977, 'ICAP 1' quickly spread to other squadrons, new-build aircraft of this marque being augmented by a CILOP project which brought the 21 surviving 'Basic' aircraft to the same standard. In the meantime, production of new-build 'ICAP 1s' continued for several years before terminating in the early 1980s with the 45th example.

Prowlers continue to roll from the Grumman production line at Calverton, however, 'ICAP 2' having supplanted 'ICAP 1' during 1983. Flown for the first

time in prototype form in June 1980, perhaps the most significant change made on this model relates to the computer, the original AYA-6 having given way to the AYK-14 which combines a memory four times that of the older unit with a processing speed three times greater. As a result the system is much more responsive to threats, being able to operate effectively across nine frequency bands. Deliveries to the Prowler training unit began in 1984 and this type is now fully operational, having made its maiden deployment with VAQ-137 in 1985. Manufacture of modest quantities of this version (probably at a rate of about six aircraft per year) seem certain to continue until about 1990-1.

Looking to the future, efforts to improve the EA-6B's already impressive talents continue and will result in the appearance of a variant known as 'ADVCAP'. Expected to be able to cope with the 10 frequency bands originally specified, it will feature a new receiver/processor group now under development by the Amecom Division of Litton Industries, as well as an advanced Passive Detection System. Other equipment which may well find its way into the 'ADVCAP' Prowler includes ASPJ, JTIDS and GPS.

Development of the 'ADVCAP' will, of necessity, be a lengthy and complex process but is expected to result in the delivery of the first of an eventual total of six systems for flight evaluation in 1987. If all goes well this should clear the way

With a variety of aerials, blade antennas and various 'lumps and bumps', the Prowler still manages to retain the essentially graceful lines of its A-6 Intruder forebear. The prominent fin-tip fairing contains ECM receivers as part of the tactical jamming system.

for the deployment of production examples of the 'ADVCAP' Prowler with fleet units in the early 1990s. By that time today's generation of ECM aircraft may well be getting rather long in the tooth since the EW field may be said to be truly dynamic in terms of growth, threats proliferating at an alarming rate and proving ever more difficult to counter.

Glossary
ADVCAP ADVanced CAPability
ASPJ Airborne Self-Protection Jammer
CILOP Conversion In Lieu Of Procurement
ECM Electronic CounterMeasures
ECMO Electronic CounterMeasures Officer
EXCAP EXpanded CAPability
EW Electronic Warfare
GPS Global Positioning System
ICAP Improved CAPability
JTIDS Joint Tactical Information Distribution System
MCAS Marine Corps Air Station
NAS Naval Air Station
TJS Tactical Jamming System

As with most US Navy aircraft, the Prowler has a wing-fold capability to reduce storage space aboard aircraft-carriers. This view also shows the prominence of the inflight-refuelling probe and the low-set 'cheek' air intakes, features adopted from the A-6 design.

Grumman EA-6B Prowler in service

United States Navy

With 12 of a planned total of 14 Prowler-equipped squadrons now active, the US Navy has almost reached its goal as far as the electronic warfare community is concerned. All the squadrons are home-based at NAS Whidbey Island, Washington State, though VAQ-136 is normally forward-based at Atsugi, Japan, this being its shore-base in support of its operations as part of CVW-5 aboard USS Midway. Though almost all the units are based on the west coast of America, they deploy with both Atlantic and Pacific Fleets, the normal complement within a Carrier Air Wing being four aircraft. Being in the sixth squadron in the wing, the Prowlers have modex numbers beginning with '6' and invariably ranging from '604' to '607'. The vast majority of aircraft are now wearing the low-visibility Tactical Paint Scheme with codes and squadron insignia severely toned down in various shades of grey or black.

The latest squadron to form on the type is VAQ-140, which will be followed by VAQ-141 and VAQ-142 in the late 1980s. As with the current units, they will be based at NAS Whidbey Island. VAQ-129 is currently tasked with Fleet Readiness Training in support of the front-line deployed units, and the aircraft of this unit follow a training unit tradition of starting their aircraft modex numbers with the last number of their squadron, e.g. '908'. The unit has a larger complement of aircraft, hence the higher numeric values.

VAQ-129 'Vikings'
Base: NAS Whidbey Island, Washington
Last tailcode: 'NJ'
Example aircraft: 159583/NJ-904, 158547/NJ-915, 158039/NJ-916

VAQ-130 'Zappers'
Base: NAS Whidbey Island, Washington
Last tailcode: 'NG' (CVW-9)
Example aircraft: none known

VAQ-131 'Lancers'
Base: NAS Whidbey Island, Washington
Last tailcode: 'NE' (CVW-15)
Example aircraft: 158810/NE-605, 161885/NE-606, 162223/NE-607

VAQ-132 'Scorpions'
Base: NAS Whidbey Island, Washington
Last tailcode: 'AG' (CVW-7)
Example aircraft: 161120/AG-604, 161242/AG-605, 161245/AG-607

VAQ-133 'Wizards'
Base: NAS Whidbey Island, Washington
Last tailcode: 'NH' (CVW-11)
Example aircraft: 161176/NH-604, 161883/NH-606, 161884/NH-607

VAQ-134 'Garudas'
Base: NAS Whidbey Island, Washington
Last tailcode: 'NL' (CVW-15)
Example aircraft: 158040/NL-604, 161119/NL-607

VAQ-135 'Black Ravens'
Base: NAS Whidbey Island, Washington
Last tailcode: 'AB' (CVW-1)
Example aircraft: 161244/AB-605, 161115/AB-606, 161243/AB-607

VAQ-136 'Gauntlets'
Base: NAS Whidbey Island, Washington, but forward-based at MCAS Atsugi, Japan
Last tailcode: 'NF' (CVW-5)
Example aircraft: 160787/NF-606, 161247/NF-607

VAQ-137 'Rooks'
Base: NAS Whidbey Island, Washington
Last tailcode: 'AC'
Example aircraft: 158801/AC-605, 161881/AC-606

VAQ-138 'Yellow Jackets'
Base: NAS Whidbey Island, Washington
Last tailcode: 'AJ' (CVW-8)
Example aircraft: 161243/AJ-606

VAQ-139 'Cougars'
Base: NAS Whidbey Island, Washington
Last tailcode: 'NK' (CVW-14)
Example aircraft: 161774/NK-605, 158033/NK-606, 158030/NK-607

VAQ-140 'Patriots'
Base: NAS Whidbey Island, Washington
Last tailcode: 'AC' (CVW-3)
Example aircraft: none known

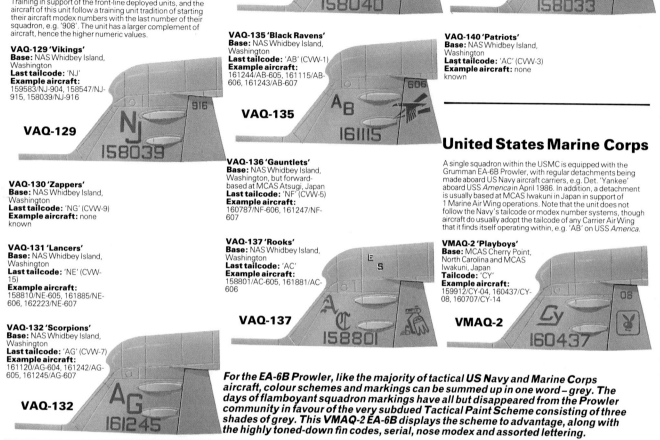

VAQ-129
VAQ-132
VAQ-134
VAQ-135
VAQ-137
VAQ-139

United States Marine Corps

A single squadron within the USMC is equipped with the Grumman EA-6B Prowler, with regular detachments being made aboard US Navy aircraft carriers, e.g. Det. 'Yankee' aboard USS America in April 1986. In addition, a detachment is usually based at MCAS Iwakuni in Japan in support of 1 Marine Air Wing operations. Note that the unit does not follow the Navy's tailcode or modex number systems, though aircraft do usually adopt the tailcode of any Carrier Air Wing that it finds itself operating within, e.g. 'AB' on USS America.

VMAQ-2 'Playboys'
Base: MCAS Cherry Point, North Carolina and MCAS Iwakuni, Japan
Tailcode: 'CY'
Example aircraft: 159912/CY-04, 160437/CY-08, 160707/CY-14

VMAQ-2

For the EA-6B Prowler, like the majority of tactical US Navy and Marine Corps aircraft, colour schemes and markings can be summed up in one word – grey. The days of flamboyant squadron markings have all but disappeared from the Prowler community in favour of the very subdued Tactical Paint Scheme consisting of three shades of grey. This VMAQ-2 EA-6B displays the scheme to advantage, along with the highly toned-down fin codes, serial, nose modex and assorted lettering.

SIR
The System Integration Receivers
detect enemy signals, and relay this data
to the central computer, which then
assigns jamming details to the
respective pod. Three sets of receivers
cover Bands 4-9

DECM
The 'beercan' antennas house a receiver
for the AN/ALQ-126 deception ECM
equipment. This delays and regenerates
radar signals to confuse and deceive
enemy radars

Formation light
A low intensity light is mounted on the
wingtip for use in night formation flying

Antennas
Mounted on the side of the tail are two
receivers for Bands 1 and 2

Slats
Leading edge slats and nearly full-span
flaps and flaperons reduce carrier
approach speed

Speed brakes
The EA-6 has inherited the split wingtip
brakes from the A-6 Intruder. These
open outwards into the airflow both
above and below the wing

Iain Wyllie

Grumman EA-6B ICAP 2 Prowler
VMAQ-2, US Marine Corps
USS America

Fin-top radome
Dubbed the 'Football', this radome houses all the SIR receivers for the ALQ-99 suite

Defensive avionics
The EA-6 is a high-priority target, and carries a suite to reflect this. Among the defence is the AN/ALQ-41 track-breaker and AN/APR-27 SAM launch warning system

Wing fence
This aerodynamic feature guides the air over the wing. It also contains an antenna for the HF system

AR

605

Equipment platform
A platform (known as the 'birdcage') hinges down from the rear fuselage undersides, mounting much special equipment, including the AN/APN-153 Doppler navigation system

Fuel tank
In practice, EA-6Bs usually carry three TJS pods and two 1136-litre (300-US gal) fuel tanks

Fuel dump
Fuel vents through this pipe. Fuel-dumping is made through two outlets at the wingtips

Chaff/flare dispenser
An AN/ALE-39 chaff/flare dispenser is mounted under the rear fuselage. Various combinations can be dispensed, and are controlled from the cockpit

TJS
Each ALQ-99 pod is thought to contain not only jammers, but a tracking receiver, exciter/processor, built-in test function equipment and a small computer which interfaces with the main onboard unit

EA-6B Prowler variants

EA-6B prototypes: three aircraft converted from two existing Grumman A-6A Intruder airframes and a single YA-6A Intruder airframe; designated M-1 to M-3 respectively, the first two aircraft were used for flight testing while the third saw use as a ground test machine; the most obvious differences from the A-6 were the addition of a (1.37-m) 54-in forward fuselage plug to provide room for a second cockpit; the addition of a large fin-top housing for electronic warfare receiver antennas and a new dorsal spine extending forward of the tail fin; the landing gear was strengthened to cope with the increased operating weights, while the main wing was also re-stressed to allow for manoeuvres up to 5.5 g; power was supplied by two Pratt & Whitney J52-P-8A turbojets, each providing 4218-kg (9,300-lb) static thrust, while four Martin Baker GRUEA 7 rocket-assisted ejector seats were provided for the crew

EA-6B pre-production aircraft: a total of five new build EA-6Bs were produced for the US Navy to conduct formal test and evaluation programmes; designated P-1 to P-5, they were similar to the prototypes and were powered by the same Pratt & Whitney turbojets

EA-6B 'Basic': the first full production model of the Prowler entered US Navy service in 1971, a total of 23 being built; the term 'Basic' refers to the original electronics suite which allowed jamming over four frequency bands via the AN/ALQ-99F Tactical Jamming System (TJS) modular unit; up to five external jamming pods could be carried on underwing/underfuselage pylons with a total of 10 jamming transmitters; the system was linked to the AN/AYA-6 solid-state digital computer; externally similar to the earlier aircraft, this model was withdrawn from front-line service in 1976

EA-6B 'EXCAP' (Expanded Capability): the second full production model of the Prowler family, 25 aircraft being built with deliveries beginning in 1973; improved and expanded equipment allowed for jamming over eight frequency bands (bands 5, 6, 8 and 9 having been added), while the on-board computer memory capacity was doubled; additional recording equipment and a greater range of computer operational modes allowed for the automatic coverage of multiple threats; powerplant was the improved Pratt & Whitney J52-P-408 turbojets, each with 5080-kg (11,200-lb) static thrust; this model was withdrawn from front-line service during 1984, survivors most likely due to be converted to 'ICAP 2' configuration; externally distinguishable by the antenna protruding from the outer wing pylons as part of the AN/ALQ-100 Deception Electronic Countermeasures (DECM) suite

EA-6B 'ICAP 1' (Improved Capability 1): a total of 45 new-build 'ICAP 1s' were produced, in addition to 21 surviving 'Basic' aircraft which underwent CILOP (Conversion In Lieu of Procurement) treatment; this model features a much greater jamming capability over eight frequency bands, the whole TJS operation having been moved to the rear cockpit; new features include improved multi-format display screens, a lower overall threat response time, an Automatic Carrier Landing System (ACLS), fully integrated computer-controlled Electronic Warfare systems, a new Deception Electronic Countermeasures (DECM) system and a new Communication-Navigation-Identification (CNI) unit; though virtually identical externally to the earlier models, the 'ICAP 1' aircraft (and subsequent models) have a small receiver for the AN/ALQ-126 DECM near the base of the inflight-refuelling probe, and a 'beer can' housing protruding aft from the rear base of the fin top bulged radome, as well as a set of antennas set low on the rudder

EA-6B 'ICAP 2' (Improved Capability 2): first flying in J[...] 1980, this model began to replace the 'ICAP 1' in front-line ser[...] during 1983; a further increase in tactical jamming capability is[...] incorporated, with an exciter in each external TJS pod, each po[...] having the ability to jam in two frequency bands simultaneous[...] exciter covers bands 1-9 while providing its own automatic tu[...] and calibration; the original AN/AYA-6 computer has been rep[...] by the AN/AYK-14 system with four times the memory capaci[...] three times the processing speed of the earlier model; additio[...] there is a Tactical Air Navigation (TACAN) data link allowing EA[...] to work together more effectively

EA-6B 'ADVCAP' (Advanced Capability): a projected m[...] which will supplant and eventually replace both 'ICAP 1' and 'I[...] 2' aircraft from the late 1980s/early 1990s onwards; fitment o[...] J-Band (10-20 Ghz) AN/ALQ-149 communications jammer sys[...] and an advanced Passive Detection System (PDS) will enable[...] greater and more effective tactical jamming over frequency ba[...] 1-10; the existing use of up to five TJS external pods will be[...] supplemented by two additional outer wing stores pylons, eac[...] which will be able to carry an extra pod, allowing a maximum o[...] seven to be carried; there is a possibility that the fin top radom[...] be redesigned, though this remains to be seen; further new[...] equipment is likely to include a Joint Tactical Information[...] Distribution System (JTIDS), a Global Positioning System (GP[...] an Airborne Self-Protection Jammer (ASPJ); the first of six[...] development aircraft is scheduled to fly in 1987/88

The vast amount of work that has to be performed by the four-man crew of the Prowler is basically split into three fields of responsibility. The pilot, seated in the port seat of the front 'office', is tasked with the flying of the aircraft, while the co-pilot/navigator seated next to him is responsible for communications, defensive ECM, navigation, and chaff/flare/expendable jammer dispensing. Officially called ECMO 1, the co-pilot has no flight controls as his existing duties occupy all his time.

The rear cockpit is occupied by ECMO 2 and 3 and is characterized by a distinct lack of forward vision and several operating consoles tied in to the on-board computer and the various individual ECM units which combine to form the TJS operation. As with the ECMO 1 position, no flight controls are provided as the TJS operators will be concentrating on detecting threat sources and then assigning, adjusting and monitoring the jammers as they work to block enemy radar.

Grumman EA-6B Prowler cutaway drawing key

1 Radome
2 APQ-92 radar antenna
3 Bulkhead
4 Rain removal nozzle
5 ALQ-126 receiver antenna fairing
6 Refuelling boom (detachable)
7 Inflight-refuelling receptacle
8 Two-piece windscreens
9 Senior EWO's panoramic/video display consoles
10 Pilot's instrument panel shroud
11 Control column
12 Rudder pedals
13 Pitot static tubes (port and starboard)
14 Power brake
15 APQ-92 transmitter
16 Anti-collision beacon
17 'L'-band antenna
18 ALQ-92 (IFF) antenna
19 Taxi/landing light
20 Nosewheel leg fairing
21 Nosewheel leg
22 Tow link (landing position)
23 Tow link (launch position)
24 Dual nosewheel assembly
25 Nosewheel retraction jack
26 Nosewheel well door
27 Approach lights
28 Shock-absorber link
29 APQ-92 high and low voltage
30 APQ-92 modulator
31 Cockpit floor level
32 Anti-skid control
33 Fuselage forward frames
34 Pilot's ejection seat
35 Senior Electronic Warfare Officer's (ALQ-99 tactical jamming) ejection seat
36 Upward-hinged forward cockpit canopy
37 Canopy mechanism
38 Aft cockpit port EWO's console

39 Handgrips
40 Security equipment
41 Splitter plate
42 Port engine inlet
43 Inlet frames
44 Aft cockpit entry ladder
45 Electric hydraulic pump
46 Manual selector valves
47 Cockpit aft bulkhead
48 Third Electronic Warfare Officer's (ALQ-92 comms jamming) ejection seat

49 Second Electronic Warfare Officer's (ALQ-99 tactical jamming) ejection seat
50 Canopy mechanism
51 Upward-hinged aft cockpit canopy
52 Starboard outer ECM pod
53 Intake
54 Pod turbine power-source
55 ALQ-41/ALQ-100 starboard spear antenna
56 Leading-edge slats (deployed)

57 Starboard inner integ[...] wing fuel cell
58 Starboard inner wing
59 Wing-fold cylinders
60 Hinge assembly
61 Wing-fold line
62 Starboard outer integ[...] wing fuel cell
63 Fuel probe
64 Wing structure
65 Starboard outer wing
66 Starboard navigation
67 Starboard formation
68 Wingtip speed-brake (open)
69 Speed-brake actuatin[...] cylinder fairing
70 Fence
71 Wingtip fuel dump ou[...]
72 Starboard single-slot flap (outer section)
73 Starboard flaperons
74 Flaperon mechanism

188

Grumman EA-6B Prowler recognition features

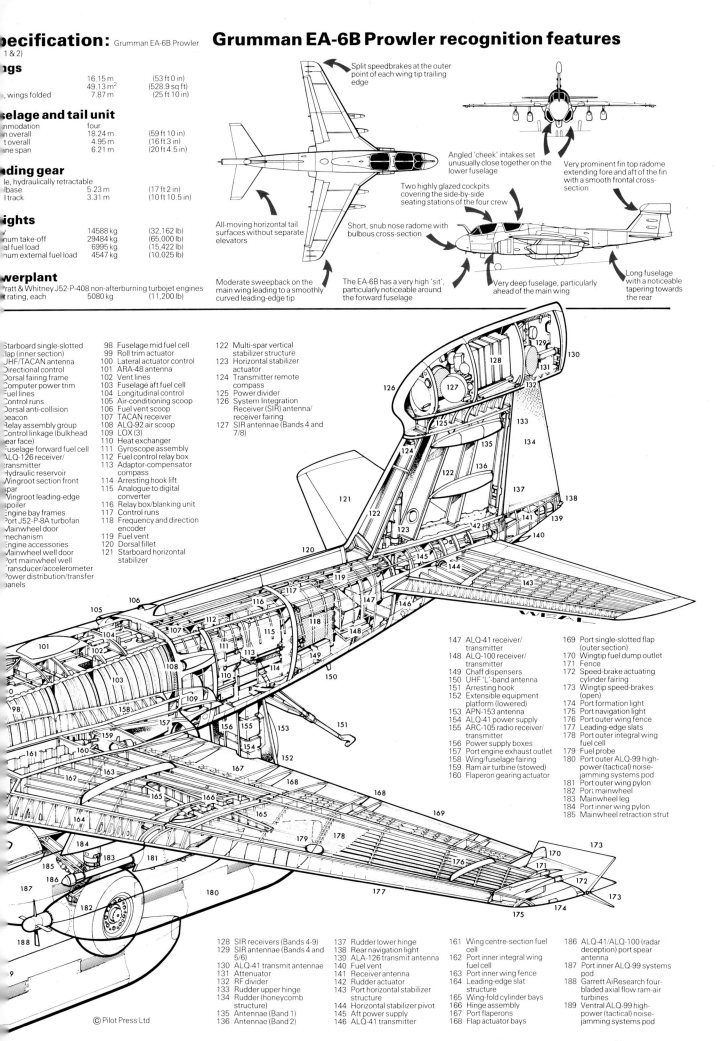

Specification: Grumman EA-6B Prowler
(1 & 2)

ings
	16.15 m	(53 ft 0 in)
	49.13 m²	(528.9 sq ft)
, wings folded	7.87 m	(25 ft 10 in)

selage and tail unit
nmodation	four	
n overall	18.24 m	(59 ft 10 in)
t overall	4.95 m	(16 ft 3 in)
ne span	6.21 m	(20 ft 4.5 in)

ding gear
le, hydraulically retractable		
lbase	5.23 m	(17 ft 2 in)
l track	3.31 m	(10 ft 10.5 in)

ights
	14588 kg	(32,162 lb)
num take-off	29484 kg	(65,000 lb)
al fuel load	6995 kg	(15,422 lb)
num external fuel load	4547 kg	(10,025 lb)

owerplant
Pratt & Whitney J52-P-408 non-afterburning turbojet engines
rating, each   5080 kg   (11,200 lb)

Recognition callouts:

Split speedbrakes at the outer point of each wing tip trailing edge

Angled 'cheek' intakes set unusually close together on the lower fuselage

Very prominent fin top radome extending fore and aft of the fin with a smooth frontal cross-section

Two highly glazed cockpits covering the side-by-side seating stations of the four crew

All-moving horizontal tail surfaces without separate elevators

Short, snub nose radome with bulbous cross-section

Moderate sweepback on the main wing leading to a smoothly curved leading-edge tip

The EA-6B has a very high 'sit', particularly noticeable around the forward fuselage

Very deep fuselage, particularly ahead of the main wing

Long fuselage with a noticeable tapering towards the rear

Parts list:

Starboard single-slotted
flap (inner section)
UHF/TACAN antenna
Directional control
Dorsal fairing frame
Computer power trim
Fuel lines
Control runs
Dorsal anti-collision
beacon
Relay assembly group
Control linkage (bulkhead
rear face)
Fuselage forward fuel cell
ALQ-126 receiver/
transmitter
Hydraulic reservoir
Wingroot section front
spar
Wingroot leading-edge
spoiler
Engine bay frames
Port J52-P-8A turbofan
Mainwheel door
mechanism
Engine accessories
Mainwheel well door
Port mainwheel well
Transducer/accelerometer
Power distribution/transfer
panels

98 Fuselage mid fuel cell
99 Roll trim actuator
100 Lateral actuator control
101 ARA-48 antenna
102 Vent lines
103 Fuselage aft fuel cell
104 Longitudinal control
105 Air-conditioning scoop
106 Fuel vent scoop
107 TACAN receiver
108 ALQ-92 air scoop
109 LOX (3)
110 Heat exchanger
111 Gyroscope assembly
112 Fuel control relay box
113 Adaptor-compensator
    compass
114 Arresting hook lift
115 Analogue to digital
    converter
116 Relay box/blanking unit
117 Control runs
118 Frequency and direction
    encoder
119 Fuel vent
120 Dorsal fillet
121 Starboard horizontal
    stabilizer

122 Multi-spar vertical
    stabilizer structure
123 Horizontal stabilizer
    actuator
124 Transmitter remote
    compass
125 Power divider
126 System Integration
    Receiver (SIR) antenna/
    receiver fairing
127 SIR antennae (Bands 4 and
    7/8)

147 ALQ-41 receiver/
    transmitter
148 ALQ-100 receiver/
    transmitter
149 Chaff dispensers
150 UHF 'L'-band antenna
151 Arresting hook
152 Extensible equipment
    platform (lowered)
153 APN-153 antenna
154 ALQ-41 power supply
155 ARC-105 radio receiver/
    transmitter
156 Power supply boxes
157 Port engine exhaust outlet
158 Wing/fuselage fairing
159 Ram air turbine (stowed)
160 Flaperon gearing actuator

169 Port single-slotted flap
    (outer section)
170 Wingtip fuel dump outlet
171 Fence
172 Speed-brake actuating
    cylinder fairing
173 Wingtip speed-brakes
    (open)
174 Port formation light
175 Port navigation light
176 Port outer wing fence
177 Leading-edge slats
178 Port outer integral wing
    fuel cell
179 Fuel probe
180 Port outer ALQ-99 high-
    power (tactical) noise-
    jamming systems pod
181 Port outer wing pylon
182 Port mainwheel
183 Mainwheel leg
184 Port inner wing pylon
185 Mainwheel retraction strut

128 SIR receivers (Bands 4-9)
129 SIR antennae (Bands 4 and
    5/6)
130 ALQ-41 transmit antennae
131 Attenuator
132 RF divider
133 Rudder upper hinge
134 Rudder (honeycomb
    structure)
135 Antennae (Band 1)
136 Antennae (Band 2)

137 Rudder lower hinge
138 Rear navigation light
139 ALA-126 transmit antenna
140 Fuel vent
141 Receiver antenna
142 Rudder actuator
143 Port horizontal stabilizer
    structure
144 Horizontal stabilizer pivot
145 Aft power supply
146 ALQ-41 transmitter

161 Wing centre-section fuel
    cell
162 Port inner integral wing
    fuel cell
163 Port inner wing fence
164 Leading-edge slat
    structure
165 Wing-fold cylinder bays
166 Hinge assembly
167 Port flaperons
168 Flap actuator bays

186 ALQ-41/ALQ-100 (radar
    deception) port spear
    antenna
187 Port inner ALQ-99 systems
    pod
188 Garrett AiResearch four-
    bladed axial flow ram-air
    turbines
189 Ventral ALQ-99 high-
    power (tactical) noise-
    jamming systems pod

© Pilot Press Ltd

EA-6B Prowler warload

[Configuration 1 legend]
☐ 5 × AN/ALQ-99F tactical jamming system external pods, one per underwing pylon and one on centreline station, each with two high-powered jamming transmitters and a tracking receiver
1 × AN/ALQ-126 deception electronic countermeasures (DECM) system carried internally, with receivers on inflight-refuelling probe and rear base of fin top radome
2 × AN/ALE-39 expendable countermeasures dispensers, one carried internally on each side of lower rear fuselage, each with a mix of chaff, infra-red flares and expendable jammers in multiples of 10

Strike Force Penetration configuration ('ICAP 1 & 2')

The penetration role is one task assigned to the Prowler within its broader task of protecting the strike force in its attacks on enemy targets. A high jammer-to-strike aircraft ratio is needed, hence the use of the maximum five jamming pods. The EA-6B enters the area of threat ahead of the strike force, getting in close to the enemy defensive systems. Pre-registered information has led to an order of battle covering radars and defensive sites, information such as positions, pulse-repetition frequencies noted before the flight. The TJS pods are linked to the receiving antennas in the fin top radome and the internally carried digital computer. The computer carries out processing for the TJS which scans in the acquisition mode, looking for threat frequencies. The ECMOs monitor their display consoles and listen for radar emissions, starting to jam by activating the 'Master Radiate' control.

[Configuration 2 legend]
☐ 3 × AN/ALQ-99F tactical jamming system external pods, one per outer underwing pylon and one on centreline station, each with two high-powered jamming transmitters and a tracking receiver
1 × AN/ALQ-126 deception electronic countermeasures (DECM) system carried internally, with receivers on inflight-refuelling probe and rear base of fin top radome
2 × AN/ALE-39 expendable countermeasures dispensers, carried internally on each side of the lower rear fuselage, each with a mix of chaff, infra-red flares and expendable jammers in multiples of 10
☐ 2 × 1136-litre (300-US gal) external fuel tanks, one per inner under wing pylon

Stand-off Jamming configuration ('ICAP 1 & 2')

A safer operational role for the Prowler, this profile is most likely to be flown in areas of reduced/degraded enemy defences where the threat level is not very high. Once again the Prowler enters the threat area ahead of the strike force, its receivers ready to pick up any emissions as the aircraft probes the enemy radar areas. Any of the threats identified will be assessed and countered, the aircraft negating the sites and loitering to maintain active jamming in the area while the strike force hits its targets, and then egressing after the strike force has left. As with all Prowlers, an AN/ALQ-92 communications jammer transmits signals via antennas in the nose radome, while an AN/ALR-67(V) radar warning system can allocate threats for the TJS and DECM. The AN/ALE-39 units can carry up to 60 loads to give protection from enemy defences.

[Configuration 3 legend]
■ 2 × AGM-88A high-speed anti-radiation missiles (HARM), one per outer underwing pylon
☐ 3 × AN/ALQ-99F tactical jamming system external pods, one per inner underwing pylon and one on centreline station
1 × AN/ALQ-126 deception electronic countermeasures (DECM) system carried internally, with receivers on inflight-refuelling probe and rear base of fin top radome
2 × AN/ALE-39 expendable countermeasures dispensers, carried internally on each side of lower rear fuselage, each with a mix of chaff, infra-red flares and expendable jammers in multiples of 10

Anti-radiation configuration ('ICAP 1 & 2')

Though the vast majority of missions flown by the EA-6B Prowler squadrons utilize only a mass of highly complex electronic equipment in the electronic warfare support role for other US Navy aircraft which will carry out the strikes, it is possible for the Prowler to carry the AGM-88A anti-radiation missile. Admittedly it is exceedingly rare to see operational aircraft so configured, but it does add to the operational versatility of the aircraft and could usefully be used in situations where the Prowler comes up against a particularly hostile radar site which poses a very major threat to both itself and the strike force, or where the particular mission requirements call for the Prowler to operate exceedingly close to enemy radar sites. For such a large aircraft, the Prowler can pull some very tight evasive manoeuvres, being stressed up to 5.5 g.

[Configuration 4 legend]
☐ 7 × AN/ALQ-99F tactical jamming system external pods, one per underwing pylon and one on centreline station, each with two high-powered jamming transmitters and a tracking receiver
1 × AN/ALQ-126 deception electronic countermeasures (DECM) system carried internally, with receivers on inflight-refuelling probe and rear base of fin top radome
2 × AN/ALE-39 expendable countermeasures dispensers, carried internally on each side of lower rear fuselage, each with a mix of chaff, infra-red flares and expendable jammers in multiples of 10

Future high-threat jamming configuration ('ADVCAP')

The 'Advanced Capability' model of the EA-6B Prowler has yet to fly and its final configuration and systems suite is still to be confirmed. There is a very good chance that two extra stores pylons will be added for the carriage of two more TJS jamming pods. This would allow for frequency coverage into bands 9 and 10 if linked in with extra transmitters being considered to extend effective jamming frequency ranges. The current AN/ALQ-92 communications jammer is to be replaced by the more effective J-band (10-20 Ghz) AN/ALQ-149 model, while an advanced passive detection system (PDS) will improve the accuracy efficiency of enemy signals detection, as well as speed up the processing and subsequent jamming response times.

Performance:

EA-6B Prowler with five ECM pods

Maximum speed at sea level	530 kts	982 km/h (610 mph)
Cruising speed at optimum altitude	418 kts	774 km/h (481 mph)
Initial rate of climb per minute	10,030 ft	(3057 m)
Service ceiling	38,000 ft	(11580 m)
Take-off run	814 m	(2,670 ft)
Range with maximum external load, five per cent reserves plus 20 minutes at sea level	1769 km	(1,099 miles)
Ferry range with maximum external fuel	3254 km	(2,022 miles)

Unrefuelled endurance

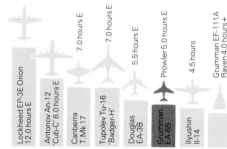

- Lockheed EP-3E Orion 12.0 hours E
- Antonov An-12 'Cub-C' 8.0 hours E
- Canberra T.Mk 17 7.0 hours E
- Tupolev Tu-16 'Badger-H' 7.0 hours E
- Douglas EA-3B 5.5 hours E
- Grumman EA-6B Prowler 5.0 hours E
- Ilyushin Il-14 4.5 hours
- Grumman EF-111A Raven 4.0 hours +

Service ceiling

- British Aerospace Canberra T.Mk 17 48,000 ft
- Grumman EF-111A Raven 45,000 ft
- Douglas EA-3B Skywarrior 41,000ft
- Tupolev Tu-16 'Badger-H' 40,350ft E
- Grumman EA-6B Prowler 38,000 ft
- Antonov An-12 'Cub-C' 33,500 ft
- Lockheed EP-3E Orion 28,300 ft
- Ilyushin Il-14 24,300 ft

Maximum speed at optimum altitude

- Grumman EF-111A Raven 1226 kts
- Grumman EA-6B Prowler 566 kts
- Tupolev Tu-16 'Badger-H' 535 kts E
- Douglas EA-3B Skywarrior 530 kts
- British Aerospace Canberra T.Mk 17 495 kts
- Antonov An-12 'Cub-C' 419 kts
- Lockheed EP-3E Orion 411 kts
- Ilyushin Il-14 232 kts

Cruising speed

- Tupolev Tu-16 'Badger-H' 455 kts E
- Douglas EA-3B Skywarrior 452 kts
- Grumman EF-111A Raven 430 kts
- British Aerospace Canberra T.Mk 17 420 kts E
- Grumman EA-6B Prowler 418 kts
- Antonov An-12 'Cub-C' 362 kts
- Lockheed EP-3E Orion 328 kts
- Ilyushin Il-14 162 kts

Range with maximum payload

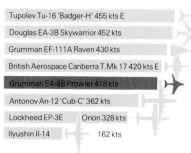

- Lockheed EP-3E Orion 4990 km
- Tupolev Tu-16 'Badger-H' 4000 km E
- Grumman EA-6B Prowler 3860 km
- Antonov An-12 'Cub-C' 3600 km
- British Aerospace Canberra T.Mk 17 3540 km
- Douglas EA-3B Skywarrior 3380 km
- Grumman EF-111A Raven 2990 km
- Ilyushin Il-14 450 km

The GRUMMAN EF-111A RAVEN

Grumman EF-111A 'Spark Vark'

The vast range of ordnance carried by today's fighting aircraft is the most tangible form of weaponry, but an equally crucial battle is fought in the field of electronic warfare. For the USA and for NATO, Grumman's EF-111A Raven is an important tool.

Although electronic warfare has been part of the military aviation world since the days of World War II, in terms of hard cash the amount of resources directed towards filling this need were, initially, relatively small, and this inevitably had some impact in both qualitative and quantitative terms. Certainly, as far as the USA was concerned, the number of units engaged in this task were spread thinly and, for the most part, EW and electronic countermeasures appear to have generally been conducted on almost a 'Cinderella' basis. For a long time modern equipment was scarce, money was hard to find and, in consequence, the few EW/ECM units that did exist had perforce to struggle along with flying hardware that was old and near-obsolescent. In time of peace this was embarrassing, but since everybody else was in pretty much the same boat it was not likely to have fatal consequences. In time of war, however, the picture was very different and it did indeed require another war to bring about much-needed change.

Vietnam was the catalyst which permanently changed the perception of EW/ECM, the multiplicity of 'threats' faced by US airmen prompting urgent reappraisal and, ultimately, the acknowledgement of the need for new and far more suitable equipment. Nevertheless, in view of the increasing complexity of the EW/ECM mission, it took several years for this equipment to filter through development channels and reach operational units. Hastily implemented modification programmes did, however, result

in some improvement, the US Navy's vintage Douglas EA-1F Skyraiders giving way to the Douglas EKA-3B Skywarrior during the mid-1960s, while the same period also witnessed deployment of a near relation of the 'whale' with the US Air Force, suitably modified examples of the B-66 Destroyer serving with distinction for virtually the entire war.

In the event, it was the Navy which first upgraded its EW/ECM capability, deploying the initial examples of the purpose-built Grumman EA-6B Prowler in the summer of 1972, shortly before the end of the US commitment to South Vietnam. The Air Force fared less well, having to wait for almost another decade before it began to take delivery of a long-overdue replacement. There was, therefore, a gap of several years between retirement of the EB-66 and the arrival of the infinitely superior and far more suitable General Dynamics/Grumman EF-111A.

Entering service shortly before the end of 1981, the EF-111A is now the USAF's principal EW/ECM platform and is operational with units in both the USA and Europe. Unfortunately, the EF-111A does not come cheap and its high cost has almost certainly militated against widespread deployment, 'production' of the EF-111A (actually a conversion process based on the original F-111A tactical fighter variant) being limited to just 42 airframes.

As far as distribution is concerned, by far the lion's share of EF-111As is located at Mountain Home AFB, Idaho, the sole European-based electronic combat

High above the mountains of North America, an EF-111A flies another training sortie. Though much of the design shows its F-111 heritage, the Raven can be easily distinguished by the fin tip antennas, radome and underfuselage 'canoe' fairing.

squadron (ECS) having just 13 examples on hand. Some of the latter, though, are 'combat-proven'; the 42nd ECS at RAF Upper Heyford furnished electronic support for attack-configured F-111Fs during the controversial US raid on Libya in April 1986.

Development hurdles

Known as the Raven, in an allusion to the electronic warfare officers who are generally called 'ravens', the EF-111A dates in development from the early 1970s, Grumman and General Dynamics each having been awarded design study contracts during 1974. In January 1975 Grumman was selected to proceed to the next stage of development, securing an $85.99 million contract calling for the conversion of two standard F-111As to serve as prototypes. Refinement of the design continued throughout 1975, one notable highlight occurring in December with the start of aerodynamic testing of the ventral canoe housing on a modified

An unusual view of a Raven during low-speed manoeuvring clearly illustrates the variable-geometry wing in the fully spread configuration. The broad forward fuselage accommodates the pilot and electronic warfare officer in side-by-side seating.

F-111A. But it was not until 10 March 1977 that the first EF-111A (66-0049) made its maiden flight from Grumman's Calverton facility on Long Island, New York.

This was, in fact, essentially an aerodynamic test specimen, being cosmetically modified in order to assess the impact of the various 'bumps' and 'bulges' on handling qualities and performance. At first glance the aeroplane certainly looked different, the most visible evidence of a changed mission role being provided by the distinctive fairing at the top of the fin, though there were many other less obvious alterations, antennae associated with the EW system having sprouted all over the airframe.

The second EF-111A (66-0041) got airborne for the first time just over two months later, on 17 May 1977, and was far more representative of the 'production' model. Incorporating the tactical jamming system earmarked for installation in full-capability aircraft, this machine was the subject of an exhaustive evaluation programme which lasted until well into 1978 and which entailed operation from Calverton as well as a number of government-owned facilities. Eventually, in March 1979, Grumman was awarded the first of a succession of modification contracts, this covering an initial batch of six aircraft, the first of which made its maiden flight on 26 June 1981, just a few days before the USAF activated the first EF-111A squadron (388th ECS) at Mountain Home.

Delivery of aircraft to the 388th ECS started in November 1981, this squadron ultimately being redesignated as the 390th ECS in December 1982. By then preparations for European deployment had also begun, the existing F-111E base at Upper Heyford in England being selected as the most suitable site for this new model. Activation of the 42nd ECS took place on 1 July 1983, but it was not until February 1984 that the first of an eventual total of 13 EF-111As arrived at Upper Heyford.

In the meantime the Calverton factory continued to produce EF-111As at a fairly modest rate, and the original modifica-

tion project terminated in 1985 with delivery of the 42nd and last example, this quantity including both of the 'prototypes' which were now brought to full-system status and turned over to the USAF as part of the deal. As noted above, the EF-111A is not cheap: the entire production programme cost in the region of $1 billion, but this investment is expected to be more than recouped if the EF-111A is called upon to go to war. In those circumstances, the protection it furnishes to strike elements is likely to more than compensate for its high cost by ensuring the survival of many more aircraft than would otherwise have been the case. Thus, to use modern vernacular, the EF-111A is what is described as a 'force multiplier'.

Jamming equipment

At the heart of the EF-111A lies the ALQ-99E tactical jamming system, itself a complex package of electronic equipment manufactured by various contractors. Essentially an improved version of the EA-6B Prowler's EW suite, the ALQ-99E system possesses the ability to deal with rather more 'threats' rather more rapidly, hostile radar emissions being detected by receivers located in the fin and countered by jamming signals from no fewer than 10 transmitters situated in the 4.88-m (16-ft) long ventral canoe fairing.

Unlike the EA-6B, which has a crew of four, the EF-111A carries only a pilot and

Mountain Home AFB, Idaho is home to the sole US-based Raven unit, namely the 390th ECS (successor to the 388th ECS). Over 25 of the 42 Ravens produced are based here for use in crew training, though they also have full front-line capabilities.

an EWO, extensive use of automation alleviating what might otherwise be an intolerable work-load. In practice, the TJS is able to first locate and then identify threat radars before initiating countermeasures aimed at rendering them inoperative. Indeed, it is possible before the mission to programme the EF-111A's integral computer to counter known threats, so leaving the EWO free to direct his attentions to looking for and dealing with previously unknown radars. Not surprisingly, details of the range of frequencies which can be countered is a closely guarded secret, but it is known that the latest version of the EA-6B can handle six specific bands and it seems reasonable to assume that the EF-111A is just as capable, or more so.

In operational terms the EF-111A is no less versatile, and present planning and training centre on three primary opera-

Visible beneath the forward fuselage of the nearest EF-111A is the prominent 'canoe' radome which covers the 10 jamming transmitters of the ALQ-99E TJS and other associated equipment carried in the large weapons bay. No armament is carried by the Raven.

Canopy
The wide main canopy is split into two sections which are partitioned by the centre brace. The separate sections hinge upwards above each of the crew members

IFR
An inflight-refuelling receptacle for the rigid 'flying boom' of the KC-135 or KC-10 tankers is covered by power-driven doors. The red markings immediately ahead of the receptacle guide the tanker boom operator to a successful connection

Self-defence receivers
Forward-facing bullet-shaped receiver antennas on each side of the wing glove are part of the AN/ALR-62(V)-4 terminal threat warning system and the Sanders AN/ALQ-137(V)-4 ECM self-protection system. These provide low, medium and high-band frequency coverage

Underbelly radome
A 4.9 m (16 ft) 'canoe' fairing covers the original bomb bay area. This is now used to house the Eaton Corporation (AIL Division) An/ALQ-99E tactical jamming system. Ten jamming transmitters, five exciters and six digitally-tuned, multi-channel receivers covering seven frequency bands are housed in the weapons bay.

Slats
The main wing has a four-part segmented slat covering the entire wing span. These are driven by torque shafts and screwjacks

Hot air dump
The large array of electronic jamming equipment in the canoe fairing produces a lot of heat. This hot air can be dumped overboard via the spill duct offset aft of the fairing

mbat Wing

Pylons
Up to four underwing pylons can be fitted (two per wing). The typical stores carried are data link pods and large 2271-litre (600-US gal) auxiliary fuel tanks (the latter for ferry flights only)

Lateral antennas (fuselage
Band 1 and 2 receiver blade ant project outwards from the low fuselage sides

Crew module
The entire cockpit can be jettisoned and fired away from the main airframe by rockets in the event of an emergency. Its descent is checked by an onboard parachute system. Such an action can be initiated by the crew while in the air, on the ground or underwater

Cockpit
The F-111A cockpit has been completely rearranged for the Raven. The two-man crew (pilot and Electronic Warfare Officer) sit side-by-side on zero-zero ejection seats. Flight controls are exclusive to the pilot, the EWO operating the very modern tactical jamming system equipment

Forward radars
Housed in the large nose radome are the AN/APQ-160 attack radar for mapping and navigation, and the AN/APQ-110 terrain following radar for operations at very low level

Pitot head
This projects ahead of the aircraft and samples air for the airspeed and air-data system

UHF/IFF
Blade antennas above and below the fuselage serve the ultra-high frequency communications and the onboard identification friend or foe radio system

Night formation panels
Strips of low-voltage strip-lighting are positioned on the forward fuselage, wing tips, rear fuselage and tail fin. In low-light or night time operations these strips facilitate formation flying by giving a basic outline of the aircraft

Grumman EF-111A Raven
42nd Electronic Combat Squadron
20th Tactical Fighter Wing/66th Electronic Co
United States Air Forces in Europe
RAF Upper Heyford

tional roles, namely stand-off, penetration and close air support. Although all three modes are principally concerned with providing protection for strike forces, they have evolved to meet differing tactical requirements; it says much for the adaptability of the basic F-111 airframe that the Raven is able to perform the three modes with near-equal facility and without the need for large forces of dedicated air-defence fighters to protect the EF-111A itself.

In the stand-off mode, the Raven or Ravens establish an orbit pattern in 'friendly' air space, well to the rear of the forward edge of the battle area and far removed from the threat posed by enemy SAMs. Once on station, the aircraft start to emit jamming signals with the object of saturating the enemy's electronic defences and masking the approach of friendly strike forces. Such stand-off jamming continues for the duration of the attack phase, the EF-111As withdrawing to safety only after the last strike aircraft has departed from the battle area.

In attacks on targets situated deep inside enemy territory, the EF-111A performs in the penetration mode, accompanying a strike package for the duration of the mission. Such sorties require continuous jamming if enemy defensive radars are to be 'knocked out' electronically and, naturally, also call for a high-performance aircraft capable of sustained flight at low-level and possessing good range. Fortunately, the EF-111A can satisfy these requirements.

Teamwork

Finally there is close air support and this, too, is essentially an escort-type mission. However, range and speed are of less importance, the Raven or Ravens working in concert with slow-moving attack aircraft like the Fairchild Republic A-10A Thunderbolt II. Although extremely rugged, the A-10A is by no means invulnerable and would be hard pressed to deal with concentrations of enemy armoured fighting vehicles in areas where the threat posed by enemy surface-to-air weaponry is high.

The EF-111A is, of course, unable to do anything about IR-homing missiles, but many battlefield weapons do require radar illumination if they are to find their target and it is in countering these that the Raven can help. Thus, close air support involves the escort of attack and/or strike aircraft to the battlefield and then the establishment of an orbit from which jamming can be undertaken while the attack/strike force goes about its business, a task which could take some time in areas where the enemy is present in quite significant numbers.

Expected to remain in front-line service until well into the 21st century, the EF-111A will undoubtedly be the subject of considerable improvement as it matures, for the electronics field is today perhaps the single most dynamic growth area in military aviation. Fortunately, development of the original system took note of the probability of the need for updating and the airframe does incorporate considerable 'growth' potential, this perhaps being best epitomized by a 25 per cent reserve in computer data-processing capability. Thus, it would appear that the USAF need have no fear of the Raven becoming outmoded in the immediate future.

With regard to the airframe itself, the fact that the F-111As which were selected for conversion to EF-111A configuration date back to the mid-1960s does, of course, mean that they are no longer in the first flush of youth. However, that is

A 42nd ECS Raven with 'everything down' clearly displays the extended full-span double-spotted flaps. Thirteen examples are assigned to this USAFE unit in support of EW operations over northern Europe.

painting rather too gloomy a picture, for present projections anticipate an operational career of the order of 35 years. Assuming that attrition is kept to minimal levels and that nothing drastic arises in the intervening period, this means that the EF-111A could still be a part of the front-line USAF inventory in the year 2010, not a bad prospect for a type which at one time was being touted as 'McNamara's Folly'.

Glossary
AFB Air Force Base
ECM Electronic CounterMeasures
ECS Electronic Combat Squadron
EW Electronic Warfare
EWO Electronic Warfare Officer
IR Infra-Red
SAM Surface-to-Air Missile
TUS Tactical Jamming System

Moments after touchdown the Raven's landing run is arrested by the large-area, all-moving tailplane being deflected down. A big and heavy beast, the Raven carries some 2722 kg (6,000 lb) of electronic warfare equipment for its vital jamming role.

EF-111A Raven in service

With a production total of just 42 examples (including the two prototypes brought up to operational configuration), front-line deployment of the Raven is, not surprisingly, somewhat limited. Just two front-line squadrons are equipped with the type, the majority serving with the 390th ECS, which is responsible for EF-111A training duties in addition to its front-line commitment. All the aircraft are basically rebuilt F-111As from Fiscal Year 1966 and 1967 allocations, most of which had served with the 366th and 474th TFWs. Deliveries to Mountain Home AFB began in late 1981, while the USAFE squadron received its first example on 3 February 1984. The latter now operates 13 EF-111As. In addition, a single aircraft is assigned to the 4485th TS for ongoing operational development. The unit is based at Eglin AFB but the aircraft is detached to Mountain Home AFB and has been noted wearing both the 'MO' and 'OT' tailcodes. One example (66-0038) is based at Fort Worth for use by General Dynamics, whilst (67-0044) is the last to undergo conversion by the Grumman Corporation.

Camouflage and markings as worn by the Raven force are hardly the most colourful in contemporary use. The two-tone blue grey scheme easily distinguishes the EF-111A from any other F-111 variant, though it is a scheme that is being adopted by Lockheed EC-130Hs operated by the 41st ECS, which will deploy aircraft to Europe for electronic warfare operations in conjunction with 42nd ECS EF-111As. Their operations are believed to come under the command of the 66th ECW at Sembach AB in West Germany (where the EC-130Hs will likely be based), though the 42nd ECS is still officially assigned to the 20th TFW. At least one Raven has been seen sporting wing crests. For both the operational units, tailcodes and serials are presented in grey on the fin, while the squadron and wing markings have been applied in both full colour and toned-down format, the latter consisting of the darker blue grey on the lighter shade which covers the forward portion of the fuselage.

Up to four underwing pylons can be fitted to carry two 2271 litre (600-US gal) fuel tanks (for ferry flights only) and a pair of data link pods. The pylons for the latter can be clearly seen in this underside view.

US Air Force
Tactical Air Command

390th ECS/366th TFW
Base: Mountain Home AFB, Idaho
Tailcode: 'MO'
Example aircraft: 60015, 60020, 60036, 60049, 70033, 70042 and 70048

4485th TS/TAWC
Base: EF-111A detachment at Mountain Home AFB
Tailcode: 'MO' or 'OT'
Example aircraft: 60013

United States Air Forces in Europe

42nd ECS/20th TFW (66th ECW)
Base: RAF Upper Heyford, Oxfordshire
Tailcode: 'UH'
Example aircraft: 60033, 60041, 60055, 60057, 70032, 70041 and 70052

390th ECS

AF 66 051

42nd ECS

AF 66 033

The Raven's radome configuration is identical to that of the Grumman EA-6B Prowler, the US Navy counterpart to the Raven, as both are equipped with the ALQ-99 TJS.

The first EF-111A Raven for the 42nd ECS arrived at RAF Upper Heyford on 3 February 1984, but it took some 18 months for all 12 units assigned to this NATO-dedicated squadron finally to arrive from the Grumman conversion line. All markings are low-visibility grey, with this aircraft carrying the crest of the 66th ECW on the forward fuselage.

Fintip aft radome
At the very rear of the large fintip fairing
is a vertical cover plate that protects the
AN/ALR-23 radar countermeasures
receiver systrem infra-red aft-facing
scanner in the upper portion, and
AN/ALQ-99E antennas in the lower
portion

TTWS receivers
Extending after from the trailing edge of
each horizontal stabilizer is a fairing
housing receiver antennas for the
AN/ALR-62(V)-4 terminal threat warning
system

Iain Wyllie

SPS receivers
A large cylindrical fairing outboard of
each engine nozzle houses receivers for
the Sanders AN/ALQ-137(V)-4 ECM
self-protection system. These receivers
operate in the low, medium, high and
omni frequency receiver bands.

Fuel jettison pipe
Located at the extreme rear of the
fuselage, this pipe allows fuel to be
dumped in flight. Dumping while the
engines are in afterburner produces a
spectacularly fiery effect.

Lateral antennas (tail fin)
In addition to the various antennas in the SIR pod, scabbed on each side of the vertical tail fin are Band 1 (upper) and Band 2 (lower) antennas that provide lateral coverage as part of the AN/ALQ-99E TJS

Spoilers
Each wing has two sections of hinged upper and surface controls which are used as roll-control spoilers in flight and lift dumpers after landing

HF communications
The long-range high-frequency communications radio is served by aerial shunt installations in the prominent spine fairing

Flaps
The trailing-edge of the main wing has a quartet of double-slotted, high-lift flaps extending across the entire span

Root pneumatic seal
Flexibile air-inflated seals on each side of the fuselage close off the compartment into which the wing moves as wing sweep is increased

Air inlet
An air inlet for the heat exchanger to the avionics air-conditioning system is immediately ahead of the horizontal stabilizer root. The air-conditioning system occupies the large box-like fairing to which the horizontal stabilizers are attached

Static dischargers
Static wicks filled with fine metallic powder to conduct electricity continuously allow static electricity to be discharged harmlessly, thus avoiding any dangerous charge build-up

Performance: (penetration role)

Maximum level speed	1226 kts; 2272 km/h	(1,412 mph)
Maximum combat speed	1196 kts; 2216 km/h	(1,377 mph)
Average speed in combat area	507 kts; 940 km/h	(584 mph)
Service ceiling	45,000 ft	(13715 m)
Combat radius	1495 km	(929 miles)
Initial climb rate	3,300 ft	(1006 m) per minute
Take-off run	1349 m	(4,425 ft)
Unrefuelled endurance	4+ hours	

Unrefuelled endurance

- Lockheed EP-3E Orion 12.0 hours E
- Antonov An-12 'Cub-C' 8.0 hours E
- Canberra T.Mk 17 7.0 hours E
- Tupolev Tu-16 'Badger-H' 7.0 hours E
- Douglas EA-3B 5.5 hours E
- Grumman EA-6B Prowler 5.0 hours E
- Ilyushin Il-14 4.5 hours
- Grumman EF-111A Raven 4.0 hours +

Service ceiling

- British Aerospace Canberra T.Mk 17 48,000 ft
- Grumman EF-111A Raven 45,000 ft
- Douglas EA-3B Skywarrior 41,000 ft
- Tupolev Tu-16 'Badger-H' 40,350 ft E
- Grumman EA-6B Prowler 38,000 ft
- Antonov An-12 'Cub-C' 33,500 ft
- Lockheed EP-3E Orion 28,300 ft

Maximum speed at optimum altitude

- Grumman EF-111A Raven 1226 kts
- Grumman EA-6B Prowler 566 kts
- Tupolev Tu-16 'Badger-H' 535 kts E
- Douglas EA-3B Skywarrior 530 kts
- British Aerospace Canberra T.Mk 17 495 kts
- Antonov An-12 'Cub-C' 419 kts
- Lockheed EP-3E Orion 411 kts
- Ilyushin Il-14 232 kts

Cruising speed

- Tupolev Tu-16 'Badger-H' 455 kts E
- Douglas EA-3B Skywarrior 452 kts
- Grumman EF-111A Raven 430 kts
- British Aerospace Canberra T.Mk 17 420 kts E
- Grumman EA-6B Prowler 418 kts
- Antonov An-12 'Cub-C' 362 kts
- Lockheed EP-3E Orion 328 kts
- Ilyushin Il-14 162 kts

Range with maximum payload

- Lockheed EP-3E Orion 4990 km
- Tupolev Tu-16 'Badger-H' 4000 km E
- Grumman EA-6B Prowler 3860 km
- Antonov An-12 'Cub-C' 3600 km
- British Aerospace Canberra T.Mk 17 3540 km
- Douglas EA-3B Skywarrior 3380 km
- Grumman EF-111A Raven 2990 km
- Ilyushin Il-14 450 km

Grumman (General Dynamics) EF-111A Raven cutaway drawing key

1 Pitot head
2 Radome
3 AN/APQ-160 navigation radar antenna (redundant attack mode)
4 Twin AN/APQ-110 terrain-following radar scanners
5 Antenna controller
6 Glideslope aerial
7 Scanner tracking mechanism
8 Radar scanner module
9 Scanner mounting bulkhead
10 Ventral ILS aerial
11 UHF comm/Tacan aerial
12 Hinged nose compartment access doors
13 Avionics equipment racks, radar
14 Forward ALQ-137 low and mid-band antenna
15 Forward avionics bay upper decking
16 Liquid oxygen converter, starboard side
17 ADF aerial
18 Windscreen rain dispersal air ducts
19 Avionics equipment, tactical jamming system (TJS)
20 Flush VOR localizer aerial
21 Cockpit pressurization relief valve
22 Angle of attack transmitter
23 Nosewheel doors
24 Twin nosewheels, forward retracting
25 Steering control jack
26 Electro-luminescent formation lighting strip
27 Nose landing gear wheel bay
28 Pressurized escape capsule joint frame
29 Underfloor impact attenuation air bags (four)
30 Rudder pedals
31 Control column
32 Instrument panel
33 Instrument panel shroud
34 Curved windscreen panels
35 Canopy arch
36 Upward hinged cockpit canopy covers
37 Electronic warfare officer's seat
38 Rear bulkhead console
39 Circuit breaker panels
40 Canopy jack
41 Headrest
42 Adjustable seat mounting
43 Pilot's seat
44 Canopy latch
45 Wing sweep control lever
46 Engine throttle levers
47 Side console panel
48 Provisions and survival equipment stowage
49 Conditioned air ducting
50 Weapons/avionics equipment bay door, open
51 Electrical system equipment

52 Forward fuselage fuel tank, total fuel capacity 18,919 litres (4,998 US gal)
53 Cockpit rear pressure bulkhead
54 Escape capsule recovery parachute container
55 Parachute attachment/release link
56 Emergency oxygen bottles (two)
57 Self righting air bag (two)
58 Air bag pressurization bottle
59 Upper UHF/IFF aerial
60 Escape capsule aft flotation bags, port and starboard
61 Stabilising and brake parachute stowage
62 Escape capsule chine section frame construction
63 Pitch stabilizers, port and starboard
64 Pressure refuelling connection
65 Fuel system control panel
66 Port navigation light
67 Boundary layer splitter plate
68 Port engine air intake
69 Movable intake spike fairing (Triple Plow 1 intake system)
70 Boundary layer duct ram air intake to conditioning system
71 Fuselage chine section integral fuel tank
72 Inflight-refuelling receptacle, open
73 ALQ-137 low/mid/high band receiver and ALR-62 forward radar warning receiver antennas, port and starboard
74 Starboard navigation light
75 UHF/Tacan aerial
76 Wing sweep control screw jacks, port and starboard
77 Anti-collision light
78 Boundary layer spill air louvres
79 Wing pivot box integral fuel tank
80 Fuselage upper longerons
81 Flap and slat drive electro-hydraulic motor
82 Wing pivot box carry-through
83 Electro-luminescent formation lighting strip
84 Starboard wing pivot bearing
85 Wing sweep control horn
86 Wing root rotating glove section, open
87 Starboard external fuel tank
88 Slat drive gearbox
89 Data link pod
90 Swivelling external stores pylons
91 Pylon attachment joints
92 Pylon angle control link

93 Fuel system piping
94 Starboard wing integral fuel tank
95 Slat drive shaft
96 Geared slat guide rails
97 Leading edge slat segments, open
98 Starboard wing fully forward (16-deg sweep) position
99 Wing tip position light
100 Electro-luminescent formation lighting strip
101 Static dischargers
102 Full-span double-slotted Fowler-type flaps, down position
103 Outboard roll control spoiler/lift dumper
104 Spoiler hydraulic actuators
105 Inboard roll control spoiler/lift dumper, de-activated at sweep angles greater than 45 degrees
106 Flap guide rails
107 Flap drive shaft
108 Screw jack
109 Wing root auxiliary flap
110 Auxiliary flap actuator
111 Angled flap drive shaft
112 Starboard engine intake trunking
113 Dorsal cable and systems ducting
114 HF aerial spine fairing
115 Diagonal rib
116 Starboard Pratt & Whitney TF30-P-3 engine
117 Fuselage flank fuel tank
118 Wing root pneumatic seal
119 Rear fuselage dorsal fuel tank
120 Starboard wing fully swept (72.5 degree) position
121 Starboard all-moving tailplane
122 Static dischargers
123 Aft ALR-62 radar warning receiver
124 Fin honeycomb leading edge panel
125 HF aerial shunt
126 Fin integral vent tank
127 Multi-spar tailfin construction
128 ALQ-99 band 2 antenna
129 ALQ-99 band 1 antenna
130 Fin tip System Integrated Receiver (SIR) pod attachment joint
131 SIR pod forward radome
132 Forward ALQ-99 receiving antennas
133 RF divider
134 ALQ-99 receivers
135 ALR-62 antenna switching unit
136 TRU-79 induction transmitters

137 ALR-23 cryogenic converter
138 Lateral ALQ-99 antennas
139 Lateral ALR-62 antennas
140 ALR-23 infra-red scanner
141 Tail position light
142 SIR pod aft radome
143 Aft-facing ALQ-99 antenna
144 Rudder
145 Electro-luminescent formation lighting strip
146 Rudder honeycomb construction
147 Starboard engine exhaust nozzle
148 Fin root attachment joint
149 Rudder hydraulic actuator
150 Tailpipe dividing fairing
151 Fuel jettison
152 Port variable area exhaust nozzle
153 Air mixing duct intakes
154 Translating primary iris afterburner nozzle
155 Chaff dispenser
156 Tailplane root fairing
157 ALQ-137 high band transmitter/receiver port and starboard
158 Port all-moving tailplane
159 ALR-62 radar warning receiver
160 Static dischargers
161 Tailplane honeycomb core construction
162 Port wing fully swept position
163 Tailplane spar construction
164 Pivot fixing
165 Tailplane hydraulic actuator
166 Afterburner ducting
167 Runway emergency arrester hook lowered
168 Ventral tail bumper, down position
169 Avionics cooling refrigerator system heat exchanger
170 Rear fuselage machined frames
171 Centre section integral fuel tank
172 Flight control mixing and feel system units

173 Pratt & Whitney TF30-P-3 afterburning turbofan engine
174 Port lateral fuel tank
175 Electro-luminescent formation lighting strip
176 Ventral fin, port and starboard
177 Engine accessory equipment gearbox
178 Port wing root pneumatic seal

179 Intake compressor face
180 Conical intake centre-body
181 Centre fuselage integral fuel tank
182 Hydraulic reservoir

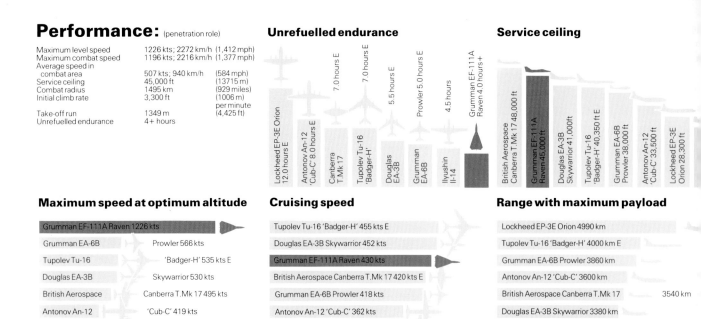

Specification: General Dynamics/Grumman EF-111A Raven

Wings

swept	9.74 m	(31 ft 11.4 in)
spread	19.20 m	(63 ft 0 in)
area, spread	48.77 m²	(525 sq ft)
limits	16° to 72° 30′	

Fuselage and tail unit

accommodation	pilot and EWO in side-by-side seating in a rocket-powered zero/zero McDonnell Douglas escape module	
length	23.16 m	(76 ft 0 in)
height overall	6.10 m	(20 ft 0 in)
tailplane span	8.94 m	(29 ft 4 in)

Landing gear

hydraulically-retractable tricycle landing gear with single wheel main units and twin-wheel nose unit

wheel track	3.06 m	(10 ft 0.4 in)
wheelbase	7.44 m	(24 ft 4.8 in)

Weights

maximum take-off	25072 kg	(55,275 lb)
combat take-off	40346 kg	(88,948 lb)
	31751 kg	(70,000 lb)
internal fuel load	14739 kg	(32,493 lb)

Powerplant

two Pratt & Whitney TF30-P-3 afterburning turbofan engines

thrust, each	8391 kg	(18,500 lb)

EF-111A Raven recognition features

The all-moving stabilators are very highly swept, their leading edge angle aligning with the wing in the fully-swept configuration

Large fin-top fairing, though surprisingly narrow in cross-section

Prominent fin antenna blisters, two each side of fin

The forward fuselage projects ahead of the highly-swept wing glove, and tapers sharply at the rear

Short quarter-cone inlets are set well back along the fuselage sides

The side-by-side cockpit arrangement is enclosed in the smoothly contoured forward fuselage

Relatively short tailfin, but very broad and with swept surfaces

The side-by-side engine configuration necessitates a very broad rear fuselage

Variable-geometry wing is long and thin with all-moving leading and trailing edges

Long nose with slight upturn, characteristic of the F-111 'Aardvark' family

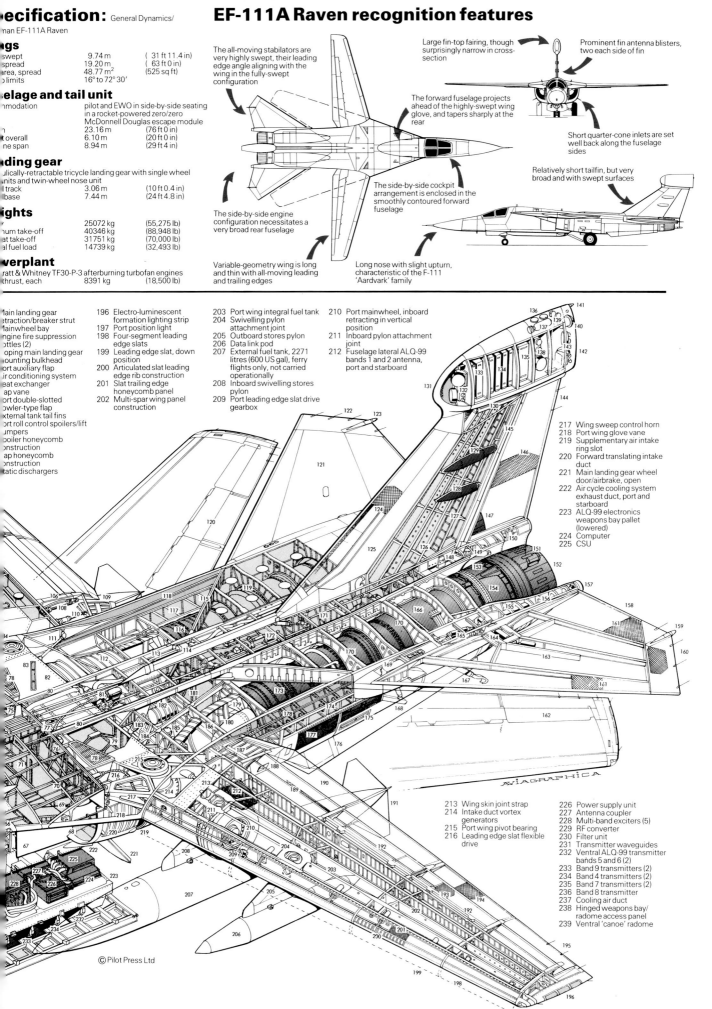

- Main landing gear retraction/breaker strut
- Mainwheel bay
- Engine fire suppression bottles (2)
- Drooping main landing gear mounting bulkhead
- Port auxiliary flap
- Air conditioning system
- Heat exchanger
- Flap vane
- Port double-slotted
- Fowler-type flap
- External tank tail fins
- Port roll control spoilers/lift dumpers
- Spoiler honeycomb construction
- Flap honeycomb construction
- Static dischargers

- 196 Electro-luminescent formation lighting strip
- 197 Port position light
- 198 Four-segment leading edge slats
- 199 Leading edge slat, down position
- 200 Articulated slat leading edge rib construction
- 201 Slat trailing edge honeycomb panel
- 202 Multi-spar wing panel construction

- 203 Port wing integral fuel tank
- 204 Swivelling pylon attachment joint
- 205 Outboard stores pylon
- 206 Data link pod
- 207 External fuel tank, 2271 litres (600 US gal), ferry flights only, not carried operationally
- 208 Inboard swivelling stores pylon
- 209 Port leading edge slat drive gearbox

- 210 Port mainwheel, inboard retracting in vertical position
- 211 Inboard pylon attachment joint
- 212 Fuselage lateral ALQ-99 bands 1 and 2 antenna, port and starboard

- 217 Wing sweep control horn
- 218 Port wing glove vane
- 219 Supplementary air intake ring slot
- 220 Forward translating intake duct
- 221 Main landing gear wheel door/airbrake, open
- 222 Air cycle cooling system exhaust duct, port and starboard
- 223 ALQ-99 electronics weapons bay pallet (lowered)
- 224 Computer
- 225 CSU

- 213 Wing skin joint strap
- 214 Intake duct vortex generators
- 215 Port wing pivot bearing
- 216 Leading edge slat flexible drive

- 226 Power supply unit
- 227 Antenna coupler
- 228 Multi-band exciters (5)
- 229 RF converter
- 230 Filter unit
- 231 Transmitter waveguides
- 232 Ventral ALQ-99 transmitter bands 5 and 6 (2)
- 233 Band 9 transmitters (2)
- 234 Band 4 transmitters (2)
- 235 Band 7 transmitters (2)
- 236 Band 8 transmitter
- 237 Cooling air duct
- 238 Hinged weapons bay/radome access panel
- 239 Ventral 'canoe' radome

AVIAGRAPHICA

© Pilot Press Ltd

The McDONNELL DOUGLAS RF-4 PHANTOM

RF-4 Phantom II: eyes in the skies

An effective fighting force cannot rely simply on massive firepower and luck in finding the enemy. It is essential that comprehensive and accurate information is available if the battle is to be won, and airborne reconnaissance platforms are an excellent source of such information. For several nations in the West, the McDonnell Douglas RF-4 is the tried and trusted vehicle for these reconnaissance tasks.

The USAF's standard tactical reconnaissance platform for close to two decades now, and likely to remain in service for a good few years to come, the McDonnell Douglas RF-4 Phantom also fulfils this important task for the US Marine Corps and for several overseas air arms, although, naturally, the number of aircraft involved is markedly fewer.

As far as quantities are concerned, production of the RF-4C for the USAF eventually terminated with delivery of the 505th example, this number including a brace of YRF-4C prototypes. Manufacture of the RF-4B for the Marines totalled 46, while a further 146 RF-4Es were completed for the export market, these serving with the air arms of West Germany (88 aircraft), Greece (8), Iran (16), Israel (12), Japan (14) and Turkey (8). In addition, four surplus USAF RF-4Cs were transferred to Spain's Ejercito del Aire, while Israel acquired three extensively modified F-4Es, these evolving from the highly sensitive RF-4X proposal and being known as F-4E(S), the 'S' signifying 'Special'.

Although consideration had been given to developing a reconnaissance version of the Phantom as early as the mid-1950s, it was not until the next decade that the decision was taken to move from the conceptual to the hardware stage. Even then, it was the Air Force and not the Navy which was the motivating service, the proposal initially being given the designation RF-110A although this was subsequently changed to RF-4C in the autumn of 1962 when the unified tri-service nomenclature system was introduced.

By then, McDonnell's reconnaissance Phantom was the subject of a firm contract, procurement having begun in May 1962 at about the same time as Specific Operational Requirement No. 196 was issued. This basically called for an all-weather aircraft capable of performing reconnaissance operations in support of air and ground forces, but retaining the secondary ability to deliver nuclear weapons.

That, however, was the limit as far as armament was concerned, the resulting RF-4C (and, indeed, all other reconnaissance Phantoms) lacking the ability to employ conventional forms of weaponry. Needless to say, some change has occurred since then, the German RF-4Es, for instance, now being able to perform a secondary bombing role with payloads of the order of 2272 kg (5,000 lb), options available presumably including both conventional and tactical nuclear weapons. Israeli RF-4Es may also carry armament, in this instance either AIM-9 Sidewinder or Shafrir IR-homing missiles for self-defence.

Initial design

The first two recce Phantoms (62-12200 and 62-12201) were essentially modifications of F-4Bs being built for the Navy, these eventually emerging from the St Louis factory as YRF-4C prototypes, and it was from St Louis that the maiden flight

Having emerged from the highly successful and versatile F-4 Phantom II design, it is not surprising that the RF-4 has proved to be an excellent and potent reconnaissance platform around the world in a service life that has so far spanned more than two decades.

took place on 9 August 1963. At the time, this first YRF-4C was fundamentally an aerodynamic test bed, being intended initially to evaluate the effect that the revised nose contours had on handling and performance qualities.

Later, however, it was fitted with the planned sensor package, with much of the investigation into reconnaissance capability being conducted from Holloman AFB, New Mexico during the course of 1964. Reconnaissance-dedicated equipment naturally included cameras: bays in the RF-4C's much redesigned nose section contain a variety of optical equipment including KS-87 cameras for forward oblique/vertical, side oblique and split vertical coverage. The RF-4C can also employ KA-55 and KA-56 panoramic cameras, coverage with these being restricted to vertical. Other equipment consisted of APQ-99 forward-look-

Though the number of RF-4 variants is somewhat modest, each possesses excellent capabilities through the three camera stations, side-looking airborne radar with 20° scan and an infra-red sensor. Equipment can also be carried on underwing/fuselage pylons.

ing radar, APQ-102 side-looking radar, IR sensors and ECM receivers, enabling it to gather a multiplicity of data on a single sortie.

Production-configured RF-4Cs began to flow from the assembly line fairly quickly although the initial Air Force order was modest, covering just two dozen airframes, the first of which took to the sky on 18 May 1964, almost a month ahead of schedule. Despite such a prompt start, this and other early production specimens lacked much of the specialized mission-related equipment that they would ultimately need to perform their task, the service being in the process of redefining its reconnaissance needs in the light of deficiencies revealed during the Cuban missile crisis and in the early stages of operations in South East Asia.

This inevitably had some impact on aircraft configuration, but despite these failings the RF-4C began to enter service with Tactical Air Command in late September 1964, the Shaw AFB, South Carolina-based 33rd Tactical Reconnaissance Training Squadron being the first unit to operate the type. Subsequently, in early 1965, the 16th Tactical Reconnaissance Squadron became the first fully-operational echelon to acquire the RF-4C and gained its combat-ready status in August 1965.

Deployment of the RF-4C to the combat zone followed rapidly, an initial batch of nine aircraft reaching Tan Son Nhut in South Vietnam at the end of October while 11 more followed in late December. Thereafter, the number assigned to PACAF rose steadily, a total of four squadrons with about 100 aircraft being present by October 1967 and engaged in direct support of combat operations from bases in South Vietnam and Thailand by October 1967. Other RF-4Cs also served with the 15th TRS, 18th TFW at Kadena AB, Okinawa.

TAC resources had also risen significantly by then, RF-4Cs being stationed at Mountain Home AFB, Idaho (67th Tactical Reconnaissance Wing); at Bergstrom AFB, Texas (75th TRW); and at Shaw AFB, South Carolina (363rd TRW). Overseas deployment was by no means confined to the Far East, USAFE's then substantial tactical reconnaissance fleet including a three-squadron wing at RAF

Alconbury (10th TRW) and another squadron with the 26th TRW at Ramstein AB.

Since then, of course, attrition (no fewer than 84 RF-4Cs were destroyed in South East Asia alone as a direct result of the war effort) and the transfer of a quite significant number of aircraft to second-line elements of the Air National Guard has played a part in bringing about a fairly marked reduction in the size of the Air Force's reconnaissance resources.

Today, Bergstrom is the principal centre for TAC operations, the 67th TRW controlling two training squadrons and two combat rated squadrons, while Shaw AFB's 363rd TFW still has one RF-4C squadron assigned. Turning to overseas bases, in the Far East, Kadena's 18th TFW still features the 15th TRS in its line-up, while in Europe the 10th TRW at Alconbury and the 26th TRW at Zweibrücken each have a single RF-4C squadron. However, European-based assets are to decline even further, the Alconbury machines being due to return to the USA in the fairly near future.

Marine Corps service

The only other element of the US armed forces to obtain reconnaissance-dedicated Phantoms was the Marine Corps which, as noted earlier, eventually took delivery of a grand total of 46 RF-4Bs. These were ordered in three separate batches, the initial quantity being limited to just nine although this contract was quickly revised to cover 36 airframes.

Fresh from another sortie to gather intelligence on Warsaw Pact force movements, an RF-4C of the 1st TRS based at RAF Alconbury starts heading for the Photo Interpretation Facility, where the sensors and cameras will be emptied for information analysis.

Eventually, attrition prompted a top-up order for a further 10 examples and about 30 remain in service at the time of writing.

Although the designation would, at first glance, seem to indicate that the RF-4B predated the Air Force model, this was not in fact the case. Work on the Marine version began as late as May 1962, this at first being known as the F4H-1P. Modification appears to have been a fairly simple and straightforward process, and, on the first 36 aircraft at least, this essentially embodied grafting of the sensor nose of the Air Force's RF-4C on to a standard Navy F-4B airframe. Contractual authorization to proceed occurred on 21 February 1963, but despite the apparent simplicity of this programme more than two years were to pass before the first RF-4B (there was no prototype in the truest sense) made a successful maiden flight from St Louis on 12 March 1965. The 10 RF-4Bs ordered later differed in

The largest operator of the RF-4 outside the United States is West Germany, with a total of 88 RF-4Es delivered in the 1970s. The fleet has received several updates over the years, including a comprehensive weapons delivery capability.

Mirrors
Mirrors are fitted to the canopy frames to enhance rear view and give the crew a greater chance of detecting hostile fighters

Rear cockpit
The rear cockpit is occupied by the Weapons Systems Operator (WSO). RF-4C crews tend to use the term 'navigator' in preference to the offici[a]l WSO. His task includes navigation, some communications, reconnaissa[nce] systems operation and managemen[t] and he shares the lookout for hostile aircraft. Although full dual controls a[re] not fitted the navigator can control th[e] throttles from the rear seat to reduce pilot workload on the run-in to the ta[rget]

STARIZE

RESCUE

Keith Fretwell

Radar mapping set
An AN/APQ-102 side-looking radar provides a high-resolution radar picture of the target area. A moving target indicator can isolate any object moving at speeds in excess of 9.25 km/h (5 kts) perpendicular to the flight path. The equipment is being replaced by a more capable, modern radar

Fuel tank
A huge, 2270-litre (600-US gal) fuel tank is often carried on the centreline of USAF RF-4Cs. Alternatively the RF-4C can carry a General Dynamics G-139 reconnaissance pod, containing a HIAC-1 high resolution long-range oblique camera with a focal length of up to 167 cm (66 in)

Flush aerial
A flush-fitting antenna atop the nose serves the ADF (Automatic Direction Finding) equipment

Pitot
A short steel probe gathers pitot static information for the flight instruments and air data system

Radome
The short radome of the RF-4C covers the scanner of the AN/APQ-99, a forward-looking radar optimized for low-altitude, all-weather operation in the J-band. A new radar is scheduled to replace this elderly equipment during the 1990s. The AN/APQ-99 provides mapping, terrain-avoidance and limited collision avoidance functions

Forward camera station
Camera station no. 1 can carry a single KS-87 forward/oblique or vertical camera with a 3-in or 6-in lens. Alternatively a KS-72 camera can be fitted

Low-altitude camera station
Camera station no. 2 has three windows to allow the use of various vertical and port/oblique and starboard/oblique cameras. A tri-camera array of KS-87s with 3-in or 6-in focal length lenses can be carried or, alternatively, a single KS-87 side-looking oblique camera with a 12-in or 18-in focal length lens. Vertical cameras that can be used include pairs of KS-72s or KS-87s or a single KA-56 low altitude panoramic camera. Early RF-4Cs have a film cassette ejection capability for use with the latter camera

High-altitude camera system
Camera station no. 3 can mount a high-altitude panoramic camera (either a KA-91 or KA-55A) or two split vertical KS-87s with lenses of between 6 and 18 in focal length. Alternatively various mapping cameras, including the KC-1A, KC-1B and T-11, can be carried in the LS-58A stabilized mount

Taxi lights
A pair of taxi lamps are fitted in the nosewheel door of USAF RF-4Cs. USMC RF-4Cs have a single light in the same location

TACAN aerial
The lower TACAN aerial is fitted to the side-opening nosewheel door

Nose landing gear unit
The nose landing gear consists of twin wheels with hydraulic steering via the rudder pedals. The steering actuator is combined with a shimmy damper and steering is limited to 70° on each side of the centreline

Infra-red reconnaissance set
The AN/AAS-18 can measure very small heat differentials and use these to produce a visual 'thermal' picture of a target

Underwing drop tank
The RF-4C's poor range makes carriage of 1400-litre (370-US gal) Sargent Fletcher fuel tanks essential for most missions. Chaff/flare dispensers can be 'scabbed' on to the underwing pylons themselves

Variable inlet ramp
A complex system of inlet ramps provides air at optimum subsonic speeds to the engine compressor. rear part of the inlet splitter plate is perforated to allow extraction of sluggish boundary layer air and prev compressor section stalls

that they were based on the RF-4C fuselage and fin, married to F-4J wing assemblies.

Once the RF-4B had entered the flight test stage, progress was rapid and deliveries to the Marines got under way later in 1965, the first example being distributed between Composite Reconnaissance Squadron Two (VMCJ-2) at MCAS Cherry Point, North Carolina and VMCJ-3 at MCAS El Toro, California. Eventually, in 1966, the RF-4B also made its combat debut when it joined VMCJ-1 at Da Nang in South Vietnam, and these three squadrons continued to operate the subtype until 1975, when Marine Corps tactical electronic warfare and tactical reconnaissance assets were rationalized. Henceforth all RF-4Bs were assigned to just one squadron at El Toro, while the ECM-dedicated Grumman EA-6A Intruders foregathered at Cherry Point.

As far as the RF-4B was concerned, control was now entrusted to VMFP-3, and this squadron continues to provide detachments on an as-needed basis to elements of the 1st, 2nd and 3rd Marine Air Wings and for occasional periods of service aboard aircraft-carriers of the Navy.

In the interval which has elapsed since the RF-4B first joined the fleet, updating of sensor systems and airframe has ensured that these aircraft have been able to remain a viable and effective entity. Perhaps the most significant undertaking of this kind was the so-called 'Project SURE' which was implemented in the latter half of the 1970s. This project entailed, in broad terms, a drastic revamping of both the airframe and associated equipment with the object of providing the Marines with an aircraft that could continue to fulfil a useful role until well into the 1980s and one that was to a near common standard. Key elements of 'Project SURE' centred around the fitment of the ASN-92 Carrier Aircraft Inertial Navigation System, ASW-25B data-link equipment, APD-10 side-looking radar, AAD-5 IR reconnaissance set and ALQ-26 defensive ECM gear.

USAF improvements

Updating has by no means been confined to the Marine Corps aircraft, those of the USAF also having been subjected to a

number of improvement and refurbishment programmes in the two decades which have elapsed since they joined TAC. Optical imagery equipment has benefited in this way, but many of the more important changes have been related to electronic systems, these perhaps being epitomized by the TEREC package installed on some aircraft.

More correctly known as ALQ-125, TEREC was conceived specifically to aid in determining the precise nature of an enemy's electronic order of battle, the system having the capability for automatic detection, classification and location of hostile ground-based emitters such as the highly mobile radars used to control SAMs and/or AAA. Capable of relaying such information on a real-time basis, TEREC can readily recognize a total of 10 types of enemy radar and may be pre-programmed to search for those deemed to represent the highest degree of 'threat'.

Once a radar has been spotlighted, tracking continues for just long enough to permit its precise location to be determined, an inbuilt data link being used to relay relevant information to ground-based intelligence facilities. These can then call upon the services of tactical aircraft to deal with the threats thus revealed.

Attention has also been paid to updating the integral radar, a new forward-looking system being under development by Texas Instruments at the present time. Assuming that this is eventually de-

*Though wearing **USAF** markings, this is in fact an **RF-4E** ordered by the Imperial Iranian Air Force. Clearly visible are the classic lines of the Phantom II, though the RF-4 family is easily distinguished by the deepened nose and camera/sensor ports.*

ployed operationally, it should significantly upgrade RF-4C capability with regard to the acquisition of vital tactical intelligence by both day and night or in bad weather conditions, the need to operate effectively under cover of darkness often being a paramount concern in ensuring survivability.

Glossary

AAA Anti-Aircraft Artillery
AB Air Base
AFB Air Force Base
ECM Electronic CounterMeasures
IR Infra-Red
MCAS Marine Corps Air Station
PACAF PACific Air Forces
SAM Surface-to-Air Missile
SURE Sensor Update and Refurbishment Effort
TAC Tactical Air Command
TEREC Tactical Electronic REConnaissance
TFW Tactical Fighter Wing
TRS Tactical Reconnaissance Squadron
TRW Tactical Reconnaissance Wing
USAFE United States Air Forces in Europe

Under the 'Peace Jack' conversion programme, three Israeli F-4Es were extensively modified for reconnaissance tasks. The revised nose houses an ultra-long focal length, high-resolution camera known as the HIAC-1 specifically for high altitude operations.

RF-4 Phantom II in service

United States Air Force
Tactical Air Command

Responsible for a large and diverse aircraft inventory commensurate with its broad operational responsibilities, both national and international, TAC originally planned for 14 tactical reconnaissance squadrons. The first operational squadron to receive the RF-4C was the 16th TRS at Shaw AFB in the mid-1960s, this following initial service acceptance work with the 33rd TRTS at Shaw AFB. Today's RF-4C units are predominantly based at Bergstrom AFB where the 67th TRW is tasked with RF-4C training duties as well as having a fully operational role. Though the fighter variants of the F-4 have been giving way to newer types such as the A-10, F-15 and F-16 for several years, the RF-4C remains a stalwart of front-line operations with no immediate replacement apparent. In fact, aircraft are currently being reassigned from USAFE's 1st TRS to TAC's 67th TRW.

12th TRS/67th TRW
Base: Bergstrom AFB, Texas
Tailcode letters: 'BA'
Tailband main colour: orange
Example aircraft: 37747, 60435, 70456, 90352

91st TRS/67th TRW
Base: Bergstrom AFB, Texas
Tailcode letters: 'BA'
Tailband main colour: red
Example aircraft: 20150, 20156, 60419, 80553

45th TRTS/67th TRW
Base: Bergstrom AFB, Texas
Tailcode letters: 'BA'
Tailband main colour: blue
Example aircraft: 37750, 60456, 70428, 90356

16th TRS/363rd TFW
Base: Shaw AFB, South Carolina
Tailcode letters: 'SW'
Example aircraft: 41009, 70464, 70465, 70467

62nd TRTS/67th TRW
Base: Bergstrom AFB, Texas
Tailcode letters: 'BA'
Tailband main colour: gold
Example aircraft: 41026, 60393, 70444, 70462

4485th TS/Tactical Air Warfare Center
Base: Eglin AFB, Florida
Tailcode letters: 'OT'
Example aircraft: 80585, 90362

This 91st TRS/67th TRW RF-4C illustrates an interim low-visibility colour scheme with the topside camouflage colours extending to the lower surfaces wraparound style, while the tailcode lettering and serial are presented in black. Note the lowered arrester hook, a legacy of the F-4 Phantom II's naval heritage.

The 'European One' camouflage of charcoal grey and two-tone green has certainly lowered the visibility of USAF RF-4Cs, but the effect is somewhat compromised on this 16th TRS/363rd TRW aircraft by the bright squadron and TAC markings.

United States Air Forces in Europe

A surprisingly small RF-4C force is assigned to USAFE, and this is gradually being reduced further with the reassignment of 1st TRS aircraft to reconnaissance units in the United States. The process of disbandment for this squadron is due to be completed during 1987. Both squadrons are assigned to NATO's 4th Allied Tactical Air Force, though they are under the operational control of the 3rd and 17th Air Forces within USAFE respectively. Both units have adopted the 'European One' camouflage with low-visibility lettering and numbering.

1st TRS/10th TRW
Base: RAF Alconbury, England
Tailcode letters: 'AR'
Example aircraft: 10259, 80561, 80563, 90363

38th TRS/26th TRW
Base: Zweibrücken AB, West Germany
Tailcode letters: 'ZR'
Example aircraft: 10249, 10254, 20153, 90366

Pacific Air Forces

Providing offensive and defensive air power for Pacific Command operations, Pacific Air Command has a single squadron of RF-4Cs operating within its largest air element, the 18th TFW. A detachment is based at Osan AB in South Korea and depot-level maintenance is now assigned to Korean Air Lines at Kimhae. Aircraft of the 15th TRS have gradually adopted the 'European One' two-tone green and dark grey 'wraparound' camouflage in favour of the old two-tone green and tan scheme, but this will gradually give way to the two-tone grey 'Egyptian One' colours.

15th TRS/18th TFW
Base: Kadena AB, Okinawa
Tailcode letters: 'ZZ'
Example aircraft: 10248, 20155, 80549, 80551

Air Force Systems Command

Within AFSC two distinct areas of flight testing occupy a small number of RF-4Cs. Test and evaluation of aircraft following development by manufacturers is often followed by continued development programmes at Edwards AFB. At Eglin AFB, flight testing of new weapons, their associated systems and operational effectiveness when combined with specific aircraft platforms is the responsibility of the Armament Division. Operations at Eglin AFB are conducted in close liaison with Tactical Air Command's 4485th TS/Tactical Air Warfare Center.

6512nd TS/Air Force Flight Test Center
Base: Edwards AFB, California
Tailcode letters: 'ED'
Example aircraft: 37744, 50941, 60384

Air National Guard

Operating the RF-4C since 1971 when the 106th TRS received its first examples, the Air National Guard now conducts approximately half of all USAF tactical reconnaissance tasks. In peacetime the individual squadrons come under the command of their respective state governors, but all would be incorporated into Tactical Air Command operations in the event of mobilization. If a squadron is based at the same location as its parent wing it will report directly, but units operating from other locations report to a co-located Group Headquarters. Not all of the squadrons apply tailcode letters, and there are still a fair few aircraft in the old two-tone green and tan camouflage, though most have adopted the 'European One' colours. This latter scheme is now giving way to a two-tone grey scheme known as 'Egyptian One'.

106th TRS/117th TRW, Alabama ANG
Base: Birmingham Municipal Airport, Alabama
Tailcode letters: 'BH'
Example aircraft: 37745, 41038, 41057, 50893

153rd TRS/186th TRG, Mississippi ANG
Base: Key Field, Mississippi
Tailcode letters: 'KE'
Example aircraft: 50931, 60418, 60425, 60428

165th TRS/123rd TRW, Kentucky ANG
Base: Standiford Field, Kentucky
Tailcode letters: 'KY'
Example aircraft: 41031, 41069, 50835, 50944

173rd TRS/155th TRG, Nebraska ANG
Base: Lincoln Municipal Airport, Nebraska
Example aircraft: 40162, 40998, 50838, 50917

189th TRTF/124th TRG, Idaho ANG
Base: Boise Air Terminal, Idaho
Example aircraft: none; aircraft drawn from the 190th TRS/124th TRG pool as and when needed for crew training duties

190th TRS/124th TRG, Idaho ANG
Base: Boise Air Terminal, Idaho
Example aircraft: 50923, 80594, 80599, 80609

192nd TRS/152nd TRG, Nevada ANG
Base: Reno International Airport, Nevada
Example aircraft: 41005, 41030, 50876, 50897

Air Training Command

Of the four Technical Training Centers within Air Training Command, two are tasked with maintenance training duties. Full use is made of a wide range of surplus airframes, their operational designations being prefixed by the letter 'G' to indicate their ground instruction tasks.

Chanute Technical Training Center
Base: Chanute AFB, Illinois
Example aircraft: 62-12201

Sheppard Technical Training Center
Base: Sheppard AFB, Texas
Example aircraft: 37751, 37763, 41000

Though allocated the tailcode letters 'KE', the 153rd TRS/186th TRG has dispensed with them as they proved all but invisible when applied to the 'European One' camouflage pattern on the tail surfaces.

Air Force Logistics Command

Operational support for USAF RF-4C operations in the form of overhaul and modification is the responsibility of the Ogden Air Logistics Center, which acts as the material manager for the type. A small test and trials fleet of various F-4 variants includes RF-4Cs, the aircraft being finished in a striking overall white with red trim scheme.

Ogden ALC
Base: Hill AFB, Utah
Example aircraft: 50905

An RF-4C of the 192nd TRS/152nd TRG, Nevada ANG, nicknamed the 'High Rollers'.

McDonnell Douglas RF-4C Phantom
1st Tactical Reconnaissance Squadron
10th Tactical Reconnaissance Wing
United States Air Force
RAF Alconbury, UK

Powerplant
The RF-4C is powered by a pair of
General Electric J79-GE-15 augmented
turbojets, each rated at 7711 kg
(17,000 lb) thrust with afterburning

Fin cap
The dielectric fin cap covers a
communications radio antenna and
serves as a mount for the white tail
navigation light

Rudder
The rudder is actuated by irreversible
dual power cylinders. A 'T'-shaped
vent/dump pipe for the fuselage fuel
tanks is located at the base of the rudder

Reconnaissance flare ejectors
This RF-4C is fitted with paired
photoflash ejectors containing 26 M112
260 million candlepower photoflash
cartridges, or 10 M123 cartridges. Later
aircraft have a single LA-429A ejector
with 20 M185 one billion candlepower
cartridges. The increasing capability of
infra-red sensors has made the use of
photoflashes something of a
disappearing art

Outer wing panel
The outer wing is angled sharply
upwards and can be folded on the
ground for storage. The leading edge
slats incorporate high-pressure engine
bleed-air blowing

Wingtip
The wingtip carries a low-voltage,
variable intensity 'glow-panel'
formation-keeping light, navigation
lights and RHAWS antennas

Aileron
All Phantom variants employ powered
ailerons. These are fitted inboard of the
wing-fold and are augmented by spoilers

Stabilator
The RF-4C is fitted with all-moving,
hydraulically actuated tailerons (US
terminology dubs them 'stabilators').
They are reverse cambered and are of
mixed steel and titanium construction
for strength and heat/noise fatigue
resistance. 23° of anhedral counteracts
the sharp dihedral on the outer wing
panels

Afterburner nozzle
The afterburner nozzle leaves are
hydraulically operated, and are
appreciably shorter than those fitted to
J79-GE-17 engined Phantom variants

Integral fuel tanks
The wing contains two integral fuel
tanks with a combined capacity of 2384
litres (630 US gal). JP-4 (NATO F-40) is
the grade of fuel usually used

Refuelling receptacle
USAF RF-4Cs are fitted with a refuelling receptacle for compatibility with the 'flying booms' of the KC-10. The Phantom's high fuel consumption makes range a problem, so inflight-refuelling is routinely practised, and an RF-4C wing is forward based at Zweibrücken, West Germany. Marines RF-4Cs can be fitted with a refuelling probe for use with the 'probe and drogue'-equipped KC-130 Hercules tankers

Fuel tanks
Six interconnected, self-sealing fuel tanks are located in the fuselage, and have a combined capacity of 4319 litres (1,141 US gal)

Aerial
This small blade antenna serves the TACAN

Pitot
A small dynamic pressure pitot on the fin leading edge serves the Q-feel system, giving the flight controls artificial 'feel' proportional to airspeed

Beacon
A high-intensity red anti-collision light is located in the fin leading edge

Inboard pylon
Defensive armament is not routinely carried by the RF-4C, although a Minnesota ANG aircraft did conduct trials during 1963 carrying a pair of AIM-9L Sidewinders on each inboard pylon. Some export RF-Cs do carry defensive AAMs

ECM jammer pod
Several different types of ECM pod can be carried by the RF-4C, including the AN/ALQ-131 shown here

Main landing gear
The main landing gear is electrically controlled and is actuated by the utility hydraulic system. It incorporates multiple disc brakes

United States Marine Corps

The sole RF-4B-equipped unit is Marine Tactical Reconnaissance Squadron Three (VMFP-3) which was activated at MCAS El Toro on 1 July 1975. Aircraft were reassigned from Marine Composite Reconnaissance Squadrons One, Two and Three (VMCJ-1, -2 and -3). Often referred to as 'The Specters', but also known as 'The Eyes of the Corps', VMFP-3 has a maximum strength of some 25 to 30 aircraft from the original 46 produced (BuNos. 151975 to 151983; 153089 to 153115; 157342 to 157351) which makes it the largest Marine Corps tactical aircraft squadron. All aircraft wear low-visibility grey-on-grey colour schemes though there are several variations within the fleet. The 'RF' (Romeo Fox) tail code has been retained, but the original fox's head and Phantom II (Specter) motifs have given way to a simple lightning bolt.

Fleet Marine Force Pacific VMFP-3/Marine Air Wing 11

Base: MCAS El Toro, California
Tailcode letters: 'RF'
Example aircraft: 151977/'02', 151983/'07', 153095/'14', 153103/'20'

The RF-4Bs of VMFP-3 have worn a variety of squadron insignia and colour schemes over years, the current tail marking being a dark grey lightning bolt.

Hellenic Air Force (Helliniki Aeroporía)

A total of eight new-build RF-4Es were supplied to the Hellenic Air Force in the late 1970s, the aircraft bearing the serials 70357 and 70358, plus 71761 to 71766. All aircraft wear the standard NATO Southern Flank two-tone green and tan camouflage with the serial carried in small black form at the base of the tail fin.

348 Mira/110 Ptérix

Base: Larissa
Example aircraft: 70358, 71763, 71765, 71766

Though currently finished in tan and two-tone green, the eight RF-4Es of the Hellenic Air Force may adopt the low-visibility grey of their F-4E counterparts.

Islamic Republic of Iran Air Force

Along with sizeable deliveries of F-4D/E fighters, the Imperial Iranian Air Force received 16 examples of the RF-4E (72-266 to -269, 74-1725 to -1736), the first of which was delivered in December 1971. A further 16 examples (78-751 to -754, 78-788 and 78-854 to -864) were ordered and in the process of construction, but the overthrow of the Shah's regime precluded their completion and delivery. One squadron was equipped with the type but its exact current status is unknown as the ravages of the long conflict with Iraq and military embargoes have all but decimated the IRIAF inventory. It is fair to assume that any surviving aircraft wear the standard tan, brown and dark green camouflage with light grey undersurfaces.

Israel Defence Force/Air Force (Tsvah Haganah le Israel-Heyl ha'Avir)

A dozen RF-4Es are known to have been delivered to the IDF/AF, their production serials being 69-7590 to -7595 and 75-418 to -423. The first example was delivered in February 1971, and it is possible that a further six examples have been acquired (75-656 to -661) though this is unconfirmed. In Israeli service the aircraft wear a three-digit serial on the tail fin, confirmed examples being 198, 216 and 234. In addition to the RF-4Es, a trio of F-4E(S) aircraft are operated, their original F-4E identities being 69-7567, -7570 and -7576.

Japan Air Self-Defence Force (Nihon Koku Jietai)

A total of 14 RF-4EJS were delivered to the JASDF from November 1974 to June 1975 to equip a single reconnaissance squadron. The aircraft are serialled 47-6901 to -6905 and 57-6906 to -6914, the full serial being carried on the tailfin and the last three digits repeated on the forward fuselage. The RF-4EJs have had several colour schemes applied over the years, originating with the light aircraft grey upper surfaces and white undersides which in turn gave way to a two-tone green and tan camouflage. The colour shading on this scheme proved to be somewhat bright so a darker, more subdued scheme was adopted. Both these schemes had light grey undersurfaces.

501 Hikotai

Base: Hyakuri AB
Example aircraft: 47-6903, 47-6905, 57-6908, 57-6914

Spanish Air Force (Ejército del Aire Español)

The sole export customer for the RF-4C with four ex-USAF examples (65-936, 937, 938 and 943) supplied for use by Esc 121 and 122 within Ala de Caza 12. The quartet bear the local designation CR.12 (CR = Caza de Reconocimiento or Fighter Reconnaissance), and all are camouflaged in two-tone green and tan upper surfaces with light grey undersides.

Combat Air Command (Mando Aéreo de Combate)

Ala de Caza 12 (12th Fighter Wing)

Base: Torrejon AB
Example aircraft: CR.12-41 to CR.12-44

Within the 501 Hikotai various camouflage schemes have been evaluated. This is one of a least two low-visibility grey schemes applied during 1986.

Turkish Air Force (Turk Hava Kuvvetleri)

Eight RF-4Es are confirmed as having been delivered to the Turkish air force (77-0309 to -0316) and there are persistent rumours that more have found their way to this southern European nation, though this remains unconfirmed. The aircraft wear a two-tone green and tan camouflage with light grey undersides. A five-digit serial is carried in black on the tail fin, the last three being repeated in a larger, white-outlined format on the engine intake nacelles and prefixed by the number '1' to identify them as residents of the 1st Jet Air Base.

1st Tactical Air Force Command
(Birinci Taktik Hava Kuvveti Komutanligi)

Base: Eskisehir
Example aircraft: 70309/'1-309' to 70316/'1-316'

1st Jet Air Base
(Birinci Ana Hava)
113 Filo

Federal German Air Force
(Luftwaffe der Bundesrepublik Deutschlands)

The first and largest recipient of export RF-4s (88 RF-4Es delivered under Operation 'Peace Rhine'), initial aircraft were assigned to AKG 51 from 20 January 1971 to replace the Lockheed RF-104G Starfighter. Deliveries to AKG 52 commenced on 17 September 1971 and these remain the only front-line RF-4E units. US production serials were 69-7448 to -7535, but the aircraft were allocated the Luftwaffe codes 35+01 to 35+88. For many years the fleet wore the standard grey/green 'splinter' camouflage, but this has now given way to a soft-line blend of two-tone green and dark grey known as 'Zitronenfalter' ('Brimstone and Butterfly'). Several RF-4Es are also assigned to EST 61 for a variety of test and training programmes.

Aufklärungs-geschwader 51
(AKG 51)
Base: Bremgarten
Example aircraft: 35+06, 35+19, 35+35, 35+68

Aufklärungs-geschwader 52
(AKG 52)
Base: Leck
Example aircraft: 35+13, 35+32, 35+60, 35+87

Erprobungs-stelle 61 (EST 61)
Base: Manching
Example aircraft: 35+01, 35+83

Both AKG 51 and AKG 52 have all but repl the 'splinter' camouflage with this wraparound scheme of greens and black

McDonnell Douglas RF 4C Phantom II cutaway drawing key

1 Pitot head
2 Radome
3 Radar scanner dish
4 Radar dish tracking mechanism
5 Texas Instruments AN/APQ-99 forward-looking radar unit
6 Nose compartment construction
7 No. 1 camera station
8 KS-87 forward oblique camera

McDonnell Douglas RF-4 Phantom II

1 Forward radar warning antennas, port and starboard
2 Camera bay access hatches
3 Vertical camera aperture KA-57 low-altitude panoramic camera
4 Lateral camera aperture alternative KS-87 installation)
5 No. 2 camera station
6 ADF sense aerial
7 Windscreen rain dispersal air duct
8 Camera viewfinder periscope
9 Nose landing gear emergency air bottles
10 Recording unit
11 No. 3 camera station
12 A-91 high-altitude panoramic camera
13 Air conditioning ram air intake
14 Landing/taxiing lamp (2)
15 Lower UHF/VHF aerial
16 Nosewheel leg door
17 Torque scissor links
18 Twin nosewheels, aft retracting
19 Nosewheel steering mechanism
20 AN/AVQ-26 'Pave Tack' laser designator pod swivelling optical package fuselage centreline pylon adaptor
21 Side-looking radar antenna (SLAR)
22 Electro-luminescent formation lighting strip
23 Canopy emergency release handle
24 Air conditioning plant, port and starboard
25 Cockpit floor level
37 Front pressure bulkhead
38 Rudder pedals
39 Control column
40 Instrument panel
41 Radar display
42 Instrument panel shroud
43 LA-313A optical viewfinder
44 Windscreen panels
45 Forward cockpit canopy cover
46 Face blind seat firing handle
47 Pilot's Martin-Baker Mk H7 ejection seat
48 External canopy latches
49 Engine throttle levers
50 Side console panel
51 Intake boundary layer splitter plate
52 APQ-102R/T SLAR equipment
53 AAS-18A infra-red reconnaissance package
54 Intake front ramp
55 Port engine air intake
56 Intake ramp bleed air holes
57 Rear canopy external latches
58 Rear instrument console
59 Canopy centre arch
60 Starboard engine air intake
61 Starboard external fuel tank, capacity 1400 litres (308 Imp gal)
62 Rear view mirrors
63 Rear cockpit canopy cover
64 Navigator/sensor operator's Martin-Baker ejection seat
65 Intake ramp bleed air spill louvres
66 Avionics equipment racks
67 Rear pressure bulkhead
68 Liquid oxygen converter
69 Variable intake ramp jack
70 Intake rear ramp door
71 Fuselage centreline external fuel tank, capacity 2273 litres (500 Imp gal)
72 Position of pressure refuelling connection on starboard side
73 ASQ-90B data annotation system equipment
74 Cockpit voice recorder
75 Pneumatic system air bottle
76 Bleed air ducting
77 Fuselage no. 1 fuel cell, capacity 814 litres (179 Imp gal)
78 Intake duct framing
79 Boundary layer spill duct
80 Control cable runs
81 Aft avionics equipment bay
82 IFF aerial
83 Upper fuselage light
84 Fuselage no. 2 fuel cell, capacity 700 litres (154 Imp gal)
85 Centre fuselage frame construction
86 Electro luminescent formation lighting strip
87 Engine intake centrebody fairing
88 Intake duct rotary spill valve
89 Wing spar attachment fuselage main frames
90 Control cable ducting
91 Inflight-refuelling receptacle, open
92 Starboard main landing rear leg pivot fixing
93 Starboard wing integral fuel tank, capacity 1191 litres (262 Imp gal)
94 Wing pylon mounting
95 Boundary layer control air duct
96 Leading edge flap hydraulic actuator
97 Inboard leading-edge flap segment, down position
98 Leading-edge dog-tooth
99 Outboard wing panel attachment joint
100 Boundary layer control air ducting
101 Hydraulic flap actuator
102 Outboard leading edge flap
103 Starboard navigation light
104 Electro-luminescent formation light
105 Rearward identification light
106 Starboard dihedral outboard wing panel
107 Wing fuel tank vent pipe
108 Starboard drooping aileron, down position
109 Aileron flutter damper
110 Starboard spoilers, open
111 Spoiler hydraulic actuators
112 Fuel jettison and vent valves
113 Aileron hydraulic actuator
114 Starboard ventral airbrake panel
115 Starboard blown flap, down position
116 TACAN aerial
117 Fuel system piping
118 No. 3 fuselage fuel cell, capacity 565 litres (122 Imp gal)
119 Engine intake compressor face
120 General Electric J79-GE-15 afterburning turbojet engine
121 Ventral engine accessory equipment gearbox
122 Wing rear spar attachment joint
123 Engine and afterburner control equipment
124 Emergency ram air turbine
125 Ram air turbine housing
126 Turbine doors, open
127 Turbine actuating link
128 Port engine bay frame construction
129 No. 4 fuselage fuel cell, capacity 759 litres (167 Imp gal)
130 Jet pipe heat shroud
131 No. 5 fuselage fuel cell, capacity 681 litres (150 Imp gal)
132 Fuel feed and vent system piping
133 Loran aerial
134 Dorsal access panels
135 Fuel pumps
136 No. 6 fuselage fuel cell, capacity 805 litres (177 Imp gal)
137 Photographic flare dispenser, port and starboard
138 Flare compartment doors, open
139 Ram air intake, tailcone venting
140 Tailcone attachment bulkhead
141 Three-spar fin torsion box construction
142 Fin rib construction
143 Electro-luminescent formation lighting strip
144 HF aerial panel
145 Anti-collision light
146 Stabilator feel system pressure head
147 Fin leading edge
148 Fin tip aerial fairing
149 Upper UHF/VHF aerial
150 Tail navigation light
151 Rudder horn balance
152 Rudder
153 Honeycomb trailing edge panels
154 Fuselage fuel cell jettison pipe
155 Rear radar warning antennae
156 Tailcone/brake parachute hinged door
157 Brake parachute housing
158 Honeycomb trailing edge panel
159 Port all-moving tailplane/stabilator
160 Stabilator mass balance weight
161 Stabilator multi-spar construction
162 Pivot sealing plate
163 All-moving tailplane hinge mounting
164 Rudder hydraulic actuator
165 Tailplane hydraulic actuator
166 Heat-resistant tailcone skinning
167 Arrester hook, lowered
168 Arrester hook stowage
169 Stabilator feel system balance mechanism
170 Artificial feel system pneumatic bellows
171 Arrester hook jack and shock absorber
172 Variable-area afterburner exhaust nozzle
173 Engine bay cooling exit louvres
174 Afterburner duct
175 Exhaust nozzle actuators
176 Hinged engine cowling panels
177 Port blown flap, down position
178 Boundary layer control air blowing slot
179 Lateral autopilot servo
180 Airbrake jack
181 Flap hydraulic jack
182 Rear spar
183 Port spoiler hydraulic jack
184 Aileron hydraulic actuator
185 Aileron flutter damper
186 Port spoiler housing
187 Aileron rib construction
188 Port drooping aileron, down position
189 Wing fuel tank jettison pipe
190 Honeycomb trailing edge panels
191 Port dihedral outer wing panel
192 Fixed portion of trailing edge
193 Rearward identification light
194 Electro-luminescent formation lighting strip
195 Port navigation light
196 Outboard leading edge flap, lowered
197 Boundary layer control air blowing slot
198 Leading edge flap actuator
199 Outer wing panel multi-spar construction
200 Outer wing panel attachment joint
201 Leading edge dog-tooth
202 Port mainwheel
203 Mainwheel multi-plate disc brake
204 Mainwheel leg door
205 Outboard wing pylon
206 Inner wing panel ouboard leading edge flap, down position
207 Leading edge flap rib construction
208 Wing pylon mounting
209 Main landing gear leg pivot fixing
210 Hydraulic retraction jack
211 Landing gear uplock
212 Port ventral airbrake panel, open
213 Main landing gear wheel bay
214 Hydraulic reservoir
215 Hydraulic system accumulator
216 Port wing integral fuel tank, capacity 1191 litres (262 Imp gal)
217 Two-spar torsion box fuel tank construction
218 Wing skin support posts
219 Leading edge boundary layer control air duct
220 Bleed air blowing slot
221 Outboard flap actuator
222 Inboard leading edge flap, lowered
223 Hydraulic flap actuator
224 Inboard wing pylon
225 AN/ALQ-101 ECM pod
226 Port external fuel tank, capacity 1400 litres (308 Imp gal)

Pilot Press Ltd

RF-4 Phantom variants

RF-110A/YRF-4C: prototype reconnaissance version for US Air Force following various unflown studies and converted from stock F-4B airframe; missile bays removed, new recce nose; this airframe later became prototype F-4E and FBW testbed; first flew 9 August 1963

RF-4C: production reconnaissance version for US Air Force, first six aircraft converted from F-4B; production aircraft had wide tyres, bulged wings and no armament apart from capability to carry nuclear weapon on centreline; some aircraft fitted with LABS; film cassette ejection system in early aircraft, distinguished by square cut nose contours, and APQ-99 radar in nose; 505 built, 23 fitted with ALQ-125 Tactical Electronic Reconnaissance System (TEREC), others with LORAN; various optical, infra-red and radar sensors in nose and forward fuselage which can include APQ-102 side-looking radar, AVD-2 laser reconnaissance set, and AAS-18 infra-red reconnaissance set; internal fuel consumption increased throughout production run; first deliveries September 1964

F4H-1P/RF-4B: reconnaissance version for US Marine Corps, basically standard F-4B with RF-4C nose; prototype first flew 12 March 1965; 46 built, last 10 were hybrids with F-4J wings, RF-4C fuselages and fins; all eventually equipped with carrier alignment INS, data link and SLAR

RF-4E: reconnaissance version of F-4E with 8119 kg (17,900 lb st) General Electric J79-GE-17 engines and updated and improved sensor package; Luftwaffe aircraft can carry external SLAR pod; one Luftwaffe RF-4E modified by E-Systems as a tactical Elint platform; Israeli aircraft carry AIM-9 Sidewinder and indigenous AAMs

RF-4E (Bomber): during 1982 the 82 surviving Luftwaffe RF-4Es (of 88 delivered) were modified by MBB to incorporate a weapons delivery system, advanced ECM systems and an infra-red linescan unit; they retain full reconnaissance capability

RF-4EJ: reconnaissance version of Japanese licence-built F-4EJ, essentially similar to RF-4E

RF-4X: several different advanced reconnaissance configurations, variously designated RF-4X, F-4X, F-4E(S), and collectively codenamed 'Peace Jack'; proposed use of water injection and new inlets providing increased thrust to counteract drag of podded HIAC 1 Long-Range Oblique Photographic camera; three F-4E(S) with nose-mounted HIAC-1 and without engine modifications delivered to Israel during late 1975

F-4M/Phantom FGR.Mk 2: some RAF Phantoms, serving with Nos 2, 31 and 41 Squadrons were equipped to carry an EMI reconnaissance pod containing a Q-band high resolution SLAR, infra-red linescan and a variety of cameras

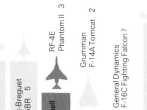

Developed by General Dynamics, the HIAC-1 high-altitude, high-resolution camera unit is a remarkable piece of equipment designed for dedicated LOROP (LOng Range Oilque Photography) tasks, though its operational application has been limited to USAF project 'Peace Eagle' flights in an underfuselage pod and in a trio of Israeli F-4E(S) aircraft. The latter carry the HIAC-1 in a new, enlarged nose and provide an excellent addition to the RF-4Es already in Israeli service.

Specification: RF-4E Phantom II

Wings
Span	11.71 m	(38 ft 5 in)
Area	49.24 m²	(530 sq ft)

Fuselage and tail unit
Accommodation	two, pilot and navigator in tandem	
Length overall	19.20 m	(63 ft 0 in)
Height overall	5.03 m	(16 ft 6 in)
Tailplane span	5.47 m	(17 ft 11.5 in)

Landing gear
Hydraulically retractable tricycle landing gear
Wheelbase	7.54 m	(24 ft 9 in)
Wheel track	5.45 m	(17 ft 10.5 in)

Weights
Empty	14111 kg	(31,110 lb)
Maximum take-off	23966 kg	(52,836 lb)
Maximum external load		
Internal fuel load	6704 litres	(1,771 US gal)

Powerplant
Two General Electric J79-GE-17 turbojets
Thrust rating, each	8119 kg	(17,900 lb)

RF-4C Phantom II recognition features

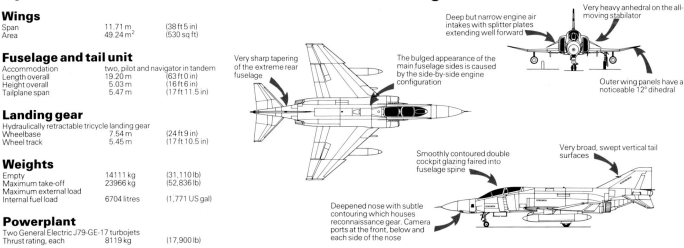

Very heavy anhedral on the all-moving stabilator

Deep but narrow engine air intakes with splitter plates extending well forward

Outer wing panels have a noticeable 12° dihedral

Very sharp tapering of the extreme rear fuselage

The bulged appearance of the main fuselage sides is caused by the side-by-side engine configuration

Smoothly contoured double cockpit glazing faired into fuselage spine

Very broad, swept vertical tail surfaces

Deepened nose with subtle contouring which houses reconnaissance gear. Camera ports at the front, below and each side of the nose

Performance

Maximum speed at 40,000 ft (12190 m)	Mach 2.25 (1290 kts)	2390 km/h (1,485 mph)
Maximum speed at sea level	Mach 1.18 (780 kts)	1445 km/h (898 mph)
Service ceiling	62,250 ft	(18975 m)
Ferry range	3034 km	(1,885 miles)
Combat radius with two 1400-litre (370-US gal) fuel tanks	1145 km	(711 miles)
Initial rate of climb per minute	61,400 ft	(18714 m)
Take-off distance to 50 ft (15 m)	1792 m	(5,880 ft)

Number of cameras carried
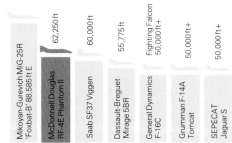

- Saab SF37 Viggen 6
- SEPECAT Jaguar S 5
- Mikoyan-Gurevich MiG-25R 'Foxbat-B' 5
- Dassault-Breguet Mirage 5BR 5
- McDonnell Douglas RF-4E Phantom II 3
- Grumman F-14A Tomcat 2
- General Dynamics F-16C Fighting Falcon ?

Service ceiling
- Mikoyan-Gurevich MiG-25R 'Foxbat-B' 88,585 ft E
- McDonnell Douglas RF-4E Phantom II 62,250 ft
- Saab SF37 Viggen 60,000 ft
- Dassault-Breguet Mirage 5BR 55,775 ft
- General Dynamics F-16C Fighting Falcon 50,000 ft+
- Grumman F-14A Tomcat 50,000 ft+
- SEPECAT Jaguar S 50,000 ft+

Maximum speed at high altitude
- Mikoyan-Gurevich MiG-25R 'Foxbat-B' Mach 3.2 E
- Grumman F-14A Tomcat Mach 2.34
- McDonnell Douglas RF-4E Phantom II Mach 2.2
- Dassault-Breguet Mirage 5BR Mach 2.2
- Saab SF37 Viggen Mach 2+
- General Dynamics F-16C Fighting Falcon Mach 2+
- SEPECAT Jaguar S Mach 1.6

Maximum speed at low altitude
- Saab SF37 Viggen Mach 1.2
- McDonnell Douglas RF-4E Phantom II Mach 1.2
- Grumman F-14A Tomcat Mach 1.2
- Dassault-Breguet Mirage 5BR Mach 1.13
- SEPECAT Jaguar S Mach 1.1
- General Dynamics F-16C Fighting Falcon Mach 1
- MiG-25R 'Foxbat-B' Mach 0.9 E

Range
- SEPECAT Jaguar S 2800 km E
- McDonnell Douglas RF-4E Phantom II 2700 km E
- Dassault-Breguet Mirage 5BR 2700 km E
- Grumman F-14A Tomcat 2600 km E
- Saab SF37 Viggen 2000 km E
- General Dynamics F-16C 2000 km E
- MiG-25R 'Foxbat-B' 1800 km E

The GRUMMAN
OV-1 MOHAWK

Grumman Mohawk: battlefield bug-eye

The enlarged cockpit canopy of the Mohawk is clearly visible on this OV-1D, one of the major features of the type. Handles on the SLAR pod allow its rapid removal if the aircraft is reconfigured to take infra-red sensors.

Mohawk! In most aviation enthusiasts' eyes the word conjures up an ungainly and awkward machine, one of the oddities of the aviation world. However, to the US Army it is its eyes and ears, providing ground commanders with up-to-the-minute information that could prove vital to their decisions regarding employment of the forces at their disposal. Grumman's bug-eyed oddity will continue in this role for many years yet.

Mention US Army Aviation and the mind immediately turns to vast swarms of helicopters, pouring load after load of troops into battle, while larger machines sling in the guns, trucks and supplies needed to fight the battle. Other helicopters cover the landings, supporting tanks on the ground to keep enemy forces at bay. But how does the commander of this huge army know where to send his troops, his helicopters and his tanks? Much of the answer lies at the door of a weird and wonderful aircraft, largely ignored in the annals of aviation except for its quirky appearance. It is the Grumman Mohawk, for many years the prime battlefield observation platform for the US Army.

The history of the Mohawk reaches back right into the 1950s, when a joint Marine Corps/Army programme looked for a STOL battlefield surveillance platform. Grumman's answer was the G-134, a twin-turboprop design with three fins and short, low-aspect ratio wings for good manoeuvrability. The Marine Corps dropped out of the programme (its aircraft would have been designated OF-1), leaving the Army to continue enthusiastically with what became known as the AO-1. The first flight took place on 14 April 1959, and the type immediately showed itself to be an excellent design able to squeeze into tight, short and rough strips, as it would be required to do when operating in the thick of battle. Nine YAO-1As were procured, followed by 64 AO-1As and the type was redesignated OV-1A in 1962. This version was configured for photographic and 'eyeball' surveillance. For the former it was fitted with KA-60 and KA-30 cameras, and for the latter the design featured an enlarged cockpit with bulged side windows and an extremely short nose. The effect on all-round view, particularly that downwards, was remarkable, as was the effect on the appearance of the machine.

Extended capabilities

The type soon proved its worth as a visual and photographic reconnaissance aircraft, and it was logical to extend its capabilities. This resulted in the OV-1B and OV-1C, which were produced in parallel. While retaining the cameras of its predecessor, the OV-1B added some 1.79 m (5 ft 10.5 in) to the span of the wing and, in addition, a large APS-94 SLAR carried in a giant canoe pod slung underneath the forward starboard fuselage. Some 101 of this version were produced. A total of 133 OV-1Cs was manufactured, these aircraft retaining the shorter wing and cameras of the OV-1A, with the important addition of UAS-4 infra-red detection gear in the lower fuselage. A dramatic increase in capabilities was realized when this pair entered service, the OV-1B permitting oblique monitoring of armoured movements and the OV-1C allowing targets to be spotted at night, in bad weather and in heavily wooded or jungle terrain.

All three of the initial versions of the Mohawk were deployed to Vietnam, to aid ground commanders, and they provided much useful intelligence. Following trials with a JOV-1A in the USA, the aircraft were cleared to fire light weapons from the wing pylons, these weapons including rockets. So armed, the Mohawks could often mark targets with smoke rockets for further attack by other systems.

The final new-build version of the Mohawk was the OV-1D, which combined the attributes of all three previous versions in a single airframe. Three rapid-access compartments in the lower fuselage were designed to take either the infra-red detector and its attendant equipment, or the control and imaging gear for the SLAR. The canoe pod for the latter could be quickly unbolted and removed, while the cockpit displays for the two systems were interchangeable, resulting in an aircraft that could be reconfigured from SLAR to IR mode in less than one hour. Photographic capability was also improved by the fitting of a new camera system with two panoramic cameras (one in the nose and one under the fuselage), and a serial frame unit under the fuselage. Some 37 OV-1Ds were built from new, and 108 examples of earlier variants were converted to the new standard. Israel was supplied with two of these aircraft in 1974.

A further diversion for the Mohawk came in the early 1970s, when the role of Elint was added to its list of surveillance regimes. As an interim measure to gain this capability, an unknown number of OV-1Cs were converted to RV-1C standard under the 'Quick Look I' programme. Housing the associated black boxes internally, the RV-1C carried the ALQ-133 Elint pod on the wing pylon to monitor WarPac radar activity. Following this was the RV-1D, of which 36 have been produced. Converted from the OV-1D, this has all the updates of the D-model, including the all-important ASN-86 INS, while still carrying the ALQ-133 Elint receiver. Known as 'Quick Look II',

One of the pair of standard OV-1Ds supplied to Israel is seen at an air show. It wears quasi-civil registrations and has unit badges carefully censored. SLAR imagery generated by the Mohawk can greatly aid Israeli knowledge of the intentions of its Arab neighbours.

the RV-1D is now in regular use with the US Army, locating and classifying radars, particularly those on mobile mounts. These aircraft have had their other reconnaissance sensors removed, and may have added further Elint sensors in recent years. Capability for either in-flight-processing or communicating the raw data to ground stations by data-link is incorporated. A final Elint version is the mysterious EV-1E, 16 of which were believed to have been converted from OV-1Bs in the 1970s. These carried Elint pods and perform a similar function to the 'Quick Look' systems on the RV-1C and RV-1D. The US Army did not take the aircraft into its inventory, and their exact fate is unknown. Frequent reports suggest that Israel received two of these aircraft, although all agencies involved deny this.

A detailed look at the OV-1D reveals a relatively simple aircraft built along traditional lines. The fuselage is of semi-monocoque construction with fuel carried in a single cell in the top of the central fuselage, although the meagre internal capacity is usually augmented by wing pods. Hydraulically-actuated divebrakes are mounted on the sides of the rear fuselage. The strong landing gear and high performance are tailored to rough field operations, and the three-finned tail and short wings cater for agility over the battlefield. Most of the electronics are carried on easily-accessed shelves in the rear fuselage.

Avionics fit

For a light battlefield reconnaissance type, the OV-1D carries a comprehensive avionics suite. Communications equipment consists of two VHF/FM sets, one UHF/AM set, one VHF/AM set and one long-range HF-SSB unit. All these are connected into the C-6533/ARC intercom system, which allows the crew to converse freely while also providing aural signals from various onboard sensors. One major advantage of the OV-1D over

earlier models is the fitment of an ASN-86 inertial navigation system, an extremely accurate unit which allows precise navigation in all weathers. INS information is also used for annotating reconnaissance data, while feeding the autopilot with data. Various other navigation aids are also carried to back up and update the INS. Among these is the AN/ARN-103 TACAN, ADF, VOR and the ASN-76 heading and attitude reference system. VORs, glide slope indicators and marker beacon indicators provide an all-weather landing system.

Other navigation avionics include the ASN-33 flight director which interfaces between the navigation system and the autopilot. The latter unit is the ASW-12, which detects slight changes in the aircraft's attitude, speed or direction and supplies correcting inputs to the flight controls. Also carried are radar altimeters, which are highly accurate up to a height of 5,000 ft (1525 m). Finally an IFF transponder broadcasts data to controllers as to the aircraft's position and altitude.

Reconnaissance data can be gathered in five main ways. Firstly, the pilot's eyes are still one of the most valuable sensors to be carried aloft. More sophisticated are the panoramic and serial frame cameras. The former scan 180° in front of and below the aircraft, photographing a wide swath of countryside as the aircraft passes

Little has been given away about the RV-1D Elint platform, and this example does not carry the 'Quick Look II' Elint pods on the wings. Most systems are similar to those of the OV-1D, except that the sensors, including cameras, have been removed.

over. The serial frame camera can be aimed to 15°, 30° or vertically from under the fuselage, and pre-fitted with four various focal length lenses to permit photography from any altitude. Night-time photography from low altitude is possible when the aircraft carries an electronic flash pod.

Infra-red and SLAR sensors can be rapidly interchanged on the OV-1D, with the cockpit console, SLAR pod, IR receiver and associated recorders all modulated to take similar connections. The AAS-24 IR system consists of a receiver in the lower fuselage, a film recorder and a cockpit display. Imagery is in real-time, and can be recorded on video, or as static frames on film. Control is undertaken from the cockpit console. IR data are recorded in a series of sweeps, so building up an image, and hot targets

Inflight close-up of the OV-1D reveals heavy-duty windscreen wipers, sharp dihedral of the wings and glazed panels in the roof of the cockpit. The large blade aerial serves the VHF/FM radio, part of an extensive onboard communications suite.

HF communications
Wire antennas serve the AN/ARC-102
HF-SSB set, which provides long-range
communications in the 2-30 MHz range

TACAN
The AN/ARN-103 TACAN system
used to update the AN/ASN-86 I
which is the principal navigation
carried by the Mohawk

Secondary VHF-FM
This blade antenna serves the secondary
AN/ARC-114 VHF/FM set. Two units
are carried for static-free retransmission

UNITED STATES ARMY

Radar altimeter
The AN/APN-171(V) altimeter is an all-
weather, pulse-type unit which is
operable up to 1525 m (5,000 ft) altitude

Airbrake
Either side of the rear fuselage is a
hydraulically-actuated airbrake

Marker beacon
Inside the blister is mounted the
AN/ARN-58 marker beacon receiver,
which is activated when the aircraft flies
overhead such a beacon during
approach

Panoramic camera
A KA-60C panoramic camera is mounte
in the fibre-glass blister under the
fuselage to provide vertical sweep
imagery

Wing tanks
A 568-litre tank carried on each inboard
pylon doubles the fuel capacity of the
OV-1

Grumman OV-1D Mohawk
73rd Combat Intelligence Company (AS)
2nd Military Intelligence Battalion
US Army in Europe
Stuttgart

VOR
The AN/ARN-82 unit operates in the 108-117.95 MHz range for VOR navigation. Above this frequency range it can be used in emergency as a communications receiver

Static wicks
These are located on the outer wings and fins to discharge static electricity into the airstream

IFF
The aft antenna for the AN/APX-72 IFF transponder is located in the base of the fin

De-icing boot
Pulses of engine bleed air are driven through rubber boots on the leading edges of wings, tailplane and fins. Two cycles are available for light or heavy conditions

Tailskid
To prevent damage to the rear fuselage in the event of over-rotation, this tailskid is fitted

Stores pylons
The two outboard pylons are used to carry a variety of stores, usually of a countermeasures nature. Simple weapons such as rocket pods were carried by Mohawks during the conflict in South East Asia

Radiac
The AN/ADR-6 radiac system is located in the bottom of the rear fuselage. This detects radiation levels underneath the aircraft's flight path. There is a cockpit alarm should radiation reach dangerous limits

IRCM
Principal defence against heat-seeking missiles and IR trackers is the Sanders AN/ALQ-147A(V)1 infra-red countermeasures pod. Known as 'Hot Brick', this pod directs IR jamming where needed

Navigation light
Navigation lights or rotating beacons are situated on both wingtips, fin-top and under the rear fuselage

Air intake
The ALQ-147 pod works on IR energy provided by burning fuel (due to a lack of power in the aircraft's electrical system), and this air scoop aspirates the small motor inside. Hot air is exhausted immediately behind

18905

Rapid access is provided to most systems for quick maintenance. This OV-1D sports the olive drab colour scheme worn for many years, and carries a Sanders AN/ALQ-147A(V)2 'Hot Brick' IRCM set on the rear of the wing drop tank.

are immediately highlighted on the cockpit screen. The operator can freeze the action at a particular point for on-the-spot analysis. The APS-94D SLAR has similar components, except that the receiver is mounted in a huge pod. Contained in the pod is the antenna for radiating and receiving radar pulses. The antenna can scan on one side only, or on both simultaneously. Imagery is processed in the fuselage units, recorded on film and displayed in the cockpit. The main targets for SLAR imagery are vehicles, and these can be detected both on the move and at rest. The entire unit is yaw-stabilized for sharp imagery, and uses variable frequencies and pseudo-pulse repetition rates to enable it to operate in enemy ECM environments.

The fifth reconnaissance-gathering method is that of radiation. In the rear fuselage is mounted the ADR-6 radiac system, which provides a constant mapping of ground radiation levels along the aircraft's flight path, allowing ground commanders to steer their troops around areas of high radiation in the event of tactical nuclear war. Should radiation levels reach dangerous levels for the

Light grey with black titling has been chosen by the US Army for its reconnaissance aircraft, giving them a clean look. Nevertheless, the Mohawk is required to operate from the mud and dust of rough strips near the front-line.

crew, a warning signal is heard through the intercom system.

All reconnaissance data is gathered on film, and each frame annotated by the AYA-10 system, which adds navigation, flight and sensor data on to each frame in either alphanumeric or binary-coded-decimal form. Some of the data can be transmitted by data-link for real- or near real-time analysis on the ground. A vital part of Mohawk operations is the TSQ-43 interpretation facility, which is truck-mounted and provides all the equipment necessary for handling and interpreting imagery generated by the OV-1. For film processing, a truck-mounted ES-38 film laboratory can process the recorded films swiftly in the field.

Self-defence

Flying over the battlefield at low level means that the Mohawk inevitably draws fire. The manoeuvrability of the type is considered to be adequate to avoid gunfire, but for missiles it requires countermeasures. ECM pods are sometimes carried to deter radar-homing missiles, fed with information from the APR-25/26 RHAW suite. Of greater threat are IR-homing missiles, and to this end the Mohawk carries the ALQ-147 'Hot Brick' pod on the wings, available either as a separate pod or as a bolt-on unit which fits the rear end of the wing fuel pod.

Mohawks are currently based in three major areas around the world. Many aircraft are based in the CONUS, often used for training but ready to support Army operations anywhere in the world they are needed. OV-1s have been used in central America to spot guerrilla operations along the Honduran border, their IR sensors being able to penetrate the heavy

vegetation to spot Nicaraguan insurgents. The two main operating locations, however, are West Germany and Korea, where a mixture of OV-1Ds and RV-1Ds keep tabs on communist military developments across the borders. In West Germany two military intelligence battalions operate about 12 OV-1Ds and six RV-1Ds each on a mixture of radar, IR and electronic surveillance, operating in concert with Beech RC-12Ds. Both RC-12D and RV-1D form a united team to eavesdrop on WarPac communications and, more importantly, monitor mobile radar movements across the border, both using data-links to provide near real-time information to ground commanders. Indeed, the equipment carried by both types is believed to be automatic. This pair performs a similar job across the north-south border in Korea. OV-1Ds maintain radar surveillance, using the APS-94 to peer across the border to keep watch on movements of enemy armour. Once again, information is available immediately on the ground thanks to the data-link.

Still going strong

Approaching 30 years since its first flight, what next for the Mohawk? The US Army has no plans for a replacement until the year 2000, when another SEMA platform will be procured. Meanwhile, ongoing update programmes of varying magnitude will keep the two species of Mohawk on top of Soviet military advances. As the Army's prime means of gathering tactical data from the air, the fleet of Mohawks will be kept busy along the borders until the end of the century, so allowing the 'bug-eyed' oddity to rack up a service career of over 40 years.

Glossary
ADF Automatic Direction Finder
CONUS CONtinental United States
ECM Electronic CounterMeasures
Elint Electronic intelligence
IFF Identification Friend or Foe
ILS Instrument Landing System
INS Inertial Navigation System
IR Infra-Red
RHAW Radar Homing And Warning
SEMA Special Electronic Mission Aircraft
SLAR Side-Looking Airborne Radar
STOL Short Take-Off and Landing
TACAN TACtical Air Navigation
VOR VHF Omni-directional radio Range

Mohawk in service

US Army

Details about the disposition of the Army's Mohawk force are sketchy to say the least, and what follows may be an incomplete listing. Force levels are maintained at around 110 OV-1Ds and 36 RV-1Ds, the latter sharing the electronic reconnaissance role with Beech RU-21s and RC-12Ds. A typical military intelligence battalion has two companies, one for aerial surveillance with some 12 OV-1Ds, and the other for electronic warfare with six RV-1Ds and six RU-21/RC-12Ds. The 1st and 2nd MIBs maintain the US Army surveillance commitment in Germany, while the 15th MIB is believed to be the Korean operating unit. The 224th MIB is the main CONUS-based unit, also supplying aircraft for surveillance duties in central America. Other units are support, reserve and training units.

This SLAR-equipped OV-1B shows the overall olive drab colour scheme worn from the mid-1960s until the early 1980s.

1st Military Intelligence Battalion
Base: Wiesbaden, West Germany
Example aircraft: 62-5865, 67-18900, 68-16993, 69-17021 (OV-1D); 62-5897, 64-14239 (RV-1D)

2nd Military Intelligence Battalion
Base: Stuttgart, West Germany
Example aircraft: 67-18921, 68-15930, 68-16996, 69-17004 (OV-1D); 62-5886, 64-14268 (RV-1D)

15th Military Intelligence Battalion (?)
Base: Korea
Example aircraft: 62-5872, 62-5890 (OV-1D); 64-14245, 64-14250 (RV-1D)

224th Military Intelligence Battalion
Base: Hunter AAF, Georgia
Example aircraft: 62-5898, 67-18932 (OV-1D)

'A' Company, 15th Military Intelligence Company
Base: Robert Grey AAF, Fort Hood, Alabama
Example aircraft: 69-17005 (OV-1D)

US Army Intelligence Corps School
Base: Libby AAF, Fort Huachuca, Arizona
Example aircraft: 67-18930, 69-17019, 69-17026 (OV-1D); 68-15965 (RV-1D)

Army Air Center
Base: Cairns AAF, Fort Rucker, Alabama
Example aircraft: not known (OV-1D)

US Army School of Transportation
Base: Felker AAF, Fort Eustis, Virginia
Example aircraft: 60-3743 (OV-1C)

Georgia Army National Guard (159th Military Intelligence Company)
Base: Dobbins AFB, Georgia
Example aircraft: 60-3753, 67-18881, 69-16998 (OV-1D)

Oregon Army National Guard (651st Military Intelligence Battalion)
Base: Salem, Oregon
Example aircraft: 67-18929 (OV-1D)

Above: This 73rd CICo OV-1D flies with the 2nd MIB at Stuttgart.

Below: US Army OV-1Ds. No aircraft in front-line service carry unit markings.

US Army AEFA
Base: Edwards AFB, California
Example aircraft: 61-2726 (OV-1C); 62-5867 (OV-1D)

US Navy Test Pilot School
Base: NAS Patuxent River, Maryland
Example aircraft: 59-2637, 62-5866 (OV-1B)

Principal countermeasures carried by the Mohawk are aimed at deterring heat-seeking missiles, which it would encounter in abundance over the battlefield. This AN/ALQ-147(V) 1 'Hot Brick' pod creates infra-red energy by burning fuel, enabling it to jam the missile's seeker head.

Israel

Israel has been supplied with at least two OV-1Ds, of which one was allocated the quasi-civil serial 4X-JRB. Persistent rumours abound as to the supply of two EV-1Es to the Israelis for electronic intelligence duties, but denials by all agencies concerned are equally persistent.

OV-1D of the Israeli air force with AN/APS-94 SLAR pod.

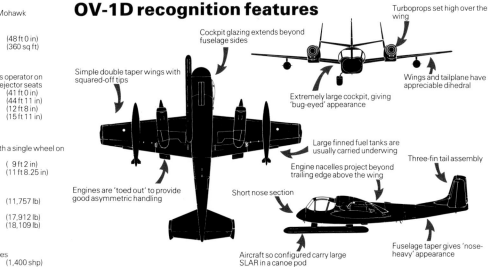

Specification: OV-1D Mohawk

Wings
Span	14.63 m	(48 ft 0 in)
Area	33.44 m²	(360 sq ft)

Fuselage and tail unit
Accommodation	pilot and systems operator on Martin-Baker J5 ejector seats	
Fuselage length	12.50 m	(41 ft 0 in)
Overall length with SLAR	13.69 m	(44 ft 11 in)
Height	3.86 m	(12 ft 8 in)
Tailplane	4.85 m	(15 ft 11 in)

Landing gear
Hydraulically retractable tricycle landing gear with a single wheel on each unit
Wheel track	2.79 m	(9 ft 2 in)
Wheelbase	3.56 m	(11 ft 8.25 in)

Weights
Empty	5333 kg	(11,757 lb)
Maximum take-off,		
with IR	8125 kg	(17,912 lb)
with SLAR	8214 kg	(18,109 lb)

Powerplant
Two Avco Lycoming T53-L-701 turboprop engines
Rating, each	1044 kW	(1,400 shp)

OV-1D recognition features

Turboprops set high over the wing

Cockpit glazing extends beyond fuselage sides

Simple double taper wings with squared-off tips

Wings and tailplane have appreciable dihedral

Extremely large cockpit, giving 'bug-eyed' appearance

Large finned fuel tanks are usually carried underwing

Three-fin tail assembly

Engine nacelles project beyond trailing edge above the wing

Engines are 'toed out' to provide good asymmetric handling

Short nose section

Aircraft so configured carry large SLAR in a canoe pod

Fuselage taper gives 'nose-heavy' appearance

Propeller
The three-blade hydromatic unit is some 3.05 m (10 ft) in diameter, and incorporates full feathering, reversing and synchronization features

Anti-icing
Propeller blades, spinners and inlet cowlings are heated from an AC generator driven by each engine

Cockpit
The sides of the cockpit are bulged outwards to give excellent sideways and downwards visibility to the crew. The drop-away nose enhances forward visibility while a glazed roof panel allows visibility upwards

Windscreen wipers
Two heavy-duty wipers keep the windscreen clear in all bad weather conditions

Windscreen
The windscreen is 1 in thick to provide protection against groundfire. Armour is located in the cockpit floor and sides, and more can be added in combat scenarios.

Pitot
A simple pitot supplies data for the air speed indicator

Nose radome
The nose radome pivots upwards to allow rapid access to the nose camera and other equipment. Cockpit equipment is accessed via the nosewheel bay, while that in the fuselage can be reached through rapid access hatches

Panoramic camera
Mounted at 20° to the horizontal is a KA-60C panoramic camera which photographs a 180° swathe ahead of the aircraft

Glide slope indicator
The AN/ARN-58 receives glide slope information from the runway glide path transmitter during landing approach

IFF
The AN/APX-72 IFF system is served by these two blade aerials. Air traffic controllers are provided with identification and altitude information in addition to position

SLAR
One of the two principal sensors carried by the OV-1D is the AN/APS-94D side-looking airborne radar, which can provide imagery on either or both sides of the flight path. Images are recorded both on photographic film for later analysis, and on a cockpit display

Intake
This air scoop atop the fuselage supplies cooling air for the electronic equipment in the rear fuselage

ADF
AN/ARN-89 is a low-frequency (100-3000 KHz) automatic direction-finding unit. Like the VOR, it can also be used for emergency communications receiving

Primary VHF-FM
The AN/ARC-114 VHF/FM set operates in the 30-75.95 MHz range, filling most of the communications requirements. The primary transceiver can also be used as a homing device

Powerplant
The engines are Lycoming T-53-L-701 turboprops, each developing some 1,400 shp at sea level, giving the propeller 1678 RPM

Fire protection
Inside each engine compartment are temperature sensors which trigger a warning in the cockpit if an engine fire develops. The crew then activates controls which cut off fuel flow and fire pressurized extinguishers containing bromotrifluoromethane

RESCUE

EXIT RELEASE

EJECTION SEAT
DANGER
DANGER DANGER

DANGER → ← DANGER

Serial frame camera
The KA-76A camera comes with four interchangeable lenses, allowing its use at any altitude. It can be rotated by a cockpit control, and navigation information is automatically exposed on to each frame

Infra-red system
An alternate sensor system to the SLAR is the AN/AAS-24 infra-red surveillance system, which can be interchanged rapidly with the SLAR (including cockpit display). The recorder and associated equipment are mounted in the lower fuselage

Fuel system
1124 litres of fuel are contained in a single fuel cell located in the top of the central fuselage. This is augmented by the wing tanks

Ejection seats
Both crew sit on Martin-Baker zero-ninety ejection seats. Ejecting automatically activates the IFF system and a seat-mounted oxygen supply

Performance

Maximum speed at
5,000 ft (1525 m)
with IR	265 kts; 491 km/h	(305 mph)
with SLAR	251 kts; 465 km/h	(289 mph)

Take-off distance to
50 ft (15 m)
with IR	349 m	(1,145 ft)
with SLAR	358 m	(1,175 ft)

Initial rate of climb,
with IR	3,618 ft (1103 m) per minute	
with SLAR	3,466 ft (1056 m) per minute	

Service ceiling	25,000 ft	(7620 m)

Range with maximum
fuel,
with IR	1626 km	(1,010 miles)
with SLAR	1518 km	(943 miles)

Combat endurance,
with IR	2.04 hours
with SLAR	1.96 hours

Initial climb rate, feet/minute

- Grumman OV-1D Mohawk 3,465 ft
- Rockwell OV-10D Bronco 3,020 ft
- Beech RC-12D 2,450 ft
- Lockheed EC-130E 1,830 ft
- Bell EH-1H 1,600 ft
- Aérospatiale AS 332B 1,395 ft
- Pilatus Britten-Norman CASTOR Islander 950 ft
- Sikorsky EH-60A 450 ft

Service ceiling

- Beech RC-12D 35,000 ft+
- Rockwell OV-10D Bronco 30,000 ft
- Grumman OV-1D Mohawk 25,000 ft
- Lockheed EC-130E 23,000 ft
- CASTOR Islander 22,000 ft
- Sikorsky EH-60A 19,000 ft
- Aérospatiale AS 332b 13,450 ft

Maximum cruising speed

- Lockheed EC-130E 320 kts
- Beech RC-12D 282 kts
- Rockwell OV-10D Bronco 250 kts
- Grumman OV-1D Mohawk 231 kts (SLAR mission)
- Pilatus Britten-Norman CASTOR Islander 150 kts
- Sikorsky EH-60A 145 kts
- Aérospatiale AS 332B 141 kts
- Bell EH-1H 110 kts

Maximum range, standard fuel

- Lockheed EC-130E 3,895 km
- Beech RC-12D 2,810 km
- Grumman OV-1D Mohawk 1,653 km (SLAR mission)
- Pilatus Britten-Norman CASTOR Islander 1,297 km
- Rockwell OV-10D Bronco 750 km
- Aérospatiale AS 332B 618 km
- Sikorsky EH-60A 600 km
- Bell EH-1H 510 km

Take-off run

- Aérospatiale AS 332B VTOL
- Bell EH-1H VTOL
- Sikorsky EH-60A VTOL
- Rockwell OV-10D Bronco 740 ft
- Grumman OV-1D Mohawk 1,175 ft
- CASTOR Islander 1,660 ft
- Beech RC-12D 1,940 ft
- Lockheed EC-130E 3,800 ft

Mohawk variants

OV-1A: initial version for photographic reconnaissance only

JOV-1A: one OV-1A involved in armament tests involving rockets and other light weapons; other armed aircraft operating in Vietnam may have adopted the JOV-1A designation

OV-1B: production variant featuring APS-94 SLAR in canoe pod slung underneath the starboard fuselage; wing span increased by 1.79 m (5 ft 10.5 in)

OV-1C: counterpart of the OV-1B featuring UAS-4 IR sensor in place of SLAR, this being carried in the lower fuselage; wings of original OV-1A span

RV-1C: electronic reconnaissance conversion of OV-1C with 'Quick Look I' Elint equipment carried in fuselage and in wing pods

YOV-1D: four OV-1C converted to serve as pre-production OV-1D

OV-1D: final basic surveillance platform with photographic capability and either SLAR or IR sensor, these being rapidly interchangeable; wings of OV-1B

RV-1D: major Elint conversion of OV-1, with photographic and other imaging capability replaced with Elint equipment under 'Quick Look II' programme

EV-1E: further Sigint conversion of older airframes, incorporating an Elint system similar to 'Quick Look II'

OV-1E: Projected version with lengthened cabin for two systems operator stations behind pilot and navigator

This trials aircraft is an RV-1D, carrying Elint equipment on the wing pods. The instrumentation boom is for evaluation.

Basic flight controls dominate the left-hand side of the OV-1D cockpit, while sensor monitors are located on the right-hand side.

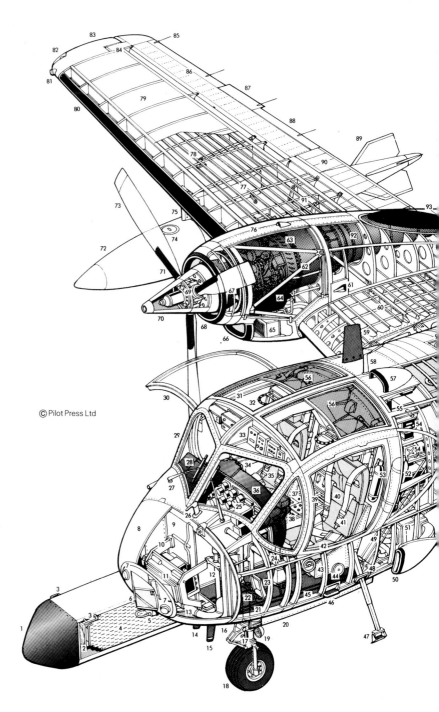

© Pilot Press Ltd

umman OV-1D Mohawk cutaway drawing key

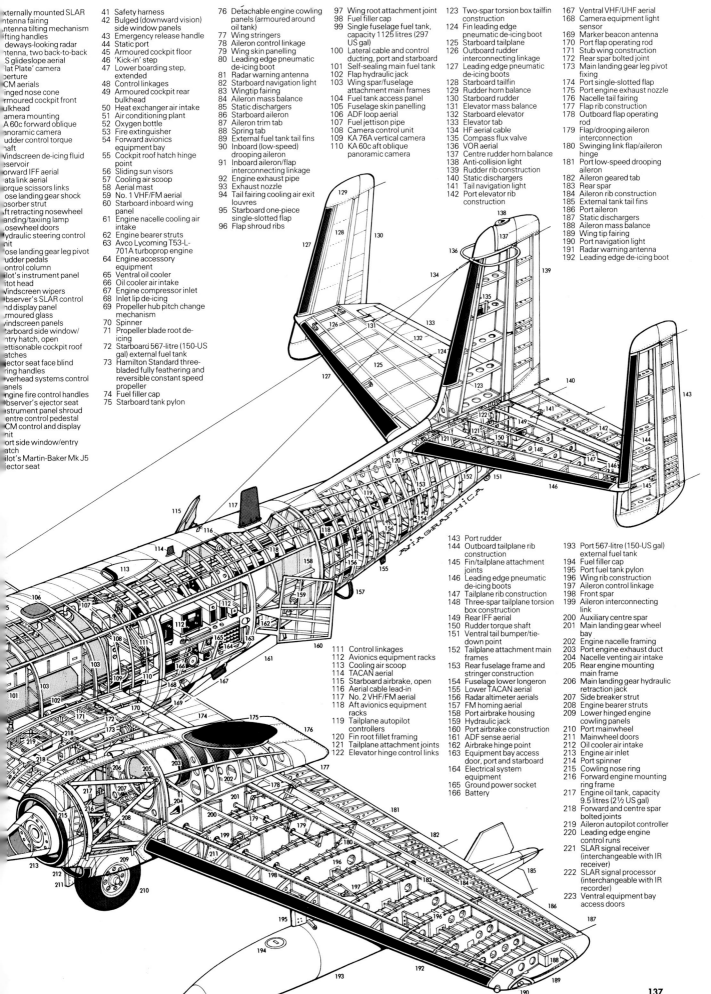

xternally mounted SLAR
ntenna fairing
fting handles
deways-looking radar
ntenna, two back-to-back
S glideslope aerial
lat Plate' camera
perture
CM aerials
inged nose cone
rmoured cockpit front
ulkhead
amera mounting
A 60c forward oblique
anoramic camera
udder control torque
haft
Vindscreen de-icing fluid
eservoir
orward IFF aerial
ata link aerial
orque scissors links
ose landing gear shock
bsorber strut
ft retracting nosewheel
anding/taxiing lamp
osewheel doors
ydraulic steering control
nit
ose landing gear leg pivot
udder pedals
ontrol column
ilot's instrument panel
itot head
Vindscreen wipers
bserver's SLAR control
nd display panel
rmoured glass
Vindscreen panels
tarboard side window/
ntry hatch, open
ettisonable cockpit roof
atches
jector seat face blind
ring handles
verhead systems control
anels
ngine fire control handles
bserver's ejector seat
nstrument panel shroud
entre control pedestal
CM control and display
nit
ort side window/entry
atch
ilot's Martin-Baker Mk J5
jector seat

41 Safety harness
42 Bulged (downward vision)
   side window panels
43 Emergency release handle
44 Static port
45 Armoured cockpit floor
46 'Kick-in' step
47 Lower boarding step,
   extended
48 Control linkages
49 Armoured cockpit rear
   bulkhead
50 Heat exchanger air intake
51 Air conditioning plant
52 Oxygen bottle
53 Fire extinguisher
54 Forward avionics
   equipment bay
55 Cockpit roof hatch hinge
   point
56 Sliding sun visors
57 Cooling air scoop
58 Aerial mast
59 No. 1 VHF/FM aerial
60 Starboard inboard wing
   panel
61 Engine nacelle cooling air
   intake
62 Engine bearer struts
63 Avco Lycoming T53-L-
   701A turboprop engine
64 Engine accessory
   equipment
65 Ventral oil cooler
66 Oil cooler air intake
67 Engine compressor inlet
68 Inlet lip de-icing
69 Propeller hub pitch change
   mechanism
70 Spinner
71 Propeller blade root de-
   icing
72 Starboard 567-litre (150-US
   gal) external fuel tank
73 Hamilton Standard three-
   bladed fully feathering and
   reversible constant speed
   propeller
74 Fuel filler cap
75 Starboard tank pylon

76 Detachable engine cowling
   panels (armoured around
   oil tank)
77 Wing stringers
78 Aileron control linkage
79 Wing skin panelling
80 Leading edge pneumatic
   de-icing boot
81 Radar warning antenna
82 Starboard navigation light
83 Wingtip fairing
84 Aileron mass balance
85 Fuselage skin panelling
86 Starboard aileron
87 Aileron trim tab
88 Spring tab
89 External fuel tank tail fins
90 Inboard (low-speed)
   drooping aileron
91 Inboard aileron/flap
   interconnecting linkage
92 Engine exhaust pipe
93 Exhaust nozzle
94 Tail fairing cooling air exit
   louvres
95 Starboard one-piece
   single-slotted flap
96 Flap shroud ribs

97 Wing root attachment joint
98 Fuel filler cap
99 Single fuselage fuel tank,
   capacity 1125 litres (297
   US gal)
100 Lateral cable and control
    ducting, port and starboard
101 Self-sealing main fuel tank
102 Flap hydraulic jack
103 Wing spar/fuselage
    attachment main frames
104 Fuel tank access panel
105 Fuselage skin panelling
106 ADF loop aerial
107 Fuel jettison pipe
108 Camera control unit
109 KA 76A vertical camera
110 KA 60c aft oblique
    panoramic camera

111 Control linkages
112 Avionics equipment racks
113 Cooling air scoop
114 TACAN aerial
115 Starboard airbrake, open
116 Aerial cable lead-in
117 No. 2 VHF/FM aerial
118 Aft avionics equipment
    racks
119 Tailplane autopilot
    controllers
120 Fin root fillet framing
121 Tailplane attachment joints
122 Elevator hinge control links

123 Two-spar torsion box tailfin
    construction
124 Fin leading edge
    pneumatic de-icing boot
125 Starboard tailplane
126 Outboard rudder
    interconnecting linkage
127 Leading edge pneumatic
    de-icing boots
128 Starboard tailfin
129 Rudder horn balance
130 Starboard rudder
131 Elevator mass balance
132 Starboard elevator
133 Elevator tab
134 HF aerial cable
135 Compass flux valve
136 VOR aerial
137 Centre rudder horn balance
138 Anti-collision light
139 Rudder rib construction
140 Static dischargers
141 Tail navigation light
142 Port elevator rib
    construction

143 Port rudder
144 Outboard tailplane rib
    construction
145 Fin/tailplane attachment
    joints
146 Leading edge pneumatic
    de-icing boots
147 Tailplane rib construction
148 Three-spar tailplane torsion
    box construction
149 Rear IFF aerial
150 Rudder torque shaft
151 Ventral tail bumper/tie-
    down point
152 Tailplane attachment main
    frames
153 Rear fuselage frame and
    stringer construction
154 Fuselage lower longeron
155 Lower TACAN aerial
156 Radar altimeter aerials
157 FM homing aerial
158 Port airbrake housing
159 Hydraulic jack
160 Port airbrake construction
161 ADF sense aerial
162 Airbrake hinge point
163 Equipment bay access
    door, port and starboard
164 Electrical system
    equipment
165 Ground power socket
166 Battery

167 Ventral VHF/UHF aerial
168 Camera equipment light
    sensor
169 Marker beacon antenna
170 Port flap operating rod
171 Stub wing construction
172 Rear spar bolted joint
173 Main landing gear leg pivot
    fixing
174 Port single-slotted flap
175 Port engine exhaust nozzle
176 Nacelle tail fairing
177 Flap rib construction
178 Outboard flap operating
    rod
179 Flap/drooping aileron
    interconnection
180 Swinging link flap/aileron
    hinge
181 Port low-speed drooping
    aileron
182 Aileron geared tab
183 Rear spar
184 Aileron rib construction
185 External tank tail fins
186 Port aileron
187 Static dischargers
188 Aileron mass balance
189 Wing tip fairing
190 Port navigation light
191 Radar warning antenna
192 Leading edge de-icing boot

193 Port 567-litre (150-US gal)
    external fuel tank
194 Fuel filler cap
195 Port fuel tank pylon
196 Wing rib construction
197 Aileron control linkage
198 Front spar
199 Aileron interconnecting
    link
200 Auxiliary centre spar
201 Main landing gear wheel
    bay
202 Engine nacelle framing
203 Port engine exhaust duct
204 Nacelle venting air intake
205 Rear engine mounting
    main frame
206 Main landing gear hydraulic
    retraction jack
207 Side breaker strut
208 Engine bearer struts
209 Lower hinged engine
    cowling panels
210 Port mainwheel
211 Mainwheel doors
212 Oil cooler air intake
213 Engine air inlet
214 Port spinner
215 Cowling nose ring
216 Forward engine mounting
    ring frame
217 Engine oil tank, capacity
    9.5 litres (2½ US gal)
218 Forward and centre spar
    bolted joints
219 Aileron autopilot controller
220 Leading edge engine
    control runs
221 SLAR signal receiver
    (interchangeable with IR
    receiver)
222 SLAR signal processor
    (interchangeable with IR
    recorder)
223 Ventral equipment bay
    access doors

The LOCKHEED
U-2/TR-1

U-2/TR-1: Burbank's Black Dragons

Since the 1950s, the mysterious shape of the Lockheed U-2 has sailed serenely over the hot spots of the Earth, recording all the activity beneath it from its perch way above the clouds. In its U-2R version, the graceful 'Dragon Lady' still goes about its business, while the TR-1 derivative has added a new dimension to tactical reconnaissance.

Lockheed's graceful but purposeful U-2 had first taken to the air on 1 August 1955, and the early U-2A to U-2G models went on to compile a remarkable service record, performing thousands of missions over hostile territory to provide the USA with most of its important intelligence throughout the late 1950s and early 1960s, while also providing a mass of scientific data on high-altitude flight, re-entry vehicles and nuclear fall-out. By the mid-1960s the ranks of the early U-2 variants had been severely depleted by losses, while the intelligence requirement had increased. More aircraft were urgently needed. Lockheed had meanwhile been investigating ways of updating the design and had come up with an enlarged version, with far greater payload and range. After receiving a request from the CIA, the 'Skunk Works' (under the direction of Kelly Johnson, Ben Rich and Fred Cavanaugh) came up with the U-2R, whose first flight took place on 28 August 1967 from Edwards North Base, where the CIA had its major U-2 facility. The first six aircraft went to the agency, a further six following to the US Air Force.

The new aircraft entered service soon after its first flight, and quickly showed itself to be superior in virtually all departments to the earlier variants. As well as the very considerable improvement in payload, range and altitude, landing was far easier, correcting a problem that had dogged the early aircraft throughout their careers. The agency aircraft were soon active in many parts of the world, especially Taiwan, where two aircraft were dispatched in 1968 to operate in ROCAF markings. This programme ended in 1974, and with it the CIA use of the aircraft, all examples then passing to the Air Force. The latter had allocated its aircraft to the 349th SRS of the 100th SRW, and these Air Force U-2Rs saw much action in South East Asia, mainly from U-Tapao RTAFB in Thailand. As well as missions flown in support of the in-theatre war, especially the 'Line-backer' raids (coded 'Olympic Torch'), 'Senior Book' missions were flown against mainland China. Throughout their South East Asia sojourn, the 100th SRW's U-2Rs set enviable safety and mission records.

Naval experiments

During late 1969 the CIA experimented with U-2R carrier operations, just as it had done earlier with the U-2As. With the high wind speed over the deck, the U-2R found no difficulty settling down on USS America (CV-66) and could lift off easily without the need for a catapult. A simple strap-on arrester hook was the only modification necessary. By folding the wings, the U-2 could just about scrape on to the deck-edge elevator and be transported to the hangar deck. So far as is known, the U-2R did not fly missions from a carrier deck as the earlier version is alleged to have done. The US Navy was interested in the possibilities of using the U-2R for long-range patrol and borrowed two aircraft from the CIA. Running throughout 1973 the EP-X programme investigated the carriage of sensors such as FLIR, periscope detection radar, maritime radar and Elint systems for high-altitude maritime monitoring and surveillance. Nothing came of the project, although studies were made regarding the possibility of fitting an anti-ship missile

This view of a TR-1A serves to illustrate the enormous wing area of the type, which gives such phenomenal performance. The simple flaps, divebrakes and undercarriage are usually deployed while cruising in the circuit. The pilot's rear view mirror is prominent.

to the aircraft.

Following the end of the war in Vietnam the U-2Rs continued their surveillance duties, and these became even more important with the cancellation of the 'Compass Cope' high-altitude RPV project. These pilotless high-fliers were designed to bring back the same type of intelligence for which the U-2 had been built, but without risk to the pilot. Lockheed had even submitted a U-2R RPV design for this project. In 1976 the USAF decided to consolidate its air-breathing high-altitude reconnaissance resources in one unit, and the aircraft of the 100th SRW joined the 9th SRW at Beale AFB, where they served alongside the Lockheed SR-71. The USAF could now make better use of the particular talents of the two types in different operations.

In 1978 the USAF announced a new programme for a tactical reconnaissance aircraft, and in 1979 the U-2R line re-opened to begin production of the TR-1A. The first aircraft from the line was a demilitarized version designated ER-2 for the NASA Ames high-altitude research centre. The ER-2 first flew on 11 May 1981

The U-2R has been in service since late 1967, at first augmenting and then totally supplanting the earlier U-2 versions. It is still employed on strategic reconnaissance duties from several operating locations around the world. This aircraft cruises without superpods.

Large 'farms' of blade, paddle and hook antennas are a common feature throughout the U-2R's career, and these have been seen several times on TR-1 aircraft, as evidenced by this 17th RW machine. Long-endurance Sigint flights are the U-2/TR-1's forte, particularly in the field of Comint.

from Palmdale and a year later the aircraft began regular research flights, which it continues today. The first TR-1A (80-1066) flew on 1 August 1981, with the first TR-1B trainer (with extra cockpit in the Q-bay area) following on 23 February 1983. The TR-1A differs little from the U-2R, featuring updated secondary systems such as communications. It is also slightly lighter thanks to the advances made in electronic components. Despite their differing designations, the U-2R and TR-1A can perform each other's tasks with little difficulty.

Shortly before the TR-1's first flight, the British government announced that a TR-1 unit would be based at RAF Alconbury, from where the aircraft could conduct operations over the entire European area. The 17th Reconnaissance Wing received its first two aircraft in February 1983 and has been highly active since then, flying mainly tactical reconnaissance missions, although also picking up some of the strategic missions which had been flown previously by U-2Rs from RAF Mildenhall. Other TR-1 aircraft, including the pair of TR-1B two-seat trainers, are on the strength of the 9th SRW at Beale in California, which also operates the remaining U-2Rs. The 9th SRW aircraft fly on strategic reconnaissance missions as part of the USAF's national security commitment. Thus the aircraft turn up

occasionally in many parts of the world, but three regular areas of interest are Korea, the Mediterranean and Central America. The first two areas are each served by single aircraft on permanent detachment to Osan AB in South Korea and RAF Akrotiri on Cyprus, while the Central American countries (especially Nicaragua) are watched from Patrick AFB, Florida and from Beale. U-2Rs are sometimes seen in Europe and the Far East when deployed on special one-off missions.

Long endurance

U-2 and TR-1 missions are generally long affairs, as a result of the types' modest transit speed. The maximum range of around 10000 km (6,215 miles) enables the TR-1 to cover most areas from its operating locations. Mission altitudes vary, but are usually around 75,000 ft (22860 m). A few low-altitude missions were flown by U-2 aircraft during the South East Asia war, pilots thus being able to enjoy the rare pleasure of flying in normal kit rather than the bulky and uncomfortable S-1010B pressure suit used for high-level flight. Mission routing does

not employ too many overflights, and these occur only where the target nation does not have SAM assets necessary to down the 'Dragon Lady'. Very few countries of note are in this position, so the U-2 goes about its business mainly outside hostile airspace, gathering optical and radar imagery in addition to Sigint.

The U-2R and TR-1 series retains the Pratt & Whitney J75 turbojet from the original versions, maintaining performance by having greater wing area ($92.9\,m^2$/1,000 sq ft compared with $52.5\,m^2$/565 sq ft) to lift the heavy payload to enormous altitudes. The fuselage is a simple semi-monocoque structure which has large internal volume for sensors, and which incorporates an airbrake on each side and a lengthened jetpipe for IR suppression. The extraordinary wing, which spans 31.39 m (103 ft 0 in) compared with 24.38 m (80 ft 0 in) for the earlier models,

The TR-1 has simple flaps sectioned to deploy each side of the superpods when they are fitted. These enormous pods can take up to 340 kg of sensors each, vastly increasing the payload of the TR-1. Prominent here is the rear-facing RHAWS receiver on the starboard wing.

Rudder
The rudder is operated mechanically and is unboosted. Travel is 30° left or right

Exhaust pipe
The exhaust pipe is lengthened to provide better infra-red suppression

Tailplane
This is rigidly connected to the fin and the whole unit pivots to provide pitch trim. The elevators are manually operated with 30° upward and 20° downward travel

Sigint antennas
Both U-2R and TR-1A aircraft are regularly seen with large 'farms' of blade, hook and spike antennas attached to the lower side of the rear fuselage

Flaps
The hydraulically-actuated flaps take up a large portion of the trailing edge and are split on each side of the superpod position. These are segmented to allow for wing flex and can deploy to 35°. They shift to 4° up when gust control is employed

Tailwheel
The forward-retracting tailwheel has two grooved solid tyres

Spoilers
The U-2R/TR-1 have two simple hydraulically-actuated spoilers mounted in each wing, those inboard used for lift dumping and those outboard for extra roll control at low speeds

'Pogo' wheel
The sprung-steel strut holds a twin-wheel, solid-tyre unit. The entire 'pogo' is held in place by a pin for taxiing, but for take-off the pins are removed, allowing the 'pogo' to drop away as the aircraft becomes airborne.

Superpod
The pod under each wing is some 8.2 m (27 ft) long and can carry 272 kg (600 lb) of stores. The pods are easily detachable but not jettisonable, and are made along traditional semi-monocoque aircraft fuselage techniques

Lockheed TR-1A
95th Reconnaissance Squadron
17th Reconnaissance Wing
Strategic Air Command
RAF Alconbury

Rear RHAWS
This large fairing in the starboard win
trailing edge is the rear hemisphere
RHAWS receiver. Together with the
wingtip antennas, it provides excelle
all-round coverage

Wing fuel tank
The giant wing is 'wet', with the wing
skin containing fuel in all but the
outermost section. Capacity is believed
to be in the region of 6435 litres
(1,700 US gal)

Wingtip RHAWS
Two receivers placed at 45° to the chord
at each end of the wingtip fairing provide
side-looking coverage for the defensive
avionics suite

Keith Fretwell.

Landing skid
A special toughened abradible and
replaceable material forms the bottom
of the wingtip skid, upon which the TR-1
rests at the end of the landing run

Stall strip
Set flush with the leading edge are s
strips which protrude about 12 mm
(0.5 in) when deployed. These impr
stall performance

is built up from a light three-spar torsion box. Despite the inherent strength in such a structure, the U-2R has a low stress factor and thus has to be flown carefully to avoid overstressing the wing. The wing has large, simple flaps which are split on each side of the 'superpods' on aircraft configured to carry them. Spoilers work for roll control and as lift dumpers, while airbrakes mounted on each side of the rear fuselage help retard the aircraft during descent and landing. Hard metal skids are incorporated in the wingtips to protect the wing during the landing run. Fuel is carried in virtually the entire wing apart from the outboard sections, which fold back for easier ground handling. Fuel dump pipes are situated in the trailing edge of both wings, while venting is accomplished through a nozzle in the tip of the tail. A mirror on the canopy frame allows the pilot to check that fuel is venting properly, and to see if he is pulling a contrail.

Undercarriage peculiarities

The U-2R has a main landing gear unit mounted in the central fuselage with two wheels, while a twin-wheel, solid-tyre arrangement is mounted in the tail. Both units are retractable. For taxiing and take-off small 'pogo' wheels are attached under the wings to give lateral stability, held in place by a removable pin. Once the aircraft is lined up on the runway the pins are removed, and the pogos are released once sufficient airspeed has been attained to hold the wings steady. On landing the aircraft comes to a halt resting on one wingtip, after the pilot has held the wings level as long as possible to prevent damage. With a good pilot and a steady, strong wind, the wingtip need never touch the ground before the aircrew can fix the pogo wheels. The landing is a tricky affair which needs much skill on the pilot's part. The immense wing requires virtually full aileron deflection at low speeds to make an impression, and the yoke-type control column keeps the pilot busy and fit during landing. There is little deceleration as the J75 engine has a high idle rate. The large vertical tail surfaces and single main wheel make the aircraft very prone to weather-cocking, and cross wind operations can be extremely hazardous. Although in much less danger during landing than the 'jockeys' of early U-2s, the U-2R and TR-1 pilot spends a long time practising circuits, keeping his landing skills as sharp as possible. Despite the phenomenal performance of the aircraft, it is very simple in basic structure and systems, and is considered very reliable and easy to maintain.

The U-2R and TR-1 carry their sensors in five main areas. The nose is completely

interchangeable and can accommodate 272 kg (600 lb) of equipment. Immediately behind the cockpit is mounted the Q-bay, which can accommodate 340 kg (750 lb) of sensors. Behind that, just in front of the main gear, is the E-bay, a small bay for light sensors. The superpods, each capable of carrying up to 340 kg, are mounted on each wing. These are optional, and some aircraft have not been converted to carry them. Other wing pods include a smaller type which does not project beyond the trailing edge, and which is usually associated with Sigint equipment. These are often seen sprouting large paddle-shaped aerials with flat sections through which peer SLARs. Finally, the spine and lower rear fuselage often play host to enormous farms of blade, spike and hook antennas for the gathering of signals.

Operational payload

Sensors carried are usually of a Sigint nature. Comint suites are common, indicated by the rows of blades and hooks mentioned above. Cameras are still carried, chief amongst these being the LOROP camera, which produces high-quality images at great oblique ranges. SLAR of various kinds are carried in the nose and wing pods. Two sensors which are primarily associated with the TR-1A are the Hughes ASARS and the PLSS. The former is a high-resolution radar which is mounted in a bulbous detachable nose section. This produces long-range oblique radar imagery for tactical use. ASARS enables the TR-1 to 'see' behind enemy lines and produce imagery of tank formations and the like which the normal reconnaissance methods cannot detect without entering hostile areas. PLSS is a precision passive emitter-locator system, developed from the 'Pave Onyx' and 'Pave Nickel' projects undertaken by U-2Cs operating from RAF Wethersfield during the mid-1970s, and by U-2Rs from Mildenhall in the late 1970s. This requires three aircraft flying along the battlefront with data-links to a ground

station. By triangulation methods, the exact position of a hostile emitter can be located in a split-second and strike detailed against it. However, this programme has run into serious technical and budgetary problems, and the USAF may look to a cheaper and less-capable derivative.

The TR-1A and U-2R are thought to have digital data-links which send real-time secure intelligence back to a ground station. Astro-inertial navigation systems are also fitted. A comprehensive RHAW system is carried to protect the aircraft and warn of impending attack by radar-guided missiles. Antennas for this system are housed in the two wingtip pods (giving near hemispherical protection) and on the trailing edge of the starboard wing for rear protection.

So the U-2R and TR-1 are equipped for service in the hostile environment of the 1980s and 1990s, using highly sophisticated sensors and systems to allow them to operate behind friendly lines and at great altitude. In the ever-spiralling race for intelligence, the mystic U-2 continues to spread its wings and soar above the rest, now adding battlefield reconnaissance to the many feathers in its cap.

Glossary
AB Air Base
AFB Air Force Base
ASARS Advanced Synthetic-Aperture Radar System
CIA Central Intelligence Agency
Comint Communications intelligence
Elint Electronic intelligence
EP-X Electronic Patrol – Experimental
FLIR Forward-Looking Infra-Red
IR Infra-Red
LOROP Long-Range Oblique Photography
NASA National Aeronautics and Space Administration
PLSS Precision Location Strike System
RHAW Radar Homing And Warning
ROCAF Republic of China Air Force
RPV Remotely-Piloted Vehicle
RTAFB Royal Thai Air Force Base
RW Reconnaissance Wing
SAM Surface-to-Air Missile
Sigint Signals intelligence
SLAR Side-Looking Airborne Radar
SRS Strategic Reconnaissance Squadron
SRW Strategic Reconnaissance Wing

Above: The display for the pilot's driftsight dominates the U-2 cockpit. This display is connected to a prism mounted outside the aircraft underneath the cockpit which is mounted in a glass bubble. The prism can be directed from inside the cockpit, giving nearly 180° vision underneath. The cockpit is that of one of NASA's two U-2Cs.

A 95th RS, 17th RW TR-1A taxis along the Alconbury runway following a landing. At the end of the landing run, the aircraft rests on one wingtip until ground crew replace the sprung-steel 'pogo' wheels, allowing the TR-1 to taxi away. The wide track of the outriggers means that some widening of taxiways has occurred to accommodate the 'Dragon Lady'.

U-2 and TR-1 in service

US Air Force

Strategic Air Command

9th Strategic Reconnaissance Wing

Home-based at Beale AFB, California, the 9th SRW operates both U-2R and TR-1 aircraft alongside the Lockheed SR-71 fleet (Boeing KC-135Qs are also flown in support of the SR-71). As well as Beale operations, the U-2s and TR-1s fly with four detachments around the world and from some 15 other OLs (operating locations). Permanent detachments are as follows:

Detachment 2: Osan AB, South Korea
Detachment 3: RAF Akrotiri, Cyprus
Detachment 5: Patrick AFB, Florida
Detachment 6: Norton AFB, California
(Detachments 1 and 4 are at Kadena and Mildenhall respectively, operating mainly the Lockheed SR-71)

Example aircraft
99th Strategic Reconnaissance Squadron
(U-2R) 68-10331, 10333, 10336, 10339
(TR-1A) 80-1067, 1071, 1074

5th Strategic Reconnaissance Training Squadron
(TR-1B) 80-1064, 80-1065

17th Reconnaissance Wing

Although assigned to USAFE duties, the 17th RW at RAF Alconbury falls under the jurisdiction of SAC. Receiving its first aircraft in February 1983, the wing will eventually have 14 aircraft on strength. Close ties are kept with the 9th SRW, and aircraft may exchange between units.

Example aircraft
95th Reconnaissance Squadron
(TR-1A) 80-1068, 1077, 1081, 1084

National Aeronautical and Space Administration
NASA Ames Research Center

Based at NAS Moffett Field, California, NASA Ames still operates two U-2Cs for scientific research, although these are rarely used. The lion's share of the workload is taken by the ER-2, ER standing for 'earth resources'.

Aircraft
(U-2C) 56-6681, 6682
(NASA 708, 709)
(ER-2) 80-1063 (NASA 706)

ctor seat
ockheed-developed ejector seat is
able of zero-zero operations. Ejection
itiated by groin release. The pilot's
s are attached to the seat by cables,
ich pull them into the correct position
mediately before firing

Fuel dump pipe
Fuel dump pipes are located between
flaps and ailerons on both wings

Ailerons
The ailerons are mechanically-operated
and unboosted. Travel is 16° up and 14°
down, and they shift to a 10° up position
when the gust control is selected.

Pressure holes
Holes in each end of the superpod allow
free passage of air, so that pressure
differential does not build up in the pod
as the aircraft gains altitude

Rear-view mirror
This is a convex mirror with wide-angle
field. It enables the pilot to see if fuel is
venting or if the aircraft is pulling a
contrail. Further mirrors are mounted on
the cockpit frame

Cockpit fan
Positioned by the pilot, the fan provides
not only comfort for pilots on 'low'
training missions where the helmet is
open, but also demists the canopy

Driftsight
Underneath the cockpit, a small glass
bubble contains the optics for the
driftsight. This gives the pilot an optical
cockpit display of the area beneath the
aircraft.

Nose section
The nose section is detachable, allowing
the quick change of various sensor fits.
Among these is a more bulbous section
which is believed to contain the ASARS
radar

ot head
o pitot heads under the nose supply
a to the flight instruments

Fuel vent
Fuel is vented through an outlet at the top of the fin

Powerplant
The powerplant of the TR-1A and U-2R is the Pratt & Whitney J75-P-13B, which is manufactured and maintained to low tolerances. The aircraft uses high-flashpoint JP-7 fuel for most operations, but can burn everyday JP-4 or JP-5 for low-altitude missions if required

Airbrake
Employed during descent, circuit operations and landing, the airbrake is a simple hydraulically-actuated unit located on each side of the rear fuselage

Communications aerial
The main communications aerial is supported by a blade aerial. This is a feature common to all current TR-1s and U-2Rs

Q-bay
Immediately behind the cockpit is a large pressurized bay for sensor carriage, with hatches in both the dorsal and ventral positions. Many of the sensor loads can be palletized for swift changes between missions. Some optical sensor fits dictate an extension to the bottom hatch with optically-flat panes

Ej
A ca
is e
le
wh
im

Main undercarriage
The twin-wheel main unit retracts forward, with simple doors enclosing the unit. A powerful landing light is mounted on the central strut

E-bay
Immediately behind the Q-bay, and in front of the main undercarriage unit is situated a small sensor-carrying bay of limited volume and weight capacity

Intake
The bifurcated intake is optimized for high-altitude flight, and is manufactured to a high standard to avoid surface anomalies. A boundary layer bleed is located between the intake and the fuselage

Portable air supply
To avoid discomfort while away from the aircraft (the suit can get extremely hot) a portable ventilation unit is carried. When the pilot is seated in the cockpit this is disconnected and the pilot plugs in to the aircraft's air system

S-1010B suit
This full-pressure suit is standard issue to U-2R, TR-1 and SR-71 pilots. Novel features include 'capstan' wrist joints which allow rotational movement. The pilot climbs into the suit from the rear

Pi
Tv
da

Lockheed U-2 and TR-1 variants

U-2A: initial version for CIA and USAF with 4763-kg (10,500-lb) J57-P-37 or 5080-kg (11,200-lb) J57-P-37A turbojet
WU-2A: U-2A used for HASP (High Altitude Sampling Program) with a forward-facing scoop on the port side of the fuselage under the equipment bay
U-2B: U-2A version with 7167-kg (15,800-lb) J75-P-13 or 7711-kg (17,000-lb) J75-P-13B turbojet
U-2C: some new builds, some conversions with enlarged inlets for J75-P-13B, extended nose and dorsal canoe; most aircraft featured a 'sugar scoop' infra-red shield fitted to jetpipe; two aircraft current with NASA

WU-2C: possible early designation for U-2R
U-2CT: one U-2C and one U-2D converted with second cockpit for training duties; aircraft 56-6953 is still present at Beale although rarely flown
U-2D: U-2A conversions with Q-bay modified to take second seat or more systems
U-2E: U-2A and U-2B conversions with advanced ECM fits for CIA work
U-2F: U-2A conversions with inflight-refuelling receptacle; two aircraft later featured 'ram's horn' Sigint antennae on rear fuselage for use over Vietnam
U-2G: two U-2Cs fitted with arrester hook and other modifications for carrier trials
U-2J: possible designation for CIA-operated carrier-capable aircraft
U-2N: possible early designation for U-2R
U-2R: retaining only the powerplant and general layout of its predecessors, the U-2R is larger in all dimensions and carries a greater sensor payload

U-2EP-X: two U-2Rs on short loan to the US Navy for the Electronic Patrol Experiment, to test the U-2 as a long-range maritime patroller; these were distinguished by a slightly shorter nose and carried slipper pods that only projected forward of the leading edge; FLIR was among the equipment carried
ER-2: demilitarized TR-1 for NASA earth resources research
TR-1: possible early designation applied to U-2Rs while testing TR-1A systems
TR-1A: almost identical to U-2R, the TR-1 differs in secondary systems only; optimized for tactical surveillance, the FY80 TR-1 production can be distinguished from early FY68 U-2Rs by having a dorsal blade antenna instead of a spike, although most current U-2Rs have been retrofitted with the blade

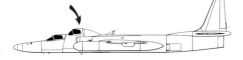

TR-1B: trainer version of TR-1/U-2R with second cockpit with raised canopy in Q-bay area

This aircraft is one of two loaned to the US Navy for the EP-X programme. The nose section is noticeably shorter, while the wing pod is of the 'slipper' variety, not projecting beyond the trailing edge.

TR-1 recognition features

Wing has zero dihedral, but flexes considerably up or down under load, especially on ground

Zero-track main landing gear

'Pogo' outrigger wheels a roughly mid-span for use ground operations

Most aircraft carry giant 'superpods' under the wings

Extremely long slender wings, with both leading- and trailing-edge taper

Wingtips have RHAW system antennas in cylindrical fairings, under which is a skid for landing

Starboard wing has prominent RHAW system antenna at roughly mid-span

Tall, upright vertical tail su

Long, slim cigar-shaped fuselage

Large airbrakes on sides of rea fuselage

Lockheed TR-1/U-2R cutaway drawing key

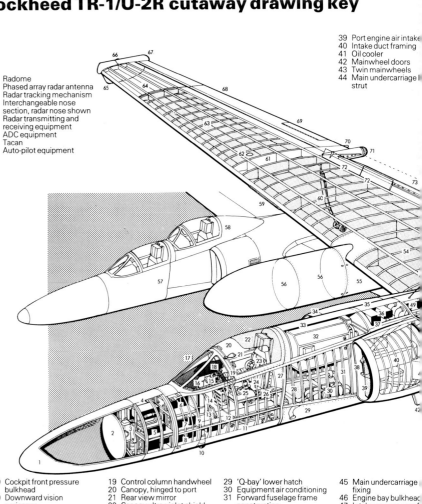

1 Radome
2 Phased array radar antenna
3 Radar tracking mechanism
4 Interchangeable nose section, radar nose shown
5 Radar transmitting and receiving equipment
6 ADC equipment
7 Tacan
8 Auto-pilot equipment

39 Port engine air intake
40 Intake duct framing
41 Oil cooler
42 Mainwheel doors
43 Twin mainwheels
44 Main undercarriage l strut

9 Cockpit front pressure bulkhead
10 Downward vision periscope
11 Underfloor control linkages
12 Cockpit pressure floor
13 Rudder pedals
14 Circuit breaker panel
15 Instrument panel
16 Instrument panel shroud
17 Windscreen panels
18 Periscope display

19 Control column handwheel
20 Canopy, hinged to port
21 Rear view mirror
22 Canopy ultra-violet shield
23 Cockpit air circulation fan
24 Pilot's ejector seat
25 Engine throttle lever
26 Side console panel
27 Cockpit rear pressure bulkhead
28 'Q-bay' mission equipment space

29 'Q-bay' lower hatch
30 Equipment air conditioning
31 Forward fuselage frame construction
32 Inertial navigation system
33 'Q-bay' upper hatch
34 Starboard air intake
35 'E-bay' hatch
36 UHF equipment
37 Boundary layer air duct
38 Air conditioning system ram air intake

45 Main undercarriage fixing
46 Engine bay bulkhead
47 Intake compressor f
48 Fuselage upper long
49 Liquid oxygen conve
50 Cockpit air condition plant
51 Heat exchanger air o
52 UHF aerial
53 Inner wing tank fuel cap

ecification: Lockheed TR-1A

gs

	31.39 m	(103 ft 0 in)
	92.90 m²	(1,000 sq ft)
t ratio	10.6:1	

elage and tail unit

mmodation	pilot seated on an ejector seat	
n overall	19.13 m	(62 ft 9 in)
t overall	4.88 m	(16 ft 0 in)

ding gear

rack retractable bicycle type with forward-retracting
wheel forward unit and steerable forward-retracting
wheel tail unit; one twin-wheel free-castoring and jettisonable
ger unit at mid-span under each wing

ights

	7031 kg	(15,500 lb)
num take-off	18733 kg	(41,300 lb)
r weight	1361 kg	(3,000 lb)
apacity	4448 litres	(1,175 US gal)
ad	3469 kg	(7,649 lb)

werplant

ratt & Whitney J75-P-13B non-afterburning turbojet

	7711 kg	(17,000 lb)

Performance

Maximum speed at		
70,000 ft (21335 m)	373 kts; 692 km/h	(430 mph)
Limiting Mach number	0.8	
Service ceiling	80,000 ft	(24385 m)
Maximum range	10058 km	(6,250 miles)
Initial climb rate about	5,000 ft	(1525 m) per minute
Climb to 65,000 ft		
(19810 m)	35 minutes	
g limits in clean		
configuration	−1.5/+3	
Take-off distance about	200 m	(650 ft)
Landing run about	760 m	(2,500 ft)

Ceiling

- MiG-25R 'Foxbat-D' 85,580 ft E
- Lockheed SR-71A 85,000 ft +
- Lockheed TR-1A 80,000 ft
- MiG-25 'Foxbat-A' 80,000 ft E
- Su-21 'Flagon' 65,600 ft E
- Canberra PR.Mk 9 57,000 ft +

Speed at high altitude

- Lockheed SR-71A Mach 3.5
- MiG-25R 'Foxbat-D' Mach 3.2 E
- MiG-25 'Foxbat-A' Mach 2.83 E
- Sukhoi Su-21 'Flagon' Mach 2.1 E
- Canberra PR.Mk 9 Mach 0.82
- Lockheed TR-1A Mach 0.7 E

Range

- Lockheed TR-1A 10058 km
- Canberra PR.Mk 9 7240 km
- Lockheed SR-71A 5300 km
- MiG-25 'Foxbat-A' 2900 km E
- MiG-25R 'Foxbat-D' 2500 km E
- Sukhoi Su-21 'Flagon' 1500 km E

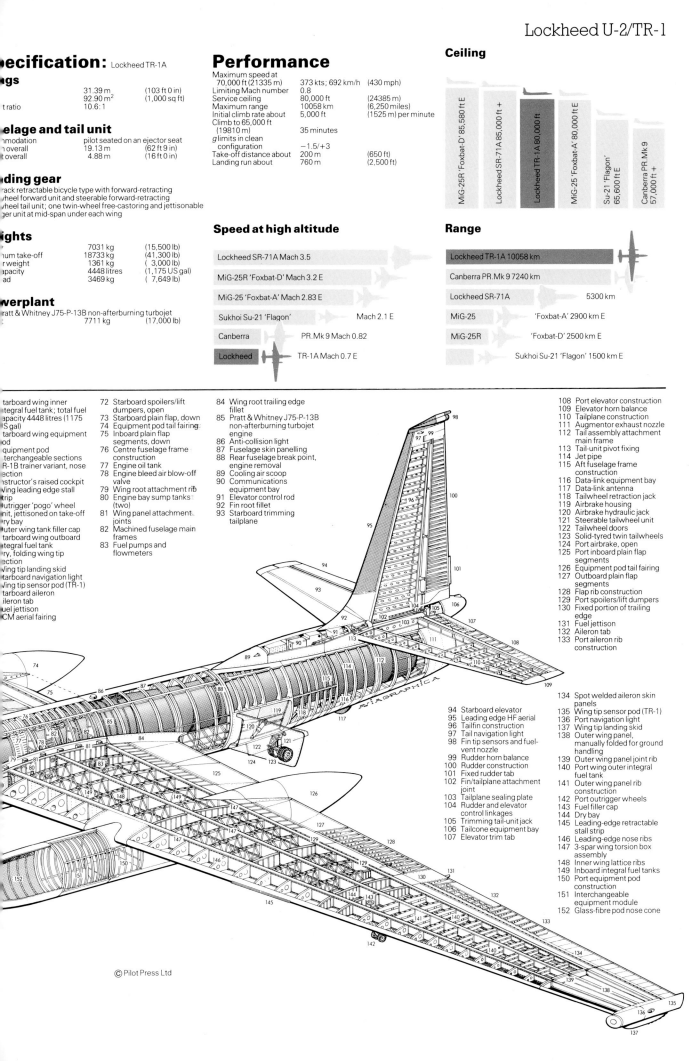

tarboard wing inner
ntegral fuel tank; total fuel
apacity 4448 litres (1175
S gal)
tarboard wing equipment
od
quipment pod
nterchangeable sections
R-1B trainer variant, nose
ection
nstructor's raised cockpit
Wing leading edge stall
trip
utrigger 'pogo' wheel
nit, jettisoned on take-off
ry bay
uter wing tank filler cap
tarboard wing outboard
ntegral fuel tank
ry, folding wing tip
ection
Wing tip landing skid
tarboard navigation light
Wing tip sensor pod (TR-1)
tarboard aileron
ileron tab
uel jettison
CM aerial fairing

72 Starboard spoilers/lift dumpers, open
73 Starboard plain flap, down
74 Equipment pod tail fairing
75 Inboard plain flap segments, down
76 Centre fuselage frame construction
77 Engine oil tank
78 Engine bleed air blow-off valve
79 Wing root attachment rib
80 Engine bay sump tanks (two)
81 Wing panel attachment joints
82 Machined fuselage main frames
83 Fuel pumps and flowmeters
84 Wing root trailing edge fillet
85 Pratt & Whitney J75-P-13B non-afterburning turbojet engine
86 Anti-collision light
87 Fuselage skin panelling
88 Rear fuselage break point, engine removal
89 Cooling air scoop
90 Communications equipment bay
91 Elevator control rod
92 Fin root fillet
93 Starboard trimming tailplane
94 Starboard elevator
95 Leading edge HF aerial
96 Tailfin construction
97 Tail navigation light
98 Fin tip sensors and fuel-vent nozzle
99 Rudder horn balance
100 Rudder construction
101 Fixed rudder tab
102 Fin/tailplane attachment joint
103 Tailplane sealing plate
104 Rudder and elevator control linkages
105 Trimming tail-unit jack
106 Tailcone equipment bay
107 Elevator trim tab
108 Port elevator construction
109 Elevator horn balance
110 Tailplane construction
111 Augmentor exhaust nozzle
112 Tail assembly attachment main frame
113 Tail-unit pivot fixing
114 Jet pipe
115 Aft fuselage frame construction
116 Data-link equipment bay
117 Data-link antenna
118 Tailwheel retraction jack
119 Airbrake housing
120 Airbrake hydraulic jack
121 Steerable tailwheel unit
122 Tailwheel doors
123 Solid-tyred twin tailwheels
124 Port airbrake, open
125 Port inboard plain flap segments
126 Equipment pod tail fairing
127 Outboard plain flap segments
128 Flap rib construction
129 Port spoilers/lift dumpers
130 Fixed portion of trailing edge
131 Fuel jettison
132 Aileron tab
133 Port aileron rib construction
134 Spot welded aileron skin panels
135 Wing tip sensor pod (TR-1)
136 Port navigation light
137 Wing tip landing skid
138 Outer wing panel, manually folded for ground handling
139 Outer wing panel joint rib
140 Port wing outer integral fuel tank
141 Outer wing panel rib construction
142 Port outrigger wheels
143 Fuel filler cap
144 Dry bay
145 Leading-edge retractable stall strip
146 Leading-edge nose ribs
147 3-spar wing torsion box assembly
148 Inner wing lattice ribs
149 Inboard integral fuel tanks
150 Port equipment pod construction
151 Interchangeable equipment module
152 Glass-fibre pod nose cone

The NORTHROP B-2

Northrop B-2: Strategy by Stealth

Northrop and the US Air Force caused something of a sensation in November 1988 when the first example of the B-2 Advanced Technology Bomber was rolled out at Palmdale. Since then the space-age bomber has been embarking on a successful flight test programme, although politicians and military commanders alike have been reviewing its increasingly threatened future.

r the past 30 years, the strategic defence of e United States has relied on the Triad con- pt with land-based strategic bombers, d-based intercontinental missiles, and bmarine-launched ballistic missiles. hile the land-based and submarine- nched components have been moder- ed several times since then, the strategic mber component has been allowed to indle. Today it is composed of only 21 uadrons, 12 with elderly Boeing B-52Gs d B-52Hs, six with B-1Bs (including a ining squadron), and three with FB-111As hich are being transferred to Tactical Air mmand), whereas in 1960 Strategic Air mmand fielded 108 bombardment squad- s, 71 with B-47s, 36 with B-52s, and one th B-58s.

For many years following curtailment of 58 production and outright cancellation of e B-70, the Strategic Air Command was left thout immediate replacement for its B-47E edium bombers, which were phased out in ly 1966, and for its B-52 heavy bombers, ich in 1991, 36 years after their entry into

service, remain SAC's most numerous bomber. As a temporary palliative until a new strategic bomber could be put into ser- vice, in 1965 the Air Force ordered enough FB-111As to equip two wings. However, the long gestation of the new bomber, which went through many iterations from the Sub- sonic Low Altitude Bomber (SLAB) in 1961, to the Extended Range Strike Aircraft (ERSA) in 1963, the Advanced Manned Precision Strategic Aircraft (AMPSA) in 1964, and the Advanced Manned Strategic Aircraft (AMSA) in the 1965-69 period, coupled with budgetary restrictions (particularly after the United States became embroiled in the South East Asia War) and the belief among many military planners that intercontinental missiles had rendered manned bombers obsolete, threatened their future with the USAF. At last, however, development of the North American Rockwell B-1A was authori- sed in June 1970.

Work on the B-1A progressed slowly as the war in South East Asia continued to drain funds and as the usefulness of manned

bombers was being bitterly debated even after the successful employment of B-52s in the closing stage of that war. In particular, many high-level strategists felt that bombers would not be able to penetrate heavily defended areas unless they could do so at minimal altitude in order to avoid detection until the very last moment. This concept eventually prevailed and in June 1977 Presi- dent Carter terminated further work on the B-1A while new alternatives were being ex- plored. While the respective merits of several alternatives were debated relatively openly, work was initiated in great secrecy on another strategic aircraft which was to rely on new technical developments,

Lifting off from the Palmdale, California, runway in front of a gallery of company employees and press, the first B-2 (82-1066) takes to the air for the first time, on 17 July 1982. The first flight ended at nearby Edwards AFB, where the main tests are being undertaken.

Powerplant
Chosen for their excellent fuel consumption, thrust/weight ratio and reliability, the four General Electric F118-GE-100 turbofans are non-afterburning developments of the F110 that powers the F-16. Each produces in the order of 8620 kg (19,000 lb) thrust for a full-weight take-off

Armament
Weapons are carried in two side-by-side bays in the central fuselage body. Each bay can accommodate a Common Strategic Rotary Launcher, which in turn can carry eight free-fall nuclear weapons (B61 or B83) or eight SRAM nuclear missiles

Test equipment
Mounted on the rear of the prototype is a rig for towing air data sensors on the end of a long cable. These measure airflow behind the aircraft, monitoring vortices

Cockpit
At present the B-2 is flown by a crew of two, both facing forward and sitting on ACES II ejection seats, these ejecting upwards through frangible roof panels. Behind on the starboard side is a frangible panel for a third seat, which may be fitted at a later date if it is decided that the workload is too much for two crew members

Crew
The B-2 breaks with tradition in having the right-hand seat Weapons System Officer as the aircraft commander, while the left-hand seat handling pilot is subordinate. This reflects the high-tech nature of the aircraft's nav/attack systems

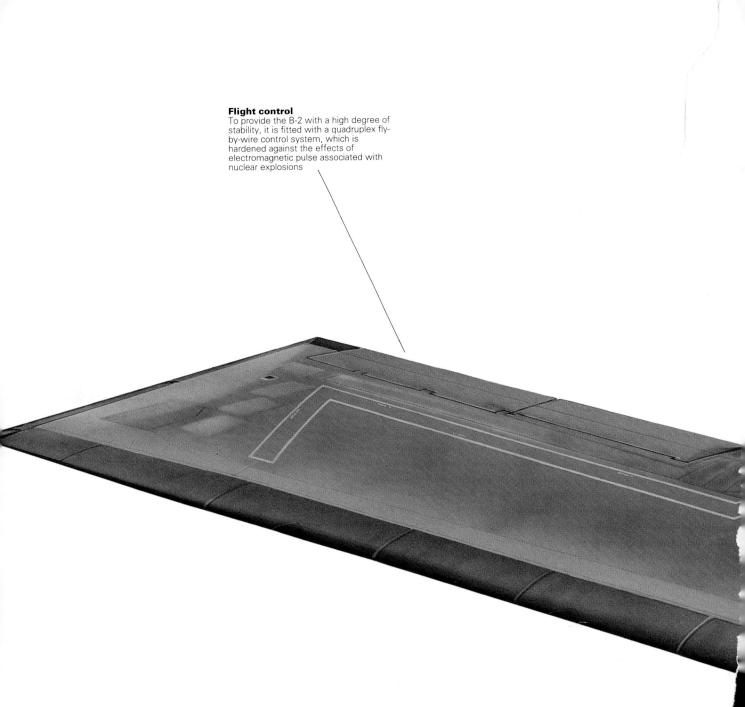

Flight control
To provide the B-2 with a high degree of stability, it is fitted with a quadruplex fly-by-wire control system, which is hardened against the effects of electromagnetic pulse associated with nuclear explosions

Northrop B-2A Advanced Technology Bomber
82-1066
Air Force Flight Test Center
Edwards AFB, California

The 3rd, 4th and 5th B-2s on the Palmdale assembly line, the delicate surface protected from engineers' shoes by large numbers of mats. Sophisticated computer technology allows the B-2 to be built to much finer tolerances than any previous generation of aircraft.

mainly in the area of stealth or 'low observables' (LO) technology, to reach target areas with relative impunity.

Funded as a 'black' programme (i.e. with expenditures of funds not revealed to taxpayers and not subject to review by Representatives and Senators except members of specially cleared committees of the House and the Senate), work on the Advanced Technology Bomber (ATB) was initiated in 1978 and eventually led to a design competition pitting a Northrop/

Boeing team against one from Lockheed and Rockwell. Notwithstanding Lockheed's greater experience with stealth technology – the A-12/SR-71 first flown in 1962 having been the first aircraft to incorporate many stealth features in its design, and the XST (Experimental Stealth Technology) prototype of the F-117 fighter having flown in 1977 – the Air Force selected the Northrop/Boeing team to proceed with the development of the ATB, and in November 1981 Northrop became the prime ATB contractor.

Bomber revelation

Although the existence of the ATB programme had first been revealed before Northrop was selected to lead the development of this highly sophisticated aircraft, no

Naturally the B-2 employs a state-of-the-art cockpit, with three large CRT displays per crew member presenting virtually all of the information they are likely to need in flight. The central fighter-style stick says much about the aircraft's performance and agility.

reliable information was allowed to lea until April 1988, when the Air Force release what turned out to be a surprisingly accurat artist's rendering, in marked contrast wit the considerable amount of disinformatio regarding the F-19/F-117 which wa distributed through various sources. Indeed photographs which became available whe the prototype of the Northrop B-2 wa publicly unveiled at Palmdale, California, o 22 November 1988, confirmed it to be a fou engined aircraft of flying wing configuratio Since then, many more photographs hav been released and the Air Force and Nortl rop have provided quite a bit of relatively i nocuous information. Notwithstanding th apparent free flow of data, hard facts remai difficult to come by.

Flying wing

The supercritical, multi-spar flying wir has an acute angle of sweepback on the lead ing edge and sharply pointed tips resultir from a change from 55 degrees of forwai sweep to 55 degrees of aft sweep. The trailir edge has a double M shape in plan and is fi ted with four-section control surfaces cor sisting of a split drag rudder and an elevon c each outboard panel and two elevons on tl next inboard panel on each side, all of whic are operated by means of a quadruple-r dundant flight control system. The inboar panels on both sides of a blended fuselage a substantially deeper and have greatly i creased chord, resulting in an almost co stant thickness-to-chord ratio.

Power is provided by four General Electr F118-GE-100 non-afterburning turbofar each with a take-off thrust of approximate 8620 kg (19,000 lb), mounted in pairs insic the wing on each side of the fuselage in suc a manner that their compressor fac

With outboard 'drag rudders' deployed to ac as airbrakes, the B-2 approaches the main runway at Edwards AFB. The markings underneath are the runways laid out on Rogers Dry Lake, part of the vast range complex.

Whereas the length of the B-2 is tiny for an aircraft of its weight, the span is enormous, as is graphically illustrated by this shot while plugged in to a KC-10 during trials. The cable trailing from the aircraft tows air data sensors for test results.

has enabled Northrop to (1) develop the world's first 'three-dimensional computing capability' combining computer-aided design and computer-aided manufacturing; (2) achieve tight manufacturing tolerances as required to obtain low-observable characterists; (3) build the prototype on production tooling; and (4) boost manufacturing productivity by a factor of 60-to-1. Moreover, without the use of computer-assisted fly-by-wire (FBW) flight controls, the B-2 would have been likely to suffer from the same lack of stability which made its piston-powered B-35 and jet-powered RB-49 forebears poor bombing and reconnaissance platforms, and caused the cancellation of these two programmes. Fortunately, the computer-assisted FBW controls appear to have solved the problem as the B-2 has proven very stable during the initial flight validation phase.

Should the B-2 be cancelled, a not unlikely occurrence in early 1991, its supporters and those favouring the Strategic Defense Initiative (SDI) ought to take comfort in the knowledge that the threat of parallel development of both the B-2 and the SDI may well have been the proverbial straw breaking the camel's back. The need to invest considerable funds in the de-velopment of defences against these two programmes is likely to have proven too much for the Soviet economy, thus contributing to the adoption of *Perestroika*.

Cruising over the Mojave desert on its first flight, the B-2 has its auxiliary engine intakes open and drag rudders partially deployed. The undercarriage is basically that of the Boeing 767 airliner.

The LOCKHEED F-117

COL TONY TOLIN

RESCUE

SSGT ROBERT EARBY
SSGT DAVE STRAWN
SGT FRANK FATA
SRA GREG KIRR

Lockheed F-117: the `black` programme

Making a radical departure in aircraft design, the F-117 'stealth' fighter proved its undoubted military value in the opening phases of the air war over Iraq. Undetected by enemy radar, it carried out pinpoint bombing raids against key Iraqi installations without loss.

Without doubt the most talked about aircraft of the late 20th Century, the Lockheed F-117A 'stealth' fighter, represents one of the best-kept military secrets in the Western world, having been in operation for five years before it was revealed to the public. It also represented another major coup for the secretive yet glamorous Advanced Development Projects division of Lockheed-California, now known as the Lockheed Advanced Development Company but universally called the 'Skunk Works'.

1967 saw the first inkling of what was going on in the Skunk Works when reports appeared of the development of an aircraft that was all but invisible to radar. In fact, this development had been going on for some time, the need for 'stealth' or low-observables (LO) technology having been heightened by the growing successes of radar-guided surface-to-air mis-

siles as demonstrated in the December 1972 'Linebacker II' raids on North Vietnam, and the October 1973 Yom Kippur war in the Middle East. Not that LO technology was new, for research into radar-absorbent material (RAM), radar-defeating meshes and aircraft shape (notably the Skunk Works' own SR-71) had been around since the 1950s.

However, in 1975 Skunk Works engineers began work on a concept known as faceting, the use of many carefully-arranged flat surfaces to produce a very weak and diffuse radar return. This showed great promise, and the dramatic increase in computing power in this period allowed a much clearer path through the three-dimensional labyrinth of positioning the surfaces so as to present minimum returns, while still retaining the necessary shape of a flying machine.

Although other companies were also

investigating LO technology, Lockheed's faceting proved sufficiently promising to pursue further. DARPA (Defense Advanced Research Projects Agency) issued a contract for two strike fighter demonstrators in early 1977 under the codename 'Have Blue', although this project was soon turned over to the US Air Force, becoming a 'black' (i.e. heavily classified) programme. Both prototypes, believed to be designated XST (eXperimental Stealth, Tactical), were hurriedly built at Burbank, California, and transported to Groom Dry Lake in Nevada, a remote and secure test site originally used by Lockheed for its U-2 and A-12 testing. Early in 1978, company pilot Bill Park took the first aircraft aloft. The second followed a couple of months later, Park being joined by Lieutenant Colonel Ken Dyson on the flight tests.

The 'Have Blue' aircraft were smaller than the F-117, and had inward-canted fins. Power came from a pair of General Electric J85 turbojets. Both aircraft were lost, the first in May 1978 with Park at the controls and the second in 1980 piloted by Dyson. Neither crash was fatal. Only after the F-117 was made public were the two pilots officially recognised for their vital

A strange shape in a barren landscape – the 37th TFW's F-117 at Tonopah. Notable features are the aircraft serial presented on the nosewheel strut, and the grille covering the air intake. The latter is considerably finer than the wavelengths of most radars, and consequently appears as a solid surface. Any radar energy penetrating the mesh is trapped by radar-absorbent material in the intake.

contributions to this major advance in aviation technology.

After only a season's flying, 'Have Blue' demonstrated extraordinary LO properties, sufficient to warrant the development of a full-scale service fighter. In November 1978 the 'Senior Trend' programme was launched, with Lockheed facing little competition from other manufacturers thanks to its 'Have Blue' experience.

Unencumbered by the normal political and technical machinations that afflict 'public' programmes thanks to its 'black' status, and energised by the small, enthusiastic and 'go-ahead' team assembled around Skunk Works boss Ben Rich, 'Senior Trend' made rapid progress. Five full-scale development pre-production aircraft were built, the first of which took to the air at Groom Lake on 18 July 1981 in the experienced hands of Hal Farley. 'Senior Trend' aircraft were designated F-117A, although all but the most informed speculations throughout the 'black' period revolved around the 'F-19' designation. Like all but the last few F-117As, the aircraft was transported to Groom Lake before final assembly and first flight.

Highly secretive types

A word about the designation: the US Air Force has never explained how the aircraft was assigned F-117, or why the fighter series leapfrogged F-19. One plausible (and attractive) theory for the former is that the USAF's MiG squadron, also based in the Nevada desert, used the F-112-F-116 designations for its Soviet equipment, and that F-117 was a logical follow-on for these highly secretive types. As for 'F-19', it suited the US Air Force to leave the number unaccounted for as it

The date: 10 November 1988; the place: Pentagon briefing room. Assistant Secretary of Defense for Public Affairs J. Daniel Howard finally ends 12 years of speculation and rumour by announcing the existence of the Lockheed F-117A and displaying this misleading photograph.

could quite truthfully deny the existence of any such aircraft! Although many nicknames have been attributed to the type, the pilots simply call it the 'Black Jet'.

In preparation for the service entry of the F-117A, the 4450th Tactical Group was established in 1980, receiving Vought A-7D Corsair IIs and ostensibly based at Nellis AFB, Nevada, on the outskirts of Las Vegas; 'LV' tailcodes were worn to reflect the unit's locality. The choice of the A-7 was deliberate, for its high subsonic performance, thrust-weight ratio, handling, manoeuvrability and low-level attack role all approximated to some degree to those of the F-117. This allowed it to operate as a daylight trainer, while also maintaining a 'cover' role for the unit's true purposes.

In October 1983 the 4450th Tactical Group was declared operational, its 18 A-7Ds being joined by 10-12 F-117As. By this time the unit had moved from Groom Lake to the northwest corner of the vast Nellis ranges to take up residence at Tonopah Test Range. Groom Lake continued in its primary role as the Air Force's most classified flight test centre.

Situated some 40 miles to the southeast of the old mining town of Tonopah, the Test Range airfield was a newly-constructed base situated on Cactus Flat, shielded by the Cactus and Karwich mountain ranges and so remote that even its circuit is totally invisible from any public highway. Only one metalled, heavily-guarded road leads from Tonopah, although when daylight operations began, hardy photographers showed that it was possible to get close to the base and its approach, but only if one was prepared to endure 30-odd miles of spine-jarring desert track.

Until the public unveiling of the F-117A, the aircraft operated exclusively at night in the interests of security. Chartered Boeing 727s of Key Air shuttled the crews and base personnel from Nellis, most staying through the weekdays at Tonopah. Adjusting the body clock to a nocturnal way of life was a major difficulty for F-117 personnel. Fatigue is likely to have caused the crashes of two F-117s, the first killing Major Ross E. Mulhare on 11 July 1986 near Bakersfield, California, and the second claiming the life of Major Michael C. Stewart on 14 October 1987. As far as is known, these were the only F-117A losses recorded by late 1990.

A misleading photograph

During the early career of the world's first operational 'stealth' fighter, it was twice nearly called upon to go into action, including (allegedly) the April 1986 raid on Libya. Whether operational circumstances or security risks precluded its use is not known.

Perhaps it was the second crash, or the increasing demands on training caused by the growing number of aircraft that forced the Pentagon into realising that daylight operations would have to be

Pilot, crew chiefs and security police pose in front of a 415th TFS, 37th TFW F-117A at Nellis AFB, Nevada. This was one of two aircraft that took part in the machine's public unveiling on 10 April 1990.

undertaken. Whatever, on 10 November 1988 a Pentagon spokesman finally admitted to the world the existence of the 'stealth' fighter, holding aloft a blurred and misleading photograph of the F-117A. This immediately allowed daylight operations to be undertaken, and reports of up to 10 F-117s in trail formation were reported from the Mojave desert and other points in the American Southwest. The first unofficial photographs filtered through, revealing the shape and equipment of the aircraft far better than the single official USAF picture.

No longer requiring a cover story or a daylight trainer, the 4450th TG relinquished its A-7Ds to other duties, receiving six Northrop AT-38B Talons in their place for fighter orientation and chase duties. All prospective F-117 pilots have long experience in jets and are graded 'above average'. Most have flown strike/attack types such as the A-7, A-10, F-4 and

This shot of the 'Black Jet' in flight highlights the faceting employed in its design. The aircraft possesses virtually no curved surfaces, including the wings and tail. Although its thrust-weight ratio cannot sustain high-g manoeuvring, the F-117 is considerably more agile than was once though, with an especially creditable roll rate.

Powerplant
Off-the-shelf engines were chosen for the F-117 on time and cost grounds, the chosen powerplant being the General Electric F404-FD2 non-afterburning low-bypass ratio turbofan, two of which are mounted side-by-side in the central fuselage

...ust
...atypus' exhaust is invisible from ...eath, and consists of a long ...gular opening with guide vanes. ...haust produces a wide, shallow ...of hot gases, which rapidly mix ...e cool air. Heat-dissipating ...c tiles are incorporated into the ...edge of the exhaust to further ...nfra-red signature

...nents
...ross-section can be considerably ...d if all the facets and edges ...n to as few alignments as ...e. Consequently many edges of ...7's structure follow similar ...nts

Brake parachute
Landing and take-off speeds of the F-117 are high due to its aerodynamic shape. A brake parachute is housed in the rear fuselage between the tails to slow the aircraft

Fins
The butterfly fins are pivoted at the bottom and provide yaw control only, all pitch and roll functions being entrusted to the wing trailing edge elevons. The fins show obvious signs of faceting as opposed to traditional camber

'Hot spots'
Radar energy is reflected best by inside corners, so where these are unavoidable, they are placed in a position that is not important when 'viewed' by radar. Consequently, the radar 'hot spots' between wings, tail and centrebody face to the rear

RAM
Radar absorbent material (RAM) covers the entire skin of the aircraft, and constantly requires attention to be kept in top condition. Originally it was supplied in cumbersome flexible sheets, but is now available as a spray, which provides better and easier coverage. RAM putty and tape can be used for localised 'finishing off'

Surface
The F-117A relies on 'faceting' to reduce its radar cross-section. This involves the use of many flat surfaces over the entire aircraft, all reflecting a small amount of radar energy in many different directions. This produces a diffuse 'sparkling' effect on radar screens, shielding the F-117s somewhere within. Even the F-117's wings employ faceting, rather than a smooth camber

Fin markings
Aircraft '790' wears markings for the 416th TFS aircraft maintenance unit, in addition to the 'TR' tailcodes (for Tonopah Range) of the 37th TFW. The outlined badge is that of Tactical Air Command

Lockheed F-117A
416th Tactical Fighter Squadron 'Ghostriders'
37th Tactical Fighter Wing
12th Air Force, Tactical Air Command
US Air Force
Tonopah Test Range, Nevada

Exha
The 'p
under
rectar
The e
plume
with t
ceram
trailir
redu

Alig
Rada
redu
confc
poss
the F
align

F-111. No F-117 trainer has been produced, pilots receiving thorough type conversion in a simulator before progressing to a first F-117 sortie, a local training hop escorted by an experienced F-117 pilot in a T-38.

Two squadrons were incorporated in the 4450th TG, the 'Grim Reapers' and the 'Nightstalkers'. In October 1989 a third suadron was added when the 4450th TG officially redesignated as the 37th Tactical Fighter Wing. This wing number had previously been assigned to an F-4E/G Phantom 'Wild Weasel' unit at George AFB, California, which amalgamated with the co-located 35th Tactical Training Wing to become the 35th TFW, carrying the 37th's old 'WW' tailcode.

Meanwhile, the new 37th adopted the 'TR' code for Tonopah Range, and consisted of the 415th Tactical Fighter Squadron 'Nightstalkers', 416th Tactical Fighter Squadron 'Ghostriders', and the 417th Tactical Fighter Training Squadron 'Bandits'. On 19 December 1989, the F-117A went into battle for the first time during Operation 'Just Cause', the invasion of Panama by US forces.

An official debut

With the aircraft made public, there was little security risk involved in using it operationally, and the chance to pit it against hostile defences as a test in battle was taken. Only one strike was undertaken, aimed at a field alongside a Panamanian barracks at Rio Hato. In all, six aircraft launched from Tonopah, although it is thought only two carried out the attack, the others having their missions cancelled mid-flight. Flying non-stop to and from their Nevada base with refuelling support, the F-117s dropped 2000 lb laser-

The F-117 has a very high landing speed, and a brake parachute is always deployed on landing to reduce the run. It is mounted in a compartment between the butterfly fins.

guided bombs into the field to cause confusion among the ground forces, paving the way for an airborne assault by Rangers.

Despite the earlier unveiling of the aircraft, and its use in Panama, it was not until 21 April 1990 that it made its official debut: a pair of F-117s arriving at Nellis AFB from Tonopah before a large crowd of press, flying a pass along the runway before landing and taxiing in for closer inspection. Subsequently, F-117s have made appearances at selected airshows, notably Andrews AFB and the Experimental Aircraft Association's convention at Oshkosh, Wisconsin. Aircraft are believed to have been deployed to Europe (possibly Spangdahlem AB, West Germany, in the early summer of 1990).

Scheduled appearances at shows in the second half of the year, including a prestigious international debut at Farnborough in England, were curtailed by world events. As part of the US response to the invasion of Kuwait by Iraq, 22 F-117s left Tonopah on 19 August in transit to Langley AFB, Virginia, with photographers being allowed on board the 9th SRW KC-135Q tankers to record the deployment. Twenty of the aircraft left Langley with KC-10 support for the non-stop flight to Saudi Arabia. Two of the aircraft stopped briefly at RAF Alconbury en route. Rumours suggested that smaller deployments were already in-theatre perhaps in Turkey.

faceted surfaces. RAM (radar absorbent material) is then applied, originally in the form of sheets but now available in a spray. This material coating needs constant attention to maintain its effectiveness.

While the shape of the aircraft and the RAM confer the bulk of the LO properties on the type, these are only effective if the facets are left clear of excrescences. The skin of operational F-117s is virtually free from any additional bulges or aerial, all the necessary equipment being contained within or under the skin. Wide, shallow exhausts, shielded from beneath and lined with ceramic tiles, present a tiny infra-red source. Defence against passive sensors involves the lack of emissions during a sortie – no radar or radio being used.

Primary control surfaces

A quadruple-redundant fly-by-wire system controls the aircraft and provides artificial stability. The problems of combining a LO shape with a flyable machine meant that FBW was a pre-requisite. Most aviation engineers believe that a practical 'stealth' aircraft with relaxed (natural) stability is virtually impossible to design, so great are the demands of LO discipline. Instead of the usual vane sensors to provide air data for the FBW system, the F-117 has four probe accelerators, these proving easier to make 'stealthy' than the conventional sensors. Large elevons and

An F-117A in flight over the Sierra Nevada. Clearly visible are the 'platypus' exhausts forward of the wing trailing edge, separated by knife-edge blades and tipped with ceramic tiles in an effort to defeat infra-red sensors.

it to the target. Bore-sighted with the DLIR is a laser designator, which 'sparkles' the target shortly after bomb release, allowing the bomb's seeker head to detect the exact impact point, and direct the weapon accordingly. The DLIR continues to track and 'lase' the target even if the aircraft has initiated evasive manoeuvres after bomb release.

This equipment was derived from the 'Pave Tack' turret employed on the F-111F and demonstrated to great effect during the raid on Libya. Although LPI (Low Probability of Intercept) radar may be added to the F-117 at a later date, the FLIR/DLIR system provides the 'Black Jet'

with a system that is 'stealthy' and supremely accurate. Weapons with optical sensors use a similar system, but rely on contrast autotrackers to follow their path to the target. The accurate INS and the use of FLIR imagery allows the precision delivery of 'dumb' (unguided) ordnance.

Upgrades seem likely

In 1990, Lockheed held a ceremony marking the delivery of the last F-117A to the US Air Force. Only 20 had been ordered originally, but the number had risen to 59 by the time production ended. With constant deferrals of funding for follow-on aircraft, such as an Air Force version of the A-12 Avenger II being developed for the US Navy, the prospects are that the F-117A will remain the only tactical low-observable penetration platform in USAF service for many years to come.

Consequently, further development and equipment upgrades seem likely.

As far as the secretive base at Tonopah goes, its days are numbered. As part of a series of budget cuts, the USAF announced in January 1990 that the base would revert to the status of a divert airfield for aircraft taking part in exercises in the Nellis ranges. No longer could the immense cost of supplying a full wing on the remote facility by air be met. In 1992, the F-117s of the 37th TFW will make the move to Holloman AFB, New Mexico, thereby removing the last vestige of secrecy from a programme which became a household name due to its very 'blackness'.

Refuelling receptacle
Behind the cockpit is a refuelling receptacle for use with KC-10 and KC-135 tankers. The doors of this have serrated edges to maintain stealth properties by channelling radar energy around the doors

Structure
Aluminium alloys are the main materials used in the F-117's structure, although titanium is used around the engines. The basic structure is a complicated skeleton, to which are attached the facet panels

Refuelling light
Forming a small pyramid at the apex of the spine, this fairing contains a rearward-facing light which illuminates the refuelling receptacle for night refuelling

of the F-117's fuel is housed in
s above the weapon bays, which
e in the lower fuselage between
ngines

LT COL JERRY CARPENTER

RESCUE

ar reflector
on-operational sorties, the F-117A
es large radar reflectors to render it
e to civilian air traffic control radars.
e lights are also fitted for
etime' ops

Fairings
These fairings scabbed on the aircraft sides are believed to house radar augmentors for peacetime operations. Radar warning and ECM equipment is all housed internally to avoid breaking up the carefully-crafted low-observable shape

Unit badge
In peacetime, the F-117s carry the 37th TFW wing badge on the intake sides, depicting a hawk striking at night. This badge was worn previously when the F-117A unit was designated the 4450th Tactical Group

Cockpit
Owing to the shape of the fuselage, the heavily-framed canopy (with radar-defeating glass) makes visibility merely adequate, and poor to the rear and above. The cockpit is very roomy lower down, although headroom is cramped. The canopy is heavy and requires explosive bolts to jettison it during ejection

HUD
A standard head-up display is provided for the pilot, which presents him with basic air data and weapon system information, and superimposed FLIR imagery. In the cockpit console are standard multi-function displays either side of a large CRT screen

FLIR
In front of the cockpit is a forward-looking infra-red turret, covered with a radar-defeating mesh and able to rotate. With this dual field-of-view sensor, the pilot can acquire and track targets in night and adverse weather conditions

Control system
The F-117A is naturally unstable, so has a quadruple-redundant fly-by-wire control system. Four prominent probes supply air data for the system, each of square section with minute pyramidal tips to preserve the stealthiness of the aircraft

DLIR
When the target has been acquired by the FLIR, it can be locked-on by the pilot. The DLIR (downward-looking infra-red) mounted under the aircraft's nose then acquires it and continues to track it while the aircraft flies towards it. Incorporated in the DLIR turret is a boresighted laser, which designates the target for laser-guided bombs

Intakes
In order to shield the compressor blades from radar energy, the intakes are covered with a fine grille. To a radar this appears as a flat surface, although air can be freely admitted

Maverick
The AGM-65 Maverick missile is a highly-accurate air-to-surface missile that is a likely load for the F-117. Available in TV-, infra-red or laser-guided versions, the Maverick fires straight from a pylon, suggesting that the F-117 has pylons that extend from the weapon bays into the airstream for launch

Armament
No gun is fitted to the F-117A, and all weaponry is carried within two bays in the fuselage. A wide variety of bombs and missiles can be carried, the most likely being 'smart' laser- or optically-guided weapons

Undercarriage
The tricycle undercarriage retracts forwards, the mainwheels rotating through 90° during the retraction sequence to lie flat. For emergency stopping on brakeless landings the F-117A has an arrester hook under the rear fuselage

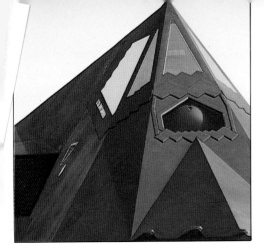

A nose close-up reveals the forward-looking infra-red turret that is the aircraft's principle low-level navigation and target acquisition sensor. A second IR unit is mounted underneath the nose, together with a bore-sighted laser, this unit controlling the attack following weapon release.

In terms of construction, the F-117 is like no other aircraft. The airframe is based on a central lifting body, to which are attached the wings and tails. Internal structure is necessarily complex to maintain integrity. A skeletal frame forms the main structure, to which are attached the rudders are the primary control surfaces, while simple inboard flaps provide extra lift at low speed.

Power is provided by a pair of non-afterburning General Electric F404 engines, a version of the powerplant employed by the F-18 Hornet. These provide sufficient thrust for the intended mission, but sustained high-g manoeuvring is more difficult due to the low thrust/weight ratio. Along with the 'platypus' exhaust, the most notable features of the propulsion system are the intakes screened by a fine grille. This has a mesh much smaller than the wavelengths of most radars, therefore appearing as 'her faceted surface. Ice is a major worry with such a fine mesh, and the grille is heated. Small lights in the cockpit allow the pilot to check each intake for icing.

Pinpoint accuracy

Weapons are housed in two bays between the engine, with fuel carried above. Precision guided weapons are the most usual load, especially laser-guided munitions. The F-117 is believed to be nuclear capable.

As shown by the operation over Panama, the forte of the F-117 is night attack with pinpoint accuracy. While the programme was completely under wraps, many commentators mentioned a reconnaissance role, but there appears little evidence of this. Similarly, the many rumours of quick and easy transportation by C-5 Galaxy appear unfounded, especially as inflight refuelling allows the type to self-deploy globally.

In fact, the F-117 is used only for attacks against what the US Air Force calls 'highly leveraged' targets, that is to say ones which have an importance out of proportion to the size. Classic examples of these are bridges, tunnels, rail junctions and operational command installations.

On an operational mission, the F-117's target would be pre-briefed. After penetrating hostile airspace undetected, the aircraft's highly accurate INS (Inertial Navigating System) would guide it towards the target. Using the FLIR (Forward-Looking Infra-Red) in a wide-scan mode, the pilot would search for the target. Once acquired, the FLIR can be switched to narrow-field, and lock-on can be achieved by aligning cross-hairs on the cockpit control system over the target. Using the contrast of the FLIR imagery, the target is locked into the weapons computer.

The FLIR is mounted above the sloping nose of the aircraft, so that as the target is neared, it falls below the look angle of the sensor. The locked-on image is transferred to another sensor, the DLIR (Downward-Looking Infra-Red) which continues to track the target, maintaining the target lock. If laser guided munitions are being used, these are released to fall into a 'basket' a theoretical cone above the target in which the weapon's controls can steer

Prominent on the dashboard of the F-117 is the HUD, which displays aircraft and weapons systems data, and presents an infra-red image for night-time flying. Note the heavy use of notching around the canopy to shield the joint, and the fine grille over the intake.

Due to its extraordinary shape, the F-117 handles like a delta-winged aircraft, flying nose-up at low speeds with speed bleeding off quickly in the turn. However, the shape has produced few handling problems, despite constant rumours concerning the erroneous 'Wobblin' Goblin' nickname.

The ADVANCED TACTICAL FIGHTER

Advanced Tactical Fighter – YF-22/23

F-15 Eagles may have acquitted themselves well in the Gulf War, but the simple fact remains that the aircraft is getting old, while Soviet fighters have begun to surpass Western types in terms of manoeuvrability and performance. To redress these problems and to maintain the US edge in systems technology, the US Air Force is looking to procure an Advanced Tactical Fighter. Here we analyse the two competing designs.

Experience in the Vietnam War graphically showed the shortcomings of US fighters when faced with manoeuvrable opposition of supposedly inferior capability. Such experience moved the fighter community back into the traditional world of agility and high performance, producing the F-15, F-16 and F-18. These three types formed the cornerstone of US fighter supremacy through the late 1970s and 1980s, but towards the end of this period, new Soviet fighters began entering service in numbers which threatened the dominance of American designs.

Although of the same generation as the US types, and in many respects inferior in terms of sophistication, the MiG-29 'Fulcrum' and Su-27 'Flanker' were ahead in basic performance and agility. Reports from the Soviet Union suggested that it would not be long before more advanced follow-on fighters were under development.

Thus the Advanced Tactical Fighter programme was born in the 1980s, chiefly as a means of providing a replacement for the F-15 Eagle, which appeared in 1975.

The three-edged chine along the forward fuselage is graphically shown in this view of the YF-23. The underslung intakes are necessary for high angle-of-attack performance, but the engines themselves are mounted above the wing line for minimum radar cross-section when viewed by radars from underneath.

Taxiing at Edwards AFB, the first Northrop/McDonnell Douglas YF-23 demonstrates the large control surfaces on the leading and trailing edges of the wing. The trough-like exhausts emit gases over a wide area, considerably cooling the exhaust and reducing infra-red cross-section.

Lockheed's second YF-22 launches from Palmdale on its first flight. The thrust-vectoring nozzles are in the standard thrust-line position, but can be deflected downwards to provide additional lift during take-off.

What was required was an aircraft which could rule the skies against any potential threat, unfettered by any air-to-ground considerations. Not only would such an aircraft have to be more powerful and more manoeuvrable than current fighters, it would also need radical improvements to its systems to meet the demands of operations well into the 21st century.

Initial concept definition study contracts were awarded in September 1983 to the main US manufacturers (Boeing, General Dynamics, Grumman, Lockheed, McDonnell Douglas, Northrop and Rockwell). All these companies submitted design proposals on 28 July 1986. On 31 October that year, two were chosen to move to the demonstration/validation phase of the programme, these being Lockheed and Northrop. Both companies felt that the programme was too large and too important to handle on their own, and selected partners for ATF, although both stayed in overall control.

Under the Dem/Val contract, two PAVs (prototype air vehicles) were to be produced for flight test, together with a ground prototype of the avionics system.

Lockheed's aircraft, in conjunction with Boeing and General Dynamics, was to be designated YF-22, while the Northrop/McDonnell Douglas submission was given the YF-23 designation. After some slippage, final proposals for the single Full Scale Development contract were required on 1 January 1991. Throughout the Dem/Val phase, the US Air Force was at pains to emphasise the fact that there was no 'fly-off' between the two types, rather a set of tests conducted separately against a standard set of criteria. At the time of writing, the award of the single FSD contract is expected in April 1991, leading to 24 FSD aircraft prior to production examples.

YF-23 into the open

Northrop/McDonnell Douglas scored the first point by revealing their YF-23 first, on 22 June 1990, and at once the considerable advances being made by these aircraft became immediately apparent. The YF-23 (unofficially called the 'Black Widow') looked like no other aircraft, although some resemblances to the Lockheed SR-71 and the mythical 'Firefox', from the Clint Eastwood movie of the same name, were noted. The airframe in profile is long and sinuous. A forward fuselage body blends into the central structure, while two large overwing bulges contain the engines. Underneath the leading edge are the engine intakes, leading to serpentine trunks which sweep the air upwards and inwards to the engines.

Exhaust from the engines is emitted from long, rectangular intakes mounted above and inboard from the leading edge. Surprisingly thrust-vectoring was not included at the final design stage: what had once been a requirement of the US Air Force had been deleted from the design criteria on grounds of acceptable weight.

In plan view the YF-23 is even stranger. Large triangular wings with cut-off tips exhibit the same angle sweep on leading and trailing edge wings. Large tail fins canted at 45° offer considerable area in plan, and join the fuselage at the same point as the trailing edge of the wing. Stealth considerations dictated the now well-known sawtooth arrangement along the trailing edges of the tails and centre-body. The forward fuselage has an SR-71-style chine along the side, this forming three distinct angles in plan. This chine forms vortices across the wing, and prevents the nose 'slicing off' at high angles of attack. Control surfaces include the all-moving tails,

One immediately noticeable feature of the Lockheed/General Dynamics/Boeing YF-22 is the size of the vertical tail surfaces. In addition to the AFSC badge under the wing, the YF-22 carries the Tactical Air Command badge on the fin, with a small Lockheed Skunk Works badge near the base of the rudder.

be shielded from radar. Each pair of engines is fed by shallow intakes with S-type inlet lip and a boundary layer splitter plate and exhaust above the wing in carbon-coated surfaces to reduce infrared signature. Further reduction in detectability is expected to result from the planned injection of chloro-fluoro-sulphonic acid in the exhaust, but this feature has not been incorporated in the prototype.

Smooth blending

The fuselage bulge, which starts immediately aft of the apex of the wing, ends short of the wing trailing edge and is smoothly blended on the upper surfaces of the wing, provides side-by-side accommodation for the crew of two, pilot and copilot/MSO, on McDonnell Douglas ACES II 'zero-zero' ejection seats. As shown on photographs of B-2s on the assembly line or during refuelling, this cockpit is quite capacious, an important consideration as mission duration is expected typically to exceed 10 hours, thus making it highly desirable to provide space for the crew to stretch out. Moreover, should the addition of a third crew member be found desirable as the result of operational testing, space will be available to install a seat immediately aft of those for the primary crew. Quite probably, space will then remain sufficient to provide inflight access to some of the electronic equipment and thus enable the crew to undertake limited troubleshooting. Probably as the re-

Control surfaces
The two main outer trailing edges of the
B-2 have large flight control surfaces.
Pitch and roll are handled by using the
surface either simultaneously for pitch
or differentially for roll in the established
way. Yaw control is more complicated,
utilising split 'drag rudders' on the outer
sections. These also can be used
simultaneously for aerodynamic braking

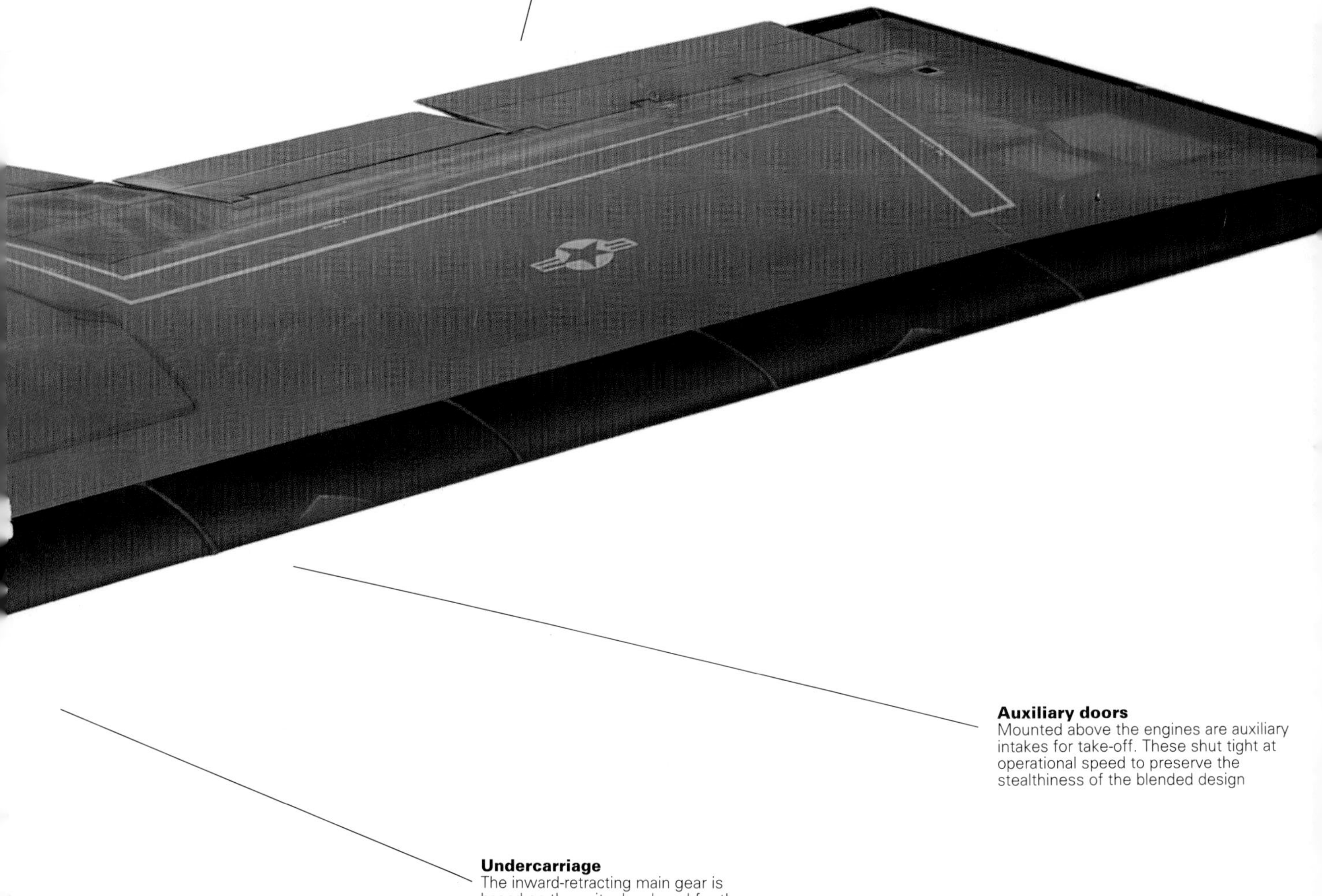

aust
oss

ıst

Auxiliary doors
Mounted above the engines are auxiliary
intakes for take-off. These shut tight at
operational speed to preserve the
stealthiness of the blended design

Undercarriage
The inward-retracting main gear is
based on the units developed for the
Boeing 767 airliner. The rearward-
retracting nosewheel has a door with
sawtooth leading and trailing edges to
make the join more stealthy

Badges
The three badges carried on the B-2 prototype represent Strategic Air Command, Air Force Systems Command and Air Force Logistics Command

Refuelling
Mounted midway along the spine is a refuelling receptacle. The B-2's 12000+ km range bestows phenomenal operational capabilities without refuelling, but with tankers it can strike anywhere on the globe

Exhausts
To significantly reduce the infra-red signature of the B-2, the engine ex[ ] is ejected from a shallow trough ac[ ] a wide section coated with carbon. CFCs may be injected into the exha[ ] to eliminate contrails

Intakes
To shield the highly radar-reflective intakes and engine compressors from radar energy, the intakes are mounted on top of the wing well back from the leading edge. A complex sawtooth arrangement further breaks up radar return, and provides a splitter plate tha[ ] separates the sluggish boundary layer from the airflow entering the engine

Radar
Peering through flush panels under the aircraft's nose is a Hughes LPI (Low Probability of Intercept) radar. This presents minimal returns to ground-based passive sensors, allowing the B-2 to acquire its target with little risk of detection

Northrop B-2: Strategy by Stealth

A 22nd Air Refueling Wing KC-10A provide the B-2 with its first inflight refuelling experience. The range performance of the is such that with one refuelling the type ca hit any spot on the globe from one of four bases.

sult of LO considerations, none of the four cockpit windows can be opened on the ground, thus leading to concern that summertime cockpit temperatures will lead to premature ageing and failure of avionics components, forcing the Air Force to plan the construction of 120 air-conditioned hangars at a cost of $1,600 million.

If credence can be given to take-off thrust, weight, and range figures which have been released, the B-2 will indeed be a spectacular performer. With a take-off thrust of 34473 kg (76,000 lb) and a take-off weight of 170100 kg (375,000 lb), giving a thrust-to-weight ratio of 0.20:1 (versus 0.26:1 for the B-1B and only 0.11:1 for the B-52G), the B-2 will be able to operate from airports suitable for Boeing 727 operations (i.e. having 3050-m/10,000-ft runways). Its low altitude penetration speed will be approximately one-third greater than that of the B-52G and about equal to the B-1B.

However, it is in terms of load-to-range that the B-2 will outshine both the B-52 and the B-1B. According to data released

The future of the B-2 is bleak, in an era when the 'peace dividend' is bringing no joy at all for defence contractors. Originally 132 bombers were required, but this seems an unlikely figure. 120, 75 and even a token squadron of 12 have been proposed as final requirements.

by the Air Force, the B-2 will have a maximum range of 10000 km (5,400 nautical miles) when carrying a 10890-km/24,000-lb load (eight AGM-131 SRAM II missiles and eight B61 bombs on two internally-carried Common Strategic Rotary Launchers, CSRLs) over an optimised high-low-high profile, the comparative figure for the B-1B being 8780 km (4,740 nautical miles).

Heavy load profile

On a similar profile, the B-2 will carry a 16920-kg/37,300-lb load (eight SRAM IIs and eight B83 bombs) over a maximum range of 9815 km (5,300 nautical miles) versus 8665 km (4,680 miles) for the B-1B. The aerodynamic efficiency of the flying wing design is further evidenced by the fact that these range figures will be achieved even though the B-2's fuel capacity (about 94625 litres/25,000 US gallons) is only three-quarters of that of the B-1B.

Reduction in detectability, not performance improvement, however, was the primary reason for the development of the B-2, as the B-1B already possess satisfactory performance in terms of penetration speed, range and runway requirements. Accordingly, the B-2 design makes extensive use of smooth blended surfaces and virtually the

entire surface is covered with radar-abs ing materials (RAM), thus enabling the craft to have a radar cross-section of a one-tenth that of the B-1B and one-hund that of the B-52G.

The first phase of the flight trials, aime verifying the aircraft's airworthiness and ploring its handling qualities, began o July 1989, when the B-2 prototype (82-1 was first flown from Palmdale to Edw AFB by Northrop Chief Test Pilot Bru Hinds and Col Richard S. Cough, the dire of the USAF combined test force. This f validation programme was completed o November 1989, when the same crew the eighth test mission to bring total f time to more than 30 hours. Principal acc plishments during that phase include speed of 650 km/h (350 knots) and altitu 10670 m (35,000 ft); (2) aerial refuelling with KC-10A tankers; (3) inflight engine start and throttling tests; (4) verificatio accuracy and performance of the air avionics display systems; (5) demonstra of handling characteristics, including pitch, roll-manoeuvres, and bank angle to 60 degrees; (6) retraction of the lan gear using the normal and 'alternate-sys (emergency back-up) systems; (7) chec the speed brake sensitivity at various sp and altitudes; and (8) verification of the craft's stability and control. Following c pletion of this phase, the first B-2 was lai for a planned maintenance and modifica downtime period which lasted until A 1990. Thereafter, seven additional basic flights were made and, after a second s duled downtime period, the aircraft be the all-important 'low observables' testi

Unsure future

Success during the LO testing phase go a long way towards assuring that the will survive both the reassessment of programme ordered by the Defense S tary Richard B. Cheney in January 1990 stepped-up criticisms by Congressi opponents of the programme (who are le Alan Cranston, one of the two senators California, the state which would be negatively affected by the cancellation o production). However, many scientist the United States and abroad now be that the development of ultra-widel (UWB) radar technology and significan creases in data processing power may render the costly LO technology obso With the threat of all-out war being cons ably reduced by changes in the Soviet U and other Warsaw Pact nations and wit United States facing serious budgetary balance of payment problems, such cl are reasons to ponder the wisdom of ceeding with the bomber.

Whether or not the B-2 will be place service at Whiteman AFB as schedule development will remain a remarkab costly, achievement. Much of it comes extensive use of computer technology w

Viewed from above the YF-23 exhibits the now accepted sawtooth arrangement of the trailing edges to defeat radars. The clipped triangle wings provide the three principal alignments for most other straight edges on the aircraft, while the snaking of the intake ducts is apparent.

large ailerons, trailing-and leading-edge s. The undercarriage retracts into the ne fairings to lie beside the intake ks.

Some time elapsed before the Lockheed team revealed their design, at the Burbank factory on 29 August 1990. A slightly more conventional design, the YF-22 (the name

The sinuous lines of the YF-23 suggest that it is tailored more to the interceptor mission, but the large control surfaces, low wing loading and fly-by-wire control system make it a highly manoeuvrable fighter.

Thrust vectoring
Each engine has a two-dimensional thrust vectoring nozzle, operating either symmetrically for pitch control in manoeuvring flight and additional unstick and lift forces during take-off and landing, or asymmetrically for additional roll control. Although the YF-22 can 'supercruise' (sustain supersonic flight without afterburner), afterburners are incorporated for high energy manoeuvring and Mach 2-plus dash speed

Auxiliary doors
Immediately above the intake a doors which open at low speed airflow through the intake. All s doors on the YF-22 are carefully present as little radar return as

Tail badge
In addition to its patriotic fin stripe, the YF-22 carries the badge of Tactical Air Command on the fin, potentially its most important user command

Undercarriage
A standard tricycle undercarriage is fitted, the nosewheel retracting rearwards to lie between the intake bodies, while the mainwheels retract forwards and inwards to lie behind the side missile bays outboard of the intake ducting. The doors of the wheel wells are crafted for minimum radar returns

Side missile bay
Located alongside the intake trunks are the short-range missile bays, accommodating two AIM-9 Sidewinder infra-red homing missiles each. As the Sidewinder ignites immediately at launch, some ejector system or extendable rail is used

Lower missile bay
Two long missile bays are incorporated into the lower structure underneath the intake trunk. These accommodate either two AIM-7 Sparrow or two AIM-120 AMRAAM radar-homing missiles each. The double-hinged doors present little radar reflection when open, and the missiles free-fall from the bay before the motors ignite

Intake trunk
Not immediately apparent fro external structure is that the ir ducts sweep upwards and inw the inlet, this serpentine trunk the engine compressors from radar beams

Lockheed/Boeing General Dynamics YF-22A PAV No. 1 N22YF
Lockheed-California
Edwards AFB, California

Registration
The two YF-22 PAVs carry civil registrations on the fins, this being required for certification purposes due to the first flights from Palmdale (a civil airfield) to Edwards. Air Force serials have been assigned. The two YF-23s carry Air Force serials as they made their first flights from Edwards, but they too have civil registrations assigned but not worn

Wings
In conjuction with the lifting qualities of the fuselage and intake bodies, the large wings of the YF-22 confer excellent agility on the type even without thrust-vectoring. It has been suggested that the carrierborne version of the YF-22 for the US Navy would feature swing-wing technology

Control system
Combining low observables technology with a demanding operational requirement necessitated the use of artificial stability in the form of fly-by-wire controls. The central computer co-ordinates the actions of leading edge flaps, trailing edge flaps, ailerons, all-moving tailplanes, rudders and thrust nozzles to provide the desired control effect. Manoeuvrability is said to be phenomenal in all three planes, and high-g manoeuvres easy to sustain. High angle-of-attack flight is far more controllable than with the current generation of aircraft

Control notches
Joints between control surfaces and wing structures exhibit an unusual notch. These have been carefully designed by computer to eradicate radar returns from the these potentially 'bright' spots

Powerplant
This is the first YF-22, powered by General Electric YF120 engines. These are variable-cycle powerplants, operating as turbofans at subsonic speeds where that mode is more efficient, but closing off bypass air at supersonic speeds to act as pure turbojets, this too proving more efficient. Features of the YF120 are a dual-spool, vaneless, counter-rotating turbine and 40 per cent fewer parts compared to the F110 jet used by current F-16s

The beautifully blended structure of the YF-23 is reminiscent of that of the same company's B-2 bomber. Careful blending of the wings and fuselage and engine bodies vastly reduces radar signature, but required the use of high-powered computers.

'Lightning II' has been mentioned) appeared considerably different in many areas, highlighting design concept differences which will be examined later. A stockier design, the profile of the YF-22 is dominated by huge twin fins, canted slightly outwards. The cockpit canopy sits high on the forward fuselage, offering exceptional visibility to the pilot.

In plan the wing is a slightly-swept trapezoidal surface, again with large manoeuvring surfaces on the leading and trailing edges (even the flaps aid roll control). An overlapping tailplane is set far back on the aircraft, offering further roll control and exceptional pitch control. However, the Lockheed team took the plunge and incorporated thrust-vectoring. Located between the tailplanes are two sawtooth nozzles with two-dimensional vectoring. Not only does this vastly increase take-off performance, but allows very rapid pitch changes and enables the type to fly very tight sustained turns.

From the front, the YF-22 demonstrates a diamond-shaped forward fuselage, with roughly diamond-shaped intakes either side. Missile bays are located on the side of the intake trunks and underneath. Again the air is ducted upwards to shield the compressor faces of the engine from radar energy. The mainwheels retract into the side of the main intake/powerplant body.

Not only did the ATF programme introduce radically improved airframe designs, but new powerplants as well. Both main engine manufacturers were invited, in 1983, to begin development of advanced powerplants for the ATF under the designations YF119 for Pratt & Whitney and YF120 for General Electric. These are variable-cycle engines, allowing them to operate as turbofans at subsonic speeds for greater efficiency, but switching to a turbojet operation with no bypass air at supersonic speeds, again offering greater efficiency. Both have thrust-vectoring ability, as demonstrated on the YF-22. One of each PAVs is powered by the P&W engine; the other by the GE engine.

ATF get aloft

Flight testing of the ATFs began at 7.15 am Pacific Daylight Time, 27 August 1990 when Northrop test pilot Paul Metz lifted the first YF-23 off from Edwards AFB, California, at the beginning of a successful first flight. Powered by P&W YF119s, 87-800 climbed to 7620 m (25,000 ft) during the flight and landed after 50 minutes airborne. The second YF-23, 87-801, flew on GE YF120 power shortly after, at the beginning of a highly successful flight test programme.

During this programme, the two YF-23s logged 65 hours on 50 missions, flown by one Northrop, one McDonnell Douglas and two Air Force pilots. A speed of Mach 1.8 and an altitude of 15340 m (50,000 ft) were achieved. The all-important 'supercruise' – the ability to fly sustained supersonic flight without afterburner – was demonstrated with flights up to Mach 1.43, although the top

'supercruise' speed remained classified. Inflight refuelling was introduced at an early stage in the programme.

Due to delays associated with its YF120 engines, the first Lockheed/Boeing/General Dynamics YF-22 (N22YF) had to wait until 29 September before it could fly. Lockheed pilot Dave Ferguson had a further delay at the end of the runway while ground telemetry equipment was repaired, so when he eventually took off from the factory at Palmdale, California, only enough fuel for a short flight to Edwards AFB was possible, this accomplished with undercarriage down. On its ninth flight, the aircraft achieved supercruise at Mach 1.23. The second YF119-powered YF-22 joined the first, and after a few minor hitches concerning gear retraction, hydraulic leaks and other problems, the two embarked on a most aggressive flight test programme in order to prepare enough flight data for the end-of-year proposal deadline.

Once again, YF-22s demonstrated inflight-refuelling at an early stage. The first weapons launch by an ATF was performed by General Dynamics pilot Jon Beesley, who fired an inert AIM-9M Sidewinder over the China Lake Naval Weapons Center range. Later Lockheed pilot Tom Morgenfeld fired an AIM-120 AMRAAM from the YF-22 on 20 December over the Pacific Missile Test Center range at Point Mugu. Late on in the flight test programme a YF-22 surpassed Mach 2 with the use of afterburner. As far as is known, the YF-23 programme did not include missile launches as this was not required by the USAF's Dem/Val needs.

As has become clear during the Dem/Val phase, what ATF offers the US Air Force is a

The YF-22's plan view reveals the aft placing of the all-moving tailplanes. Allied to the thrust-vectoring, these give phenomenal rates of change in both pitch and roll. Note the tailplanes overlapping the wings, and the strange cut-out sections between moving surfaces, presumably to reduce radar reflections from these joints.

Canopy
The YF-22 features a beautifully crafted one-piece canopy which sits high on the fuselage. This high position gives superb all-round vision, a major consideration for air combat. The canopy is treated to not be reflective to radar energy

Cockpit
Little has been released as to the precise nature of the YF-22's cockpit, but it can be assumed to be dominated by large multi-function CRTs (cathode ray tubes) which can display relevant flight, navigation and targetting data. The salient items are displayed on the head-up display to allow the pilot to receive information while keeping his head 'out of the cockpit'

Gun
If chosen for production, the YF-22 will feature an internal cannon for short range work. This will be derived from the trusty M61A1 Vulcan 20-mm six-barrel rotary weapon carried by most US fighters

Radar
Giving first-look, first-launch, first-kill capability, the YF-22's radar has long range and high resolution for the early detection of opposing fighters. It has a low passive detection signature, which allied to the aircraft's own very low radar cross-section, allows the YF-22 to approach very close to its quarry before being detected, thereby dramatically increasing the chance of a kill

Air data probe
In common with most prototypes and test vehicles, the YF-22 has a large nose probe with highly sensitive air data measuring vanes. A standard pitot tube is mounted further back on the lower nose

Avionics
VHSIC (very high speed integrated circuit) technology is at the heart of the YF-22's avionic system, which is being tested on a Boeing 757 flying test-bed and a ground-based prototype. Several systems can share processing and antenna functions, while common processors cater for rapid maintenance and reduced complexity of replacement stocks. A comprehensive threat warning and analysis system is incorporated

Fins
Huge fins are fitted to the YF-22, canted outwards to follow the alignments of the forward fuselage. These are not all-moving slabs as in the YF-23, but feature standard rudders

Communications
Two small blade antennae spoil the otherwise stealthy lines of the YF-. The onboard communications suite features many jam-resistant and stealthy features

Intake
The diamond-shaped intakes follow the same alignments as the forward fuselage and canted tail fins. A pronounced lip above the intake aids air ingestion at high angles of attack, while the intake is set proud from the fuselage to incorporate a splitter plate which separates the sluggish boundary layer of air next to the fuselage

Forward fuselage
Characterised by its diamond cross-section, the forward fuselage has a distinct chined edge which provides great stability for high angle of attack flight

LOCKHEED BOEING
GENERAL DYNAMICS

The first missile launch from an ATF involved an AIM-9M Sidewinder fired from a YF-22. The Sidewinder missiles are carried in bays along the side of the intake body and thrust through open bay doors as the motor is fired.

Beyond visual range kill capability for the ATF will largely be entrusted to the AIM-120 AMRAAM missile, seen here being launched by a YF-22 and closely watched by an F-16. AMRAAMs are housed underneath the intake body, hidden behind double-hinged doors. The missile drops before igniting.

most significant upgrade of fighter capabilities in every department. Performance from the engine/airframe design offers exceptional agility and sustained turn performance, allied to previously unheard-of high speed cruise and acceleration figures. Key areas addressed by the design teams are reliability and maintenance. ATF offers much quicker turn-round times between missions than current generation fighters, while maintenance requirements are drastically cut by the use of advanced materials and vastly reduced numbers of components.

Sophisticated systems

Another extremely important area of ATF advances is the avionics and weapon systems. Comprehensive electronic counter-

measures are integrated into the overall system, which for the first time uses common processors for differing systems, allowing great system flexibility, redundancy and ease of replacement. In addition to the ground prototype for the avionics system, both ATF teams produced airborne test vehicles for key components of the system. Boeing provided the prototype 757 for integration of the YF-22's equipment, while the Northrop/McDonnell Douglas team used a Westinghouse BAC 1-11.

Principal among the components are new radars, developed to present minimal returns to a passive detection system, allowing the ATF to use its radar more freely in air combat without risking detection of the aircraft itself. Processing of data is significantly

improved compared with current genera fighters, allowing swift interpretation an sponse to threats.

While these mission considerations v paramount, a requirement of the US Force was for an extremely stealthy airc Central to the ATF's projected effectiver is its ability to operate undetected. Ste properties allow the ATF to approach its get much closer before it is detected, therefore increase the probability of scori kill. The need for stealth has played a g part in defining the shapes of the fight Combining the need for stealth with other operational considerations has b one of the greatest challenges in aviation sign in recent years, and would not be sible without the aid of fly-by-wire con systems and 3-D computer design.

Design comparison

Comparing the two ATF designs h lights different design configurations. W exact performances remain classified, an sis of the outward appearances would gest that the YF-23 is stealthier and proba faster, while the YF-22 is more manoe able. Certainly the inclusion in the Lockh design of thrust-vectoring has given it edge in the latter department. Northrop's sign is more tailored to an intercept r whereas the YF-22 is more of a fighter.

Different approaches to design are parent. Northrop appears to have create sophisticated stealth design (incorpora many of the features of the B-2 bomber) which have been grafted the operational quirements of the fighter mission, w Lockheed have begun with a fighter des and then integrated low observable featu

From what can be gleaned from publi released information, both flight test grammes proceeded exceptionally we Lockheed being able to recapture any ground at the start of the programme wit aggressive flight test schedule. Northrop sued a more measured but no less succes programme.

As both aircraft appear to have perfor

Illustrating the advances made in stealth technology, two of the Skunk Works' low-observable designs line up at Palmdale. T F-117 is considerably more angular than th YF-22, but is probably more stealthy as it h less operational considerations to accommodate.

Both YF-22s refuel from a 93rd Bomb Wing Boeing KC-135A during a test mission from Edwards AFB. The far aircraft (PAV No. 1) has a spin parachute attached to the rear fuselage.

exceptionally, the Air Force's decision will hinge as much on other considerations as the individual merits of each design. Certainly cost will be a factor, as might political considerations. Without doubt combat reports from the Gulf War against Iraq will help point the way. However, the bottom line is that the Air Force has to make the choice as to whether it wants a fighter or an interceptor.

Naval interest

Closely watching the ATF programme is the US Navy, which is considering the ATF design for an F-14 Tomcat replacement, suitably navalised as the NATF (Naval Advanced Tactical Fighter). Unlike the F-16/F-17 competition, it seems highly unlikely that one competitor will win the Air Force order and the other the Navy contract. Just as ATF is facing competition from advanced F-15 derivatives, so Grumman is pushing new Tomcat variants as a much cheaper alternative to NATF.

Following the award of an FSD contract, the winning ATF design faces an uphill

Both YF-23 Prototype Air Vehicles formate for the camera, illustrating two potential camouflage schemes for the type if it is chosen for production. Both aircraft carry the Aeronautical Systems Division badge on the central fuselage.

struggle for funding, although again the war in the Gulf may ease matters considerably in this area. Pro-ATF politicians will be quick to point out that Allied air superiority in the conflict was achieved so successfully chiefly by the use of high-technology warplanes, and that the United States should not slip behind again as it had done with the MiG-29/Su-27 generation. The US Air Force requirement is for 750 aircraft to replace its active-duty fleet of F-15s.

In service the ATF will provide a rapidly-deployable asset that can achieve air superiority against any opposition. Initial purchase costs may be high, but the ATF's advances in materials, systems and construction will dramatically cut maintenance costs. More importantly, its performance, stealth properties and kill-capability will maintain the US fighter as the best in the world, a weapon able to defeat any potential enemy.

The TUPOLEV
Tu-142 'BEAR'

Tupolev `Bear` Murmansk Monster

For 30 years, the skies over the world's oceans have reverberated to the growl of the 'Bear'. It has kept pace with scientific advances, adding more and more roles to its repertoire as time passes. It is still in production and will threaten naval forces around the world for many years to come.

Seven monster turboprop aircraft flew over Moscow's Red Square on Aviation Day 1955, and caused fresh consternation in the West. Nothing like them had been seen before. Clearly more powerful than any previous propeller aircraft, they had swept wings and tail! Dubbed 'Bear', they were assessed as having considerable range, but their propellers (giant eight-blade counter-rotating units of 5.6 m/18 ft 4.5 in diameter) caused them to be regarded slightly as freaks. Certainly the 'Bear' was undervalued, whereas in contrast the Pentagon grossly over-reacted to the four-jet 'Bison' first seen the previous year.

Nobody was in the least prepared for continued production of the giant turbo-prop for 30 years. Equally curiously, ever since 1955 the 'Bear' has been the subject of speculation and controversy. Even today its size is a matter for estimation, as is its capability. And even its true designations are not known. The Tupolev OKB number was Tu-95, and reasonably enough it was given the V-VS (air force) designation Tu-20 when it entered service in 1956. Much later it entered service with the AV-MF (naval air force), and it is

these versions with which this article is concerned. When a new ASW version appeared in 1973, dubbed 'Bear-F' by NATO, it was learned that this is the Tu-142. Today it is generally believed that all AV-MF versions are Tu-142s. And to confuse matters further, since 1979 the Soviet SALT 2 negotiators have used the designation Tu-95 for the V-VS versions, despite the fact that odd numbers were always reserved for fighters!

Here we are concerned with the AV-MF variants, and except for the 'Bear-F' and subsequent models it is believed that all are rebuilds of the 300-odd original bomber versions built in 1955-61. The first to be seen, called 'Bear-B', was the carrier of the biggest-ever cruise missile, given the NATO name AS-3 'Kangaroo'. A swept-wing turbojet of fighter size, this mighty weapon has always been officially assessed as having beam-riding followed by terminal pre-programmed autopilot guidance, possibly the most ridiculous combination of methods that could be invented. Such guidance would preclude operation against surface vessels. In any case most 'Bear-B' aircraft have been

rebuilt, either for reconnaissance with a blister on the right side of the rear fuselage, or to carry the later AS-4 'Kitchen' missile described under the 'Bear-G'. The biggest modification of the original 'Bear-B' was the reconstruction of the nose to accommodate a giant surveillance and target-acquisition radar (NATO 'Crown Drum'), in place of the glazed bomb-aiming station. From 1962 inflight-refuelling probes were added above the nose, with the supply pipe along the outside of the fuselage along the right side.

In 1964 the 'Bear-C' appeared, dedicated to Elint missions in a maritime environment. At first some retained 'Kangaroo' missile capability, but this was not the primary role. The nose remained as that of the 'Bear-B', the probe being standard, but the tail turret was sometimes replaced by a long fairing housing large electronics systems (thought to be mainly passive receivers, though almost certainly also including aft-hemisphere defensive jammers). This tail section is the same as that used on the Tu-126 'Moss' AEW platform, which is a rebuild of the commercial Tu-114, itself a passenger derivative of the 'Bear'. Another feature of the 'Bear-C' is that there is a reconnaissance blister on each side of the rear fuselage. Usually the weapon bay is occupied by auxiliary fuel tanks, of about 19000 litres (4,180 Imp gal), and most 'Bear-C' aircraft have the same EW blister radomes along the ventral centreline as the Tu-16 'Badger-H'.

The 'Bear-D' is the most common variant; it is a general-purpose maritime reconnaissance, Elint, missile targeting and patrol aircraft. About 45 are thought to be in service with the AV-MF, based mainly in the Kola Peninsula, around the Black Sea and on the south-eastern corner of the USSR.

First seen in 1967, the 'Bear-D' has probably been photographed by Western aircraft more than any other version, though it is not the most numerous version in service (which is the V-VS Long-Range Aviation 'Bear-A' followed by the naval 'Bear-F'). The 'Bear-D' is a versatile multi-sensor maritime reconnaissance platform, without weapons capability (though one of its avowed tasks is to provide inflight course-correction and target update data to cruise missiles fired from Soviet warships). The nose remains the same as that of the original bomber, with the addition of an inflight-refuelling probe and a very large chin radar (NATO 'Mushroom') and a colossal surveillance radar under the weapons bay (NATO 'Big Bulge'). Both these installations operate in I-band wavelengths, and their main function is to find and pinpoint targets (mainly surface ships) for missiles fired by Soviet ships (including submarines) and aircraft which are too far away and at too low a level to have a view of the enemy. To do this over a long period demands an extremely high standard of defensive electronics, and the 'Bear-D' is covered with warning receivers and defensive jamming and dispensing systems. The tail-warning radar is the larger 'Box Tail' also seen on AV-MF Tupolev Tu-26 'Backfires', while the tailplane carries on each tip a streamlined pod which the author has always believed to be a chaff dispenser. Twin canoe strakes above the fuselage, aft of the main pressurized crew compartment, appear to contain exhaust stacks for an auxiliary electric generating plant. A reconnaissance blister appears on each side of the rear fuselage, and sometimes the tail turret is replaced by the long ECM fairing.

The only pure maritime reconnais-sance version is the 'Bear-E', basically similar to the 'Bear-D' but without the surveillance/targeting capability. This frees the aft bomb bay for fuel and six or seven large optical cameras plus either IR linescan or a SLAR, all mounted on a giant demountable pallet conforming to the fuselage curvature and forming the external skin when installed. There is a small navigation radar under the nose, and some of this type have two small radomes under the forward weapon bay. This variant is used in small numbers, but in wartime would be used only for post-attack assessment where it would be un-likely to encounter hostile forces.

Continuing production

The appearance in 1973 of the new version called 'Bear-F' (the first to be positively identified as a Tu-142) was a major surprise. This was no rebuild but a new aircraft, and instead of being regarded as obsolescent, the venerable 'Bear' was suddenly regarded as very much an on-going production programme. Indeed, though rate of output from the former Beriev location at Taganrog was only about one per month during the 1970s (since increased), the fact that 'Bear' was being built at all was quite an eye-opener.

Though sometimes described as a re-connaissance aircraft, the 'Bear-F' is in fact a dedicated ASW platform, and the biggest in the world. Previously the AV-MF's only long-range aircraft for ASW missions was the Ilyushin Il-38 'May', and compared with this the new Tu-142 offers greatly increased mission radius and endurance. One of its major airframe modifications is redesign of the fuselage to have a completely pressurized rear section without turrets (except in the tail) but devoted to sonobuoy stowage and

launch, and many other equipment items. The forward fuselage is also totally rearranged, and is lengthened by a plug section which puts the crew compartment farther ahead of the propellers. Fuel capacity is increased, better crew rest facilities are provided, and the avionics have been completely revised. Along the dorsal centreline are dual satellite communications terminals and tandem ADF sense aerials (instead of one or none). On the underside, from the nose, are the usual communications and ILS, then a radome which hardly breaks the profile of the fuselage but is of considerable size (this is not always present), then a very large bulged radome (in the size inter-mediate between the front and rear radomes of the 'Bear-D'), then a tandem weapon bay with front and rear pairs of doors, and under the rear fuselage the various sizes of sonobuoy tube and retro-launcher. There are no tailplane con-tainers, but nearly all 'Bear-F' aircraft have a MAD installation aft of the tip of the fin (not the same as that fitted to the Il-38).

A curious feature is that when they were first seen, aircraft of this family had bulged doors over the nose landing gear and grossly enlarged fairings aft of the inboard engines. The seemingly obvious inference was that with the increase in gross weight the landing-gear tyres had been considerably increased in size, but this is now thought not to be the case.

'Bear-D' carries two main radars, the 'Mushroom' under the chin and the 'Big Bulge' under the centreline. Both operate in the I/J-band (previously X-band) and are used for over-the-horizon targeting for anti-ship missiles launched by other aircraft or ships. Defensive electronics are comprehensive.

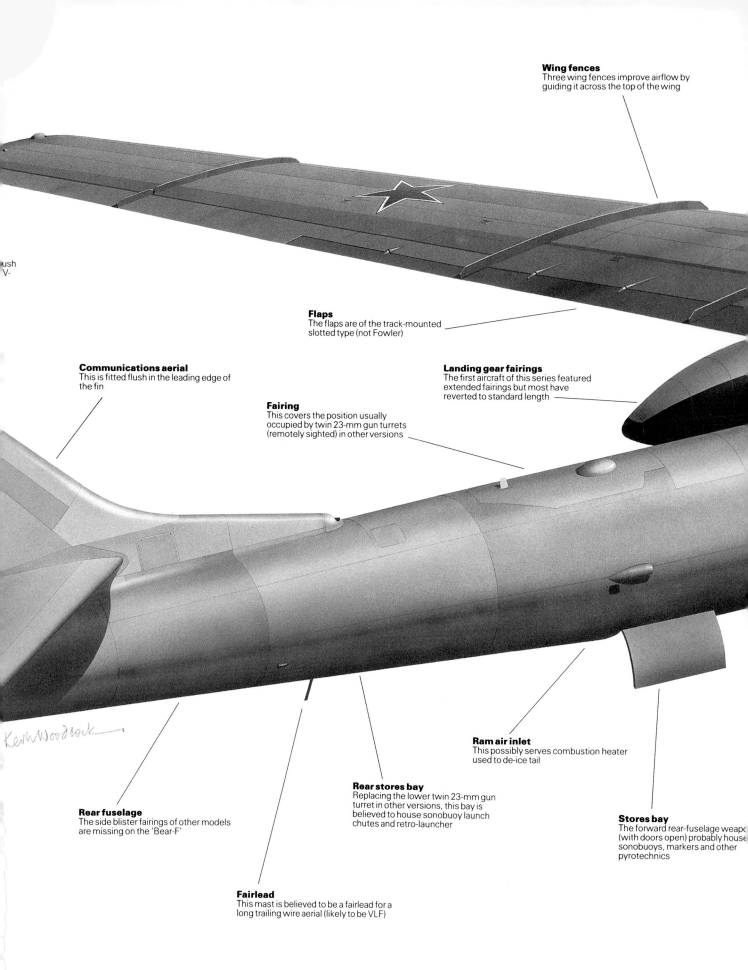

Wing fences
Three wing fences improve airflow by guiding it across the top of the wing

ush
V-

Flaps
The flaps are of the track-mounted slotted type (not Fowler)

Communications aerial
This is fitted flush in the leading edge of the fin

Landing gear fairings
The first aircraft of this series featured extended fairings but most have reverted to standard length

Fairing
This covers the position usually occupied by twin 23-mm gun turrets (remotely sighted) in other versions

KeithWoodcock

Ram air inlet
This possibly serves combustion heater used to de-ice tail

Rear stores bay
Replacing the lower twin 23-mm gun turret in other versions, this bay is believed to house sonobuoy launch chutes and retro-launcher

Stores bay
The forward rear-fuselage weapo (with doors open) probably house sonobuoys, markers and other pyrotechnics

Rear fuselage
The side blister fairings of other models are missing on the 'Bear-F'

Fairlead
This mast is believed to be a fairlead for a long trailing wire aerial (likely to be VLF)

Tupolev Tu-142 `Bear-F´
Soviet Naval Aviation (AV-MF)

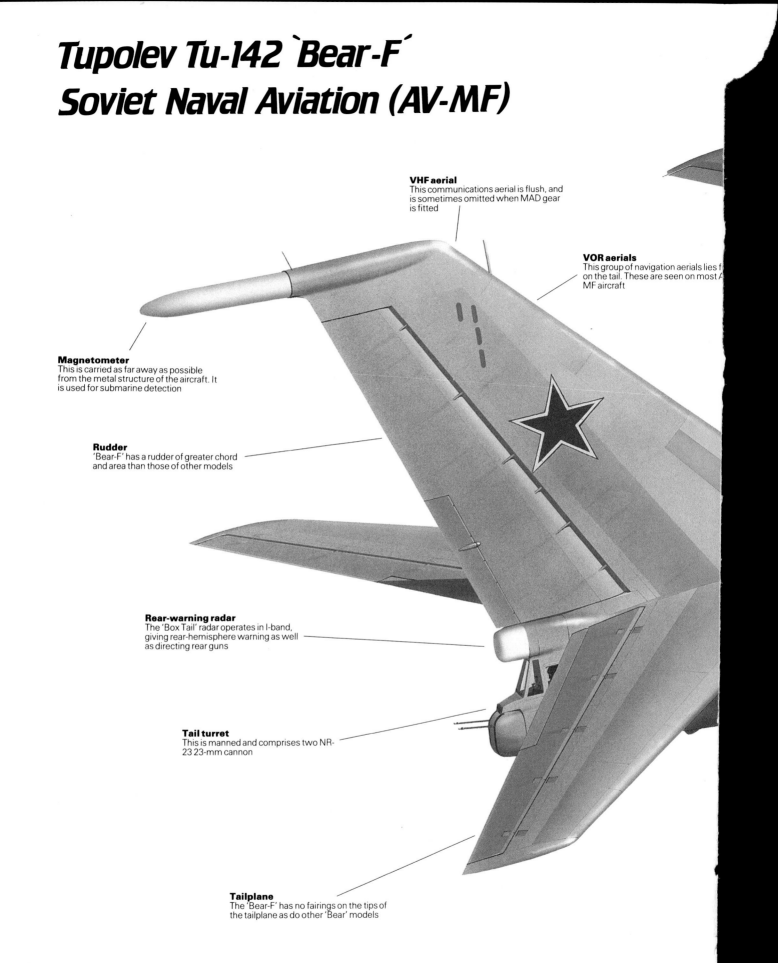

VHF aerial
This communications aerial is flush, and is sometimes omitted when MAD gear is fitted

VOR aerials
This group of navigation aerials lies f
on the tail. These are seen on most A
MF aircraft

Magnetometer
This is carried as far away as possible from the metal structure of the aircraft. It is used for submarine detection

Rudder
'Bear-F' has a rudder of greater chord and area than those of other models

Rear-warning radar
The 'Box Tail' radar operates in I-band, giving rear-hemisphere warning as well as directing rear guns

Tail turret
This is manned and comprises two NR-23 23-mm cannon

Tailplane
The 'Bear-F' has no fairings on the tips of the tailplane as do other 'Bear' models

Current production aircraft have reverted to the original inboard nacelles. There is thought to have been an aerodynamic reason for the bigger nacelles, though in view of the exhaustive aerodynamic testing done in the early 1950s this seems unlikely. There has been no mention in Western analyses of the extended nacelles having been used to dispense chaff and other payloads removed from the tailplanes. Of course, this variant does not have the rear-fuselage lateral radomes and other sensors of the reconnaissance and Elint versions.

New missiles for old aircraft

The missile-carrier called 'Bear-G' by NATO was first identified as recently as 1980. These aircraft are almost certainly former carriers of AS-3 'Kangaroo' rebuilt to launch the AS-4 'Kitchen'. This cruise missile is smaller than its predecessor, but it is still a massive vehicle, having a tailed delta configuration with a length of some 11.3 m (37 ft). Launch weight is certainly well in excess of 6000 kg (13,228 lb), and a rocket engine gives a range varying up to at least 300 km (186 miles), depending on the selected flight profile. The warhead is either a large conventional charge or a thermonuclear type, variable from 350- to 800-kiloton yield. Such devastating yields would be used either against land targets, such as ports and naval bases, or against an entire surface fleet. The weapon appears to have a liquid-propellant engine (with main and cruise thrust chambers) and cruciform tail surfaces, sometimes with the ventral fin folded sideways until shortly before the release. There are several versions of this large supersonic missile, but the usual form of guidance is thought to be inertial, with terminal homing by active radar in the case of missiles fired against surface fleets. As far as is known, the 'Bear-G' carries only one missile, recessed under the fuselage.

In the final 'Bear' variant identified in the West, the new-build airframe is mated with the new long-range cruise missile dubbed as AS-X-15. In view of its estimated range of 3000 km (1,864 miles), this weapon is almost certainly of a strategic nature, and it may be used mainly or entirely against land targets. Thus, the new carrier aircraft, the 'Bear-H', may be used only by Long-Range Aviation of the

V-VS and not by the AV-MF. Indeed, it may be designated as a Tu-20 or Tu-95 rather than as a Tu-142.

In any case, very little is known about either it or the new missile. Artwork published in Washington in 1984 showed the AS-X-15 missile as looking rather like a BGM-109 Tomahawk only much larger, with a tubular fuselage and mid-mounted untapered wings. A crude drawing in the 1985 *Soviet Military Power* annual published by the US Department of Defense purports to give a more detailed idea of the 'Bear-H', but the only feature of this drawing that can be regarded as new and apparently reliable is that instead of carrying one missile under the fuselage the new bomber carries pairs (or clusters of three) missiles under pylons beneath the inner wings. The artist has in fact merely drawn B-52G ALCM launch pylons and folded missiles and hung them under a 'Bear'. The accuracy of this representation cannot yet be judged. Of course with such an installation the missiles must all drop well clear before engine light-up, because if a missile were to accelerate straight ahead it might encounter adjacent propellers.

'Bear-H' photographed

In early May 1985 a photograph of a new 'Bear' version, said to be the 'Bear-H', was published in the West. Taken by 331 Skv of the Royal Norwegian air force (which flies General Dynamics F-16s), the photograph was secured over the Barents Sea. Thus, though the aircraft appeared to be in natural metal finish, it is probably flown by the AV-MF. The fuselage is of the original length, and in fact there are several features which suggest that this particular machine is not new but a conversion. There are no tailplane tip pods, but a small ram inlet or blister is visible on the right side of the rear fuselage. The obvious new feature is the nose, which carries a large forward-looking surveillance radar of a type not seen previously, with a 180° azimuth scanner of considerable size and depth, though smaller than that of the 'Crown Drum', with a small projection beneath it. A dark line was seen running from this radar back almost to the wing. It has been surmised that this might be an identifying strakelet, demanded for all strategic cruise-missile carrier aircraft by the unratified SALT 2

The specialized anti-submarine version is the 'Bear-F', which carries a smaller centreline radar than the 'Bear-D'. The most notable features are the extended forward fuselage and the MAD projection from the fin tip. The 'Bear-F' has comprehensive communications systems to keep in contact with both its own base and Soviet submarines and surface forces.

treaty. The missiles and pylons, if present, were completely hidden by the wing; presumably the Norwegian pilot took photographs from below which have not yet been released for publication.

Altogether Tupolev's great 'Bears' form a family without parallel in aviation. Boeing's B-52 has comparable dimensions, and its capabilities are also in many ways similar, and it has been around for as long; but it has never been anything but a strategic bomber and missile carrier, and the last one came off the line more than 23 years ago. A further contrast is that, except during the Vietnam War, the B-52 has never been based outside the USA (and Guam). The 'Bear', on the other hand, routinely covers much of the globe, operating not only from the Soviet Union's vast land mass but also from Cuba, Guinea, Angola, Somalia and the former US base at Cam Ranh Bay in Vietnam. The AV-MF's Tu-142s have never been subject to any SALT restrictions, though many of them are nuclear-capable and with their tremendous range can cover about half the politically interesting areas of our planet including the entire USA. The low rumbling snarl of the 'Bear' will certainly be heard into the next century.

Glossary

ADF Automatic Direction Finding
AEW Airborne Early Warning
ASW Anti-Submarine Warfare
ECM Electronic Countermeasures
Elint Electronic intelligence
EW Electronic Warfare
ILS Instrument Landing System
IR Infra-Red
MAD Magnetic Anomaly Detection
OKB experimental construction bureau (in fact, design bureau)
SLAR Side-Looking Airborne Radar

Current production aircraft have reverted to the original inboard nacelles. There is thought to have been an aerodynamic reason for the bigger nacelles, though in view of the exhaustive aerodynamic testing done in the early 1950s this seems unlikely. There has been no mention in Western analyses of the extended nacelles having been used to dispense chaff and other payloads removed from the tailplanes. Of course, this variant does not have the rear-fuselage lateral radomes and other sensors of the reconnaissance and Elint versions.

New missiles for old aircraft

The missile-carrier called 'Bear-G' by NATO was first identified as recently as 1980. These aircraft are almost certainly former carriers of AS-3 'Kangaroo' rebuilt to launch the AS-4 'Kitchen'. This cruise missile is smaller than its predecessor, but it is still a massive vehicle, having a tailed delta configuration with a length of some 11.3 m (37 ft). Launch weight is certainly well in excess of 6000 kg (13,228 lb), and a rocket engine gives a range varying up to at least 300 km (186 miles), depending on the selected flight profile. The warhead is either a large conventional charge or a thermonuclear type, variable from 350- to 800-kiloton yield. Such devastating yields would be used either against land targets, such as ports and naval bases, or against an entire surface fleet. The weapon appears to have a liquid-propellant engine (with main and cruise thrust chambers) and cruciform tail surfaces, sometimes with the ventral fin folded sideways until shortly before the release. There are several versions of this large supersonic missile, but the usual form of guidance is thought to be inertial, with terminal homing by active radar in the case of missiles fired against surface fleets. As far as is known, the 'Bear-G' carries only one missile, recessed under the fuselage.

In the final 'Bear' variant identified in the West, the new-build airframe is mated with the new long-range cruise missile dubbed as AS-X-15. In view of its estimated range of 3000 km (1,864 miles), this weapon is almost certainly of a strategic nature, and it may be used mainly or entirely against land targets. Thus, the new carrier aircraft, the 'Bear-H', may be used only by Long-Range Aviation of the

V-VS and not by the AV-MF. Indeed, it may be designated as a Tu-20 or Tu-95 rather than as a Tu-142.

In any case, very little is known about either it or the new missile. Artwork published in Washington in 1984 showed the AS-X-15 missile as looking rather like a BGM-109 Tomahawk only much larger, with a tubular fuselage and mid-mounted untapered wings. A crude drawing in the 1985 *Soviet Military Power* annual published by the US Department of Defense purports to give a more detailed idea of the 'Bear-H', but the only feature of this drawing that can be regarded as new and apparently reliable is that instead of carrying one missile under the fuselage the new bomber carries pairs (or clusters of three) missiles under pylons beneath the inner wings. The artist has in fact merely drawn B-52G ALCM launch pylons and folded missiles and hung them under a 'Bear'. The accuracy of this representation cannot yet be judged. Of course with such an installation the missiles must all drop well clear before engine light-up, because if a missile were to accelerate straight ahead it might encounter adjacent propellers.

'Bear-H' photographed

In early May 1985 a photograph of a new 'Bear' version, said to be the 'Bear-H', was published in the West. Taken by 331 Skv of the Royal Norwegian air force (which flies General Dynamics F-16s), the photograph was secured over the Barents Sea. Thus, though the aircraft appeared to be in natural metal finish, it is probably flown by the AV-MF. The fuselage is of the original length, and in fact there are several features which suggest that this particular machine is not new but a conversion. There are no tailplane tip pods, but a small ram inlet or blister is visible on the right side of the rear fuselage. The obvious new feature is the nose, which carries a large forward-looking surveillance radar of a type not seen previously, with a 180° azimuth scanner of considerable size and depth, though smaller than that of the 'Crown Drum', with a small projection beneath it. A dark line was seen running from this radar back almost to the wing. It has been surmised that this might be an identifying strakelet, demanded for all strategic cruise-missile carrier aircraft by the unratified SALT 2

The specialized anti-submarine version is the 'Bear-F', which carries a smaller centreline radar than the 'Bear-D'. The most notable features are the extended forward fuselage and the MAD projection from the fin tip. The 'Bear-F' has comprehensive communications systems to keep in contact with both its own base and Soviet submarines and surface forces.

treaty. The missiles and pylons, if present, were completely hidden by the wing; presumably the Norwegian pilot took photographs from below which have not yet been released for publication.

Altogether Tupolev's great 'Bears' form a family without parallel in aviation. Boeing's B-52 has comparable dimensions, and its capabilities are also in many ways similar, and it has been around for as long; but it has never been anything but a strategic bomber and missile carrier, and the last one came off the line more than 23 years ago. A further contrast is that, except during the Vietnam War, the B-52 has never been based outside the USA (and Guam). The 'Bear', on the other hand, routinely covers much of the globe, operating not only from the Soviet Union's vast land mass but also from Cuba, Guinea, Angola, Somalia and the former US base at Cam Ranh Bay in Vietnam. The AV-MF's Tu-142s have never been subject to any SALT restrictions, though many of them are nuclear-capable and with their tremendous range can cover about half the politically interesting areas of our planet including the entire USA. The low rumbling snarl of the 'Bear' will certainly be heard into the next century.

Glossary
ADF Automatic Direction Finding
AEW Airborne Early Warning
ASW Anti-Submarine Warfare
ECM Electronic Countermeasures
Elint Electronic intelligence
EW Electronic Warfare
ILS Instrument Landing System
IR Infra-Red
MAD Magnetic Anomaly Detection
OKB experimental construction bureau (in fact, design bureau)
SLAR Side-Looking Airborne Radar

Tupolev Tu-142 `Bear-F´
Soviet Naval Aviation (AV-MF)

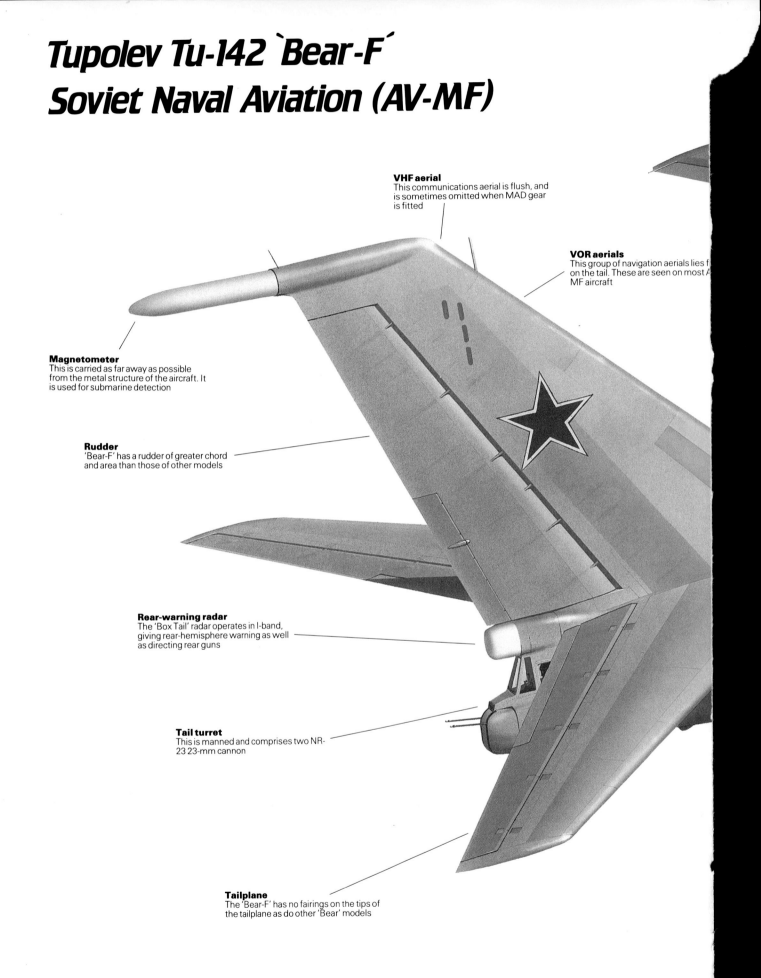

VHF aerial
This communications aerial is flush, and is sometimes omitted when MAD gear is fitted

VOR aerials
This group of navigation aerials lies f[...] on the tail. These are seen on most [AV-]MF aircraft

Magnetometer
This is carried as far away as possible from the metal structure of the aircraft. It is used for submarine detection

Rudder
'Bear-F' has a rudder of greater chord and area than those of other models

Rear-warning radar
The 'Box Tail' radar operates in I-band, giving rear-hemisphere warning as well as directing rear guns

Tail turret
This is manned and comprises two NR-23 23-mm cannon

Tailplane
The 'Bear-F' has no fairings on the tips of the tailplane as do other 'Bear' models

Tu-142 'Bear-F' performance (estimated)

Maximum speed at 41,000 ft (12500 m)	500 kts	925 km/h	575 mph
Maximum speed at low altitude	450 kts	834 km/h	518 mph
Service ceiling	41,000 ft	12500 m	
Maximum range with 11340-kg (25,000-lb) weapon load	12550 km	7,800 miles	

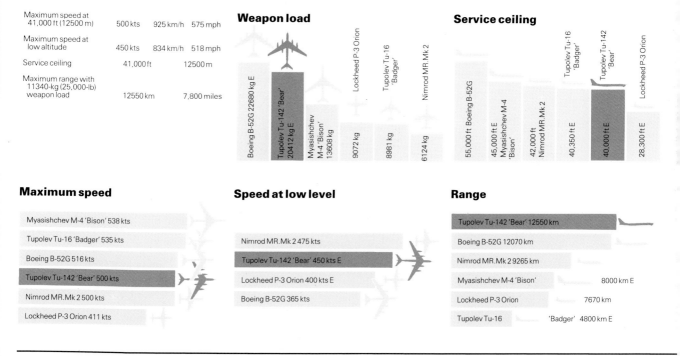

Weapon load

Boeing B-52G 22680 kg E
Tupolev Tu-142 'Bear' 20412 kg E
Myasishchev M-4 'Bison' 13608 kg
Lockheed P-3 Orion 9072 kg
Tupolev Tu-16 'Badger' 8981 kg
Nimrod MR.Mk 2 6124 kg

Service ceiling

55,000 ft Boeing B-52G
45,000 ft Myasishchev M-4 'Bison'
42,000 ft Nimrod MR.Mk 2
40,350 ft Tupolev Tu-16 'Badger'
40,000 ft Tupolev Tu-142 'Bear'
28,300 ft Lockheed P-3 Orion

Maximum speed

Myasishchev M-4 'Bison' 538 kts
Tupolev Tu-16 'Badger' 535 kts
Boeing B-52G 516 kts
Tupolev Tu-142 'Bear' 500 kts
Nimrod MR.Mk 2 500 kts
Lockheed P-3 Orion 411 kts

Speed at low level

Nimrod MR.Mk 2 475 kts
Tupolev Tu-142 'Bear' 450 kts E
Lockheed P-3 Orion 400 kts E
Boeing B-52G 365 kts

Range

Tupolev Tu-142 'Bear' 12550 km
Boeing B-52G 12070 km
Nimrod MR.Mk 2 9265 km
Myasishchev M-4 'Bison' 8000 km E
Lockheed P-3 Orion 7670 km
Tupolev Tu-16 'Badger' 4800 km E

Tupolev Tu-142 'Bear' recognition points

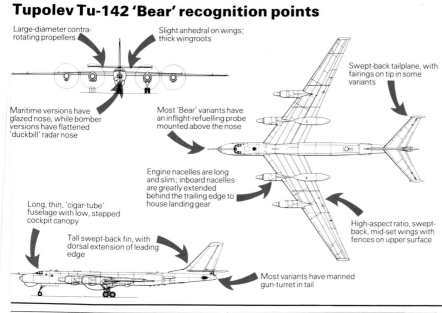

Large-diameter contra-rotating propellers

Slight anhedral on wings; thick wingroots

Swept-back tailplane, with fairings on tip in some variants

Maritime versions have glazed nose, while bomber versions have flattened 'duckbill' radar nose

Most 'Bear' variants have an inflight-refuelling probe mounted above the nose

Engine nacelles are long and slim; inboard nacelles are greatly extended behind the trailing edge to house landing gear

Long, thin, 'cigar-tube' fuselage with low, stepped cockpit canopy

High-aspect ratio, swept-back, mid-set wings with fences on upper surface

Tall swept-back fin, with dorsal extension of leading edge

Most variants have manned gun-turret in tail

Specification:
Tupolev Tu-95 'Bear-C' (estimated)

Wings
Span	51.10 m	167 ft 7.8 in
Area	295.00 m²	3,175.46 sq ft

Fuselage and tail unit
Length overall	49.50 m	162 ft 4.8 in
Height overall	12.12 m	39 ft 9.2 in
Tailplane span	14.90 m	48 ft 10.6 in

Landing gear
Wheelbase	15.85 m	52 ft 0 in
Wheel track	12.95 m	42 ft 5.8 in

Weights
Empty	80000 kg	176,370 lb
Normal take-off	170000 kg	374,786 lb
Maximum take-off	188000 kg	414,469 lb

All 'Bears' feature many radomes, blisters and aerials housing radar, communications and listening gear. The 'Bear' is not easily confused with any other aircraft apart from the Boeing B-52, which features a similar planform. The size of the 'Bear' sets it apart from all aircraft except the B-52 and Myasishchev M-4 'Bison', which does not have engine pods or nacelles. Although a lot smaller, the same manufacturer's Tu-16 'Badger' is sometimes confused with 'Bear' on account of its similar anhedral wings and tail

The 'Bear-A' is the original free-fall bomber version, and did not carry any large radar. A small radar unit is located under the nose.

This 'Bear-B' shows the 'Top Crown' radar in the nose and the pipe leading from the inflight-refuelling probe back to the fuel tanks.

'Bear-C' is a dual reconnaissance and bomber version. It is distinguished from the 'Bear-B' by having a blister on both sides of the rear fuselage.

'Bear-D' is the major maritime general purpose version, with 'Mushroom' chin radar and the enormous 'Big Bulge' under the belly.

Several 'Bear-C' and 'Bear-D' aircraft have appeared with a faired tailcone, which is believed to house various electronic sensors and ECM gear.

'Bear-H' is the new-build aircraft for cruise missile carriage. The nose is of similar type to the 'Top Crown' of the 'Bear-B' and 'Bear-C'.

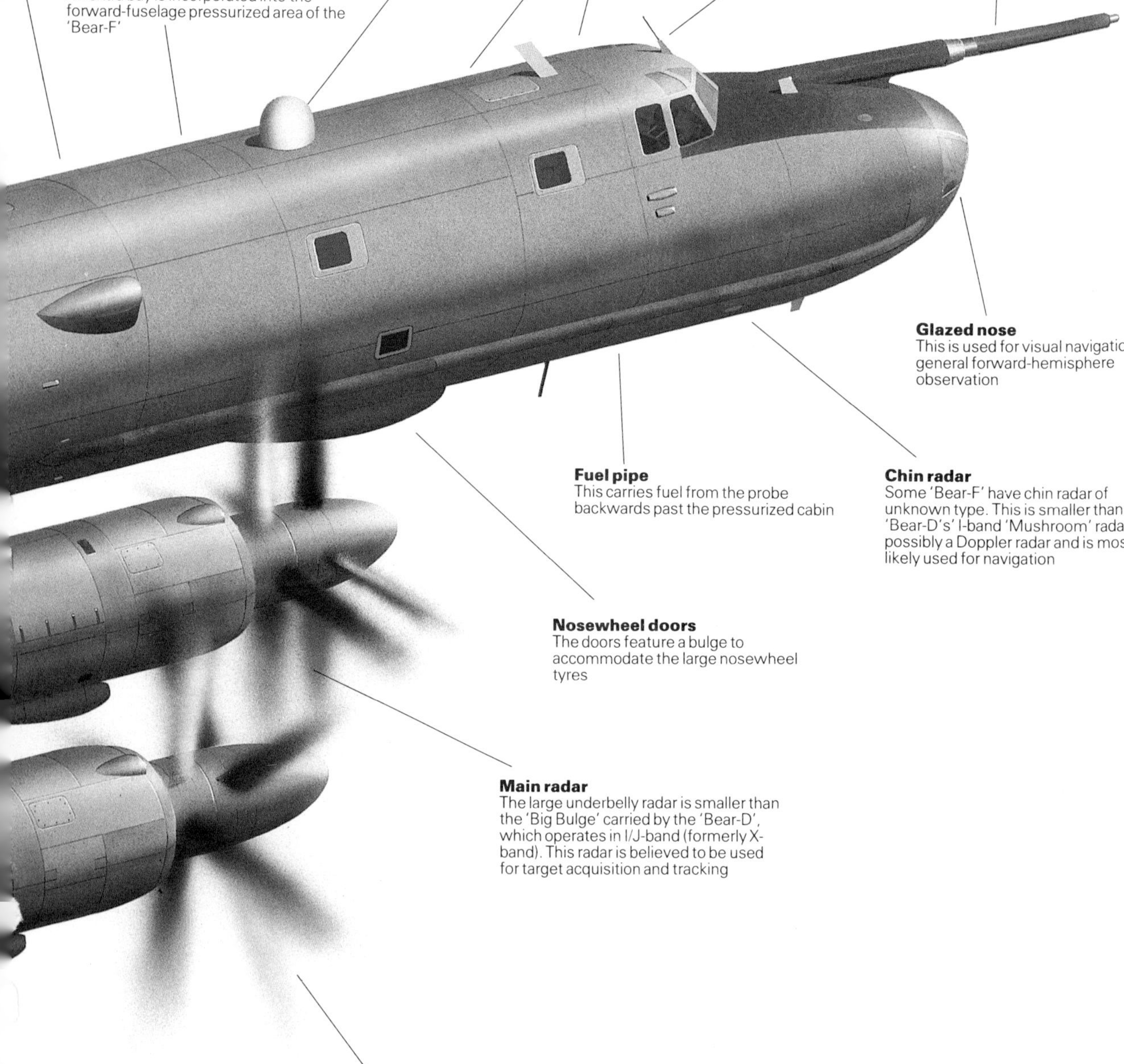

m air inlet
s possibly serves the automatic
ver unit

Fuselage 'plug'
An extra bay is incorporated into the
forward-fuselage pressurized area of the
'Bear-F'

Observation dome

Lateral observation windows

VHF whip aerial

Refuelling probe
The probe is fixed and is carried by all
'Bear-F' and most other AV-MF 'Bears'

Glazed nose
This is used for visual navigation and
general forward-hemisphere
observation

Fuel pipe
This carries fuel from the probe
backwards past the pressurized cabin

Chin radar
Some 'Bear-F' have chin radar of
unknown type. This is smaller than the
'Bear-D's' I-band 'Mushroom' radar. It is
possibly a Doppler radar and is most
likely used for navigation

Nosewheel doors
The doors feature a bulge to
accommodate the large nosewheel
tyres

Main radar
The large underbelly radar is smaller than
the 'Big Bulge' carried by the 'Bear-D',
which operates in I/J-band (formerly X-
band). This radar is believed to be used
for target acquisition and tracking

Propellers
The AV-60N eight-blade, contra-rotating
propellers have a diameter of 5.6 m
(18.37 ft)

coolers
se are mounted in low-drag fairings

Exhaust stacks
These two outlets are believed to be exhaust stacks for the automatic power unit (APU)

R
Th
pc

HF aerials
These long aerials are used for global HF communications. In some versions these are in 'towel-rail' form

Fuselage
The fuselage of the 'Bear-F' is much 'cleaner' than other variants, which are covered with avionics aerials of many forms

Main weapons bay
A heavy load of anti-submarine weapons is carried, including at least eight torpedoes and nuclear depth charges

Jetpipes
These are of the twin (inner and outer) bifurcated type

C
T

Leading edge
These are thermally de-iced by air heated in gas/air heat exchangers. Jetpipe flow can be partly diverted through these in very icy conditions

Tupolev Tu-142 warload

■ 1 × AS-3 'Kangaroo' strategic nuclear missile on
fuselage centreline
2 × NR-23 23-mm cannon in tail turret
4 × NR-23 23-mm cannon in retractable dorsal and
ventral remote turrets

■ 1 × AS-4 'Kitchen' strategic cruise missile under
fuselage
2 × NR-23 23-mm cannon in tail turret
4 × NR-23 23-mm cannon in retractable dorsal and
ventral remote turrets

■ 2 × NR-23 23-mm cannon in tail turret
4 × NR-23 23-mm cannon in retractable ventral and
dorsal remote turrets
4/6 × AS-X-15 cruise missiles

■ 2 × NR-23 23-mm cannon in tail turret
4 × NR-23 23-mm cannon in retractable dorsal and
ventral remote turrets

□ 6/7 × large optical cameras SLAR or IR linescan
small navigation radar under nose

Nuclear strike with 'Kangaroo'
('Bear-B')
The mighty AS-3 is terribly inaccurate, but with a
yield approaching 800 kilotons is deadly enough
against area targets such as carrier battle
groups. The 'Kangaroo' is also thought to have
been carried by the 'Bear-C', although this
variant is primarily used for maritime Elint duties.

Nuclear strike with 'Kitchen'
('Bear-G')
The 'Bears' modified to carry the 'Kitchen' are
almost certainly converted 'Bear-Bs' which had
previously carried the 'Kangaroo'. The 'Kitchen'
may also be carried under the wings of the 'Bear-
G', although this cannot be confirmed.

Cruise missile carrier
('Bear-H')
No photographs are known to exist of the 'Bear-
H'/AS-X-15 combination, and the number and
position of weapons carried must remain a
matter for speculation.

Maritime photo-recon
('Bear-E')
The cameras and linescan, or SLAR if carr
the 'Bear-E' are mounted on an enormous
which conforms to the fuselage contours
fitted.

Tupolev Tu-95/142 variants

Tu-95 'Bear-A': basic strategic bomber version which entered
service 1955-6; only a small number remain in service

Tu-95 'Bear-B': generally similar to 'Bear-A', but a missile-
launching version equipped to carry the subsonic AS-3 'Kangaroo'
weapon of aeroplane form; became operational from 1961

Tu-95 'Bear-C': first identified during NATO exercises in
September 1964, this is similar to 'Bear-B' (carrying the AS-3
'Kangaroo') except that it has a streamlined blister fairing on each
side of the rear fuselage and a nose refuelling probe

Tu-142 'Bear-D': first identified in August 1967 when overflying
US Coast Guard icebreakers operating in the Soviet Arctic;
maritime reconnaissance and missile-guidance version with an
undernose radar scanner, a large underbelly radome and, like 'Bear-
C', a nose refuelling probe

Tu-142 'Bear-E': maritime reconnaissance version; basically
similar to 'Bear-A' but with the refuelling probe and rear blister
fairings of the 'Bear-C'; has camera installations in the weapons
bay
Tu-142 'Bear-F': ASW version first identified in 1973 and seen
with several variations of radar; has two stores bays in rear
fuselage, resulting in deletion of the rear ventral gun turret; some
have been seen with a MAD (magnetic anomaly detection) sting
extending rearward from the fin tip; about 50 believed to be in
operation in 1984

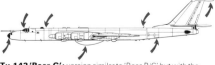

Tu-142 'Bear-G': version similar to 'Bear-B/C' but with the
subsonic AS-3 'Kangaroo' replaced by the supersonic AS-4
'Kitchen' air-to-surface missile
Tu-142 'Bear-H': production version, first reported officially in
1984, which is equipped to carry the AS-X-15 air-launched cruise
missile that will provide low-level and stand-off attack capability

Tupolev Tu-142 'Bear-D' cutaway drawing key

1 Fixed inflight-refuelling probe
2 Observer/bomb aimer's compartment nose glazing
3 Nose radome
4 Avionics equipment bay, port and starboard
5 'Odd-Rods' IFF aerials
6 Cockpit enclosure, pilot and co-pilot
7 Nose undercarriage pivot mounting
8 Retractable landing/taxiing lamps, port and starboard
9 Nosewheel steering jacks
10 Aft retracting twin nosewheels
11 Nosewheel doors
12 Pitot tubes
13 Cockpit roof escape hatch
14 Forward pressurized crew compartment
15 Observation hatch
16 Wing root attachment joint
17 Wing centre section carry-through
18 Inboard wing panel
19 Starboard engine nacelles
20 AV-60N eight-bladed contra-rotating propellers
21 Propeller spinners
22 Wing fences
23 Outboard wing panel
24 Wing tip lighting
25 Starboard aileron
26 Aileron tab
27 Outboard tracked, slotted flap, lowered
28 Flap guide rails
29 Nacelle tail fairing
30 Aerodynamically extended tail fairing (some 'Bear-F' aircraft)
31 Mainwheel doors
32 Inboard flap, lowered
33 Satellite communications antennae
34 ADF sense aerial

35 Circular section unpressurized fuselage
36 Retractable dorsal cannon barbette, 2 x 23-mm cannon, remotely controlled

37 Fuselage profile 'Bear-E' & 'F'
38 Raised cockpit section
39 Extended crew compartment fuselage plug
40 Search radar
41 Two-section weapons bay ('Bear-F')
42 Weapons bay camera and reconnaissance pallet ('Bear-E')

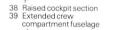
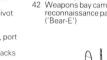

2 × NR-23 23-mm cannon in tail turret

various sonars and depth charges stowed in new, pressurized rear fuselage
various unidentified radomes and aerials
MAD stinger on tail

i-submarine/Elint

('Bear-F')

'Bear-F' is probably the world's largest dedicated ASW ...m. It features two weapons bays, and a completely ...rized rear fuselage section. The forward fuselage is ...ened.

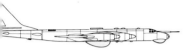

4 × NR-23 23-mm cannon in retractable dorsal and ventral remote turrets

'Mushroom' I-band radar under chin
'Big Bulge' surveillance radar under weapons bay
'Box Tail' threat-warning radar on tail
tailplane-tip chaff/ECM pods
tail turret replaced by ECM tail

tail turret replaced by long fairing housing passive and active ECM equipment

EW blister radomes along centreline
reconnaissance blisters on rear fuselage as standard

Elint/Electronic warfare

('Bear-C')
The 'Bear-C' is essentially similar to the 'Kangaroo'-toting 'Bear-B', and early aircraft retained the capability to carry this missile.

Missile guidance/Elint

('Bear-D')
The 'Bear-D' finds and pinpoints targets for missiles fired by friendly platforms such as ships and low-flying aircraft. It can provide inflight course-correction and target-update data for cruise missiles. The 'Bear-D' is also a versatile multi-sensor reconnaissance and Elint platform.

This 'Bear-B' shows the missile carriage of the huge AS-3 'Kangaroo'. This is the largest air-launched missile in service, with the dimensions of a small fighter. It does not have terminal guidance and is therefore inaccurate, but overcomes this by carrying a huge nuclear or conventional warhead.

... root fillet
...arboard tailplane
...lfin
...ort-wave ground control
...mmunications antennae

47 HF aerial cable
48 Fin tip aerial fairing
49 Magnetic Anomaly Detection (MAD) boom ('Bear-F')

50 Rudder
51 Rudder tab
52 Sensor equipment tail fairing (some 'Bear-D' aircraft)

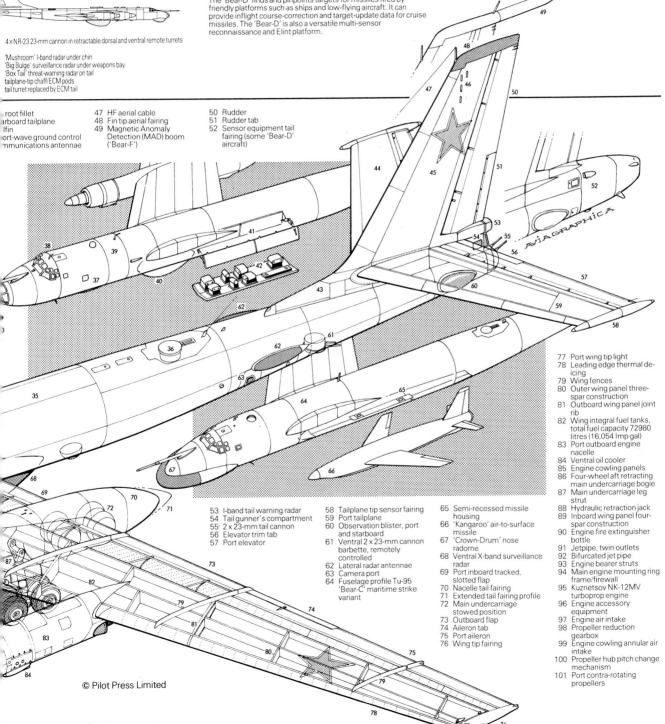

53 I-band tail warning radar
54 Tail gunner's compartment
55 2 × 23-mm tail cannon
56 Elevator trim tab
57 Port elevator

58 Tailplane tip sensor fairing
59 Port tailplane
60 Observation blister, port and starboard
61 Ventral 2 × 23-mm cannon barbette, remotely controlled
62 Lateral radar antennae
63 Camera port
64 Fuselage profile Tu-95 'Bear-C' maritime strike variant

65 Semi-recessed missile housing
66 'Kangaroo' air-to-surface missile
67 'Crown-Drum' nose radome
68 Ventral X-band surveillance radar
69 Port inboard tracked, slotted flap
70 Nacelle tail fairing
71 Extended tail fairing profile
72 Main undercarriage stowed position
73 Outboard flap
74 Aileron tab
75 Port aileron
76 Wing tip fairing

77 Port wing tip light
78 Leading edge thermal de-icing
79 Wing fences
80 Outer wing panel three-spar construction
81 Outboard wing panel joint rib
82 Wing integral fuel tanks, total fuel capacity 72980 litres (16,054 Imp gal)
83 Port outboard engine nacelle
84 Ventral oil cooler
85 Engine cowling panels
86 Four-wheel aft retracting main undercarriage bogie
87 Main undercarriage leg strut
88 Hydraulic retraction jack
89 Inboard wing panel four-spar construction
90 Engine fire extinguisher bottle
91 Jetpipe, twin outlets
92 Bifurcated jet pipe
93 Engine bearer struts
94 Main engine mounting ring frame/firewall
95 Kuznetsov NK-12MV turboprop engine
96 Engine accessory equipment
97 Engine air intake
98 Propeller reduction gearbox
99 Engine cowling annular air intake
100 Propeller hub pitch change mechanism
101 Port contra-rotating propellers

© Pilot Press Limited

GLOSSARY

AAA	Anti-Aircraft Artillery		MCAS	Marine Corps Air Station
AAM	Air-to-Air Missile		NAS	Naval Air Station
ACM	Air Combat Manoeuvre		NAVWAS	NAVigation and Weapon-Aiming System
AFB	Air-Force Base		NWDS	Navigation and Weapons Delivery System
AFRes	Air Force Reserve		OAS	Offensive Avionics System
ANG	Air National Guard		OCU	Operational Conversion Unit
AHRS	Attitude and Heading Reference System		OTEAF	Operational Test and EvaluAtion Force
ALARM	Air-Launched Anti-Radiation Missile		PGM	Precision-Guided Munition
ALCM	Air-Launched Cruise Missile		Photint	Photographic intelligence
ARM	Anti-Radiation Missile		QRA	Quick-Reaction Alert
ASM	Air-to-Surface Missile		RAAF	Royal Australian Air Force
ASMP	Air-Sol Moyenne Portee (medium-range surface-to-air)		RDT&E	Research, Development, Test and Evaluation
AMRAAM	Advanced Medium-Range Air-to-Air Missile		RIO	Radio Intercept Officer
AV-MF	Soviet Naval Aviation		RNAS	Royal Naval Air Station
BW	Bomber Wing		RWR	Radar Warning Receiver
CBU	Cluster Bomb Unit		SAC	Strategic Air Command
CILOP	Conversion In Lieu Of Procurement		SACEUR	Supreme Allied Commander EURope
CITS	Central Integrated Test System		SACLANT	Supreme Allied Commander AtLANTic
COMED	COmbined Map and Electronic Display		SAM	Surface-to-Air Missile
CRT	Cathode Ray Tube		SAR	Search And Rescue
DARIN	Display, Attack, Ranging and Inertial Navigation		SEAM	Sidewinder Expanded-Acquisition Missile
DME	Distance Measuring Equipment		SIOP	Single Integrated Operational Plan
ECM	Electronic CounterMeasures		SLEP	Service Life Extension Program
Elint	Electronic Intelligence		SNOE	Smart Noise Operation Equipment
EMP	Electro-Magnetic Pulse		SOR	Specific Operational Requirement
EO	Electro-Optical		SRAM	Short-Range Attack Missile
ESM	Electronic Support Measures		Tacan	Tactical air navigation
EVS	Electro-optical Viewing System		TAC	Tactical Air Command
EW	Electronic Warfare		TERCOM	TERrain COntour Matching
FLIR	Forward-Looking Infra-Red		TFR	Terrain Following Radar
GP	General Purpose		TFS	Tactical Fighter Squadron
GSFG	Group of Soviet Forces in Germany		TFW	Tactical Fighter Wing
HARM	High-speed Anti-Radiation Missile		TFX	Tactical Fighter eXperimental
HUD	Head-Up Display		TISL	Target Indicator System - Laser
HUDWAS	Head-Up Display and Weapon-Aiming System		TRAM	Target Recognition and Attack Multi-sensor
IFF	Identification Friend or Foe		TRIM	Trails, Roads, Interdiction Multi-sensor
ILS	Instrument Landing System		TTTE	Trinational Tornado Training Establishment
INS	Inertial Navigation System		UHF	Ultra High Frequency
IOC	Initial Operational Capability		VG	Variable Geometry
IR	Infra-Red		VHF	Very High Frequency
IRCM	Infra-Red CounterMeasures		VOR	VHF Omni-directional Range
JATO	Jet-Assisted Take-Off		VTAS	Visual Target-Acquisition System
LID	Lift-Improvement Device		VTOL	Vertical Take-Off and Landing
LLLTV	Low-Light-Level TV		V-VS	Soviet air force
LRMTS	Laser Ranger and Marked-Target Seeker		WAC	Weapon-Aiming Computer
			WSO	Weapons System Officer